KU-768-236

THE BLUE GUIDES

Albania
Austria
Belgium and Luxembourg
China
Cyprus
Czech and Slovak Republics
Denmark
Egypt

FRANCE
France
Paris and Versailles
Burgundy
Loire Valley
Midi-Pyrénées
Normandy
South West France
Corsica

GERMANY
Berlin and Eastern Germany
Western Germany

GREECE
Greece
Athens and environs
Crete

HOLLAND
Holland
Amsterdam

Hungary
Ireland

ITALY
Northern Italy
Southern Italy
Florence
Rome and environs
Sicily
Tuscany
Umbria
Venice

Jerusalem
Jordan
Malta and Gozo
Mexico
Morocco
Moscow and St Petersburg
Portugal

SPAIN
Spain
Barcelona
Madrid

Sweden
Switzerland

TURKEY
Turkey
Istanbul

Tunisia

UK
England
Scotland
Wales
London
Museums and Galleries
    of London
Oxford and Cambridge
Country Houses of England
Gardens of England
Literary Britain and Ireland
Victorian Architecture in Britain
Churches and Chapels of
    Northern England
Churches and Chapels of
    Southern England
Channel Islands

USA
New York
Museums and Galleries of New York
Boston and Cambridge

The eye-catching view of the Buda skyline, dominated by the Matthias Church, as seen from Pest

BLUE GUIDE

Budapest

Bob Dent

A & C Black
London

WW Norton
New York

First edition 1996

Published by A & C Black (Publishers) Limited
35 Bedford Row, London WC1R 4JH

ISBN 0-7136-4077-4

A CIP catalogue record of this book is available from the British Library

Published in the United States of America by
WW Norton and Company, Inc
500 Fifth Avenue, New York, NY 10110

Published simultaneously in Canada by
Penguin Books Canada Limited
2801 John Street, Markham, Ontario L3R 1B4

ISBN 0-393-3422-7 USA

The author and the publishers have done their best to ensure the accuracy of all the information in Blue Guide Budapest; however, they can accept no responsibility for any loss, injury or inconvenience sustained by any traveller as a result of information or advice contained in the guide.

British journalist **Bob Dent** has lived in Budapest since 1986. His articles on Hungary have appeared in *The Guardian, The European, Independent on Sunday, New Statesman & Society, The Scotsman, Times Educational Supplement* and many other publications, and have been distributed around the globe by Gemini News Service. He has reported from Budapest for the BBC World Service, IRN and Blue Danube Radio (Vienna), and has often worked as a research consultant for ITN crews filming in Hungary. Bob Dent is the author of Blue Guide Hungary (1990, new edition in preparation) and Budapest for Children (1992).

Maps and plans by Carto Graphics, © A & C Black
Illustrations © Jim Urquhart, 1996

The publishers invite readers to write in with their comments, suggestions and corrections for the next edition of the Blue Guide. Writers of the best letter will be awarded a free Blue Guide of their choice.

Printed and bound by William Clowes Ltd, Beccles and London

PREFACE

Beautiful Budapest—it is no exaggeration. The Hungarian capital straddles the River Danube in a breathtaking setting, unparalleled elsewhere in Europe. On the right bank the Buda Hills reach almost to the riverside, with Castle Hill and Gellért Hill offering splendid panoramas. Pest, on the left bank and connected to Buda by a series of impressive bridges, with its predominant mixture of late 19C Eclectic and early 20C Art Nouveau architecture, is still very much a 'turn-of-the-century' city.

For over 50 years up to the Second World War, Budapest was one of the outstanding cultural capitals of Central Europe, on a par with, and in some ways ahead of, Vienna and Prague. Some of that old atmosphere has returned, helped by the fact that Hungary had a head start in the east European transition of the 1990s. Today Budapest is one of the most vibrant cities in the region.

With its marvellous views, attractive architecture, rich history, long hours of summer sunshine, unique thermal baths and swimming pools, its excellent public transport system, street cafés and multitude of restaurants (still cheap by Western standards), Budapest is a fascinating place to visit and an easy place in which to relax.

The aim of this work is to be a comprehensive, detailed, serious English-language guidebook to Budapest's history and culture and in particular its architecture and monuments. 'Serious' here should not be taken too seriously. While detail and accuracy are all-important (corrections are welcome), the goal has been to provide historical, political and other information in the text in such a way as to make the buildings, streets, squares and statues of the city 'come alive'.

Among the many people in an official capacity who have kindly helped in the preparation of this guidebook, Ágnes Padányi and her staff at Tourinform, Hungary's central tourist information office, deserve special thanks. Their services can be highly recommended to all visitors.

In addition, a number of individuals have gone out of their way in helping to track down information. Many thanks to them: Judit Acsádi, János Gerle, Elizabeth Ibbetson, Andrew Lenard, Éva Lihovay, Gabriella Markgraf, András Szilágyi, Renilde Vervoort, Francis Wheen and Jo Wiggans.

Judy Tither of A&C Black has carefully applied her editorial skills to the manuscript with the result that the text has been greatly improved.

Finally, a special thanks is due to Katalin Rácz, not only for providing the section on Hungarian food, but also for much help with research, translations and constructive criticism.

CONTENTS

Maps and plans

EXPLANATORY NOTES

Hungarian names
In Hungarian, surnames come first (Kovács Anna, Tisza Róbert, etc.). In this guide they are written in English stye (Anna Kovács, etc.) except when people's names are used as names of streets or squares. In these cases the text follows the order which appears on the street sight (Kovács Anna utca, etc.). Usually the Hungarian form of names has been retained and not anglicised (e.g. János and not John). One major exception is King (St) Stephen, Hungary's first monarch. Due to common usage, he is referred to as Stephen throughout, rather than by his Hungarian name of István.

Hungarian terms and abbreviations used in the text
fasor   boulevard
hegy   hill
köz   alley or mews
krt/körút   ring boulevard
lépcső   steps
sétány   walkway
sor   row
tér/tere   square
u./utca   street
út/útja   road

Using this book
The **index** is comprehensive and should prove useful in tracking down any building or location irrespective of whether you are following a set route or not.

Before visiting any museum it is worth consulting the **Museums Checklist** p 190, particularly for the notes there are about opening times and other practical matters.

History is all-important in getting to grips with Hungarian culture and society. Readers are therefore advised to glance through the historical **In a Nutshell** section (p 187) for an idea of the major names and periods in Hungary's history—references to these appear many times throughout the text.

PRACTICAL INFORMATION

Planning your trip

Gathering information

The Hungarian Tourist Board has a representative office in **London** which deals with tourist enquiries. The office is not open to personal callers but can be contacted via post, fax or 24-hour telephone (premium rate) which offers a menu of recorded information for various categories of enquiry. Additional enquiries for personal help can be made Mon–Fri, 09.00–12.00 on 0181–871 4009. Hungarian National Tourist Board, PO Box 4336, London SW18 4XE, tel: 01891–171 200, fax: 01891-669 970.

A similar office operates in **New York**. Hungarian Tourist Board, c/o Hungarian Commercial Consulate, 150 East 58th Street, 33rd Floor, New York, NY 10155, tel: (212) 355-0240, fax: (212) 207–4103.

Other Hungarian Tourist Board offices can be found in: **Austria:** A-1010 Vienna 1, Parkring 12. III Stiege, 6 Stock, tel: 513-9122, fax: 513-1201. **Germany:** D-60311 Frankfurt am Main, Berliner Strasse 72, tel: 929119-0, fax: 929119-18. **Italy:** Via Dei Monti Parioli 38, 00197 Rome, tel: 32 12 409, fax: 32 11 373. **The Netherlands:** Postbus 91644, 2509 EE Den Haag, tel: 385-3985, fax: 347-8963. **Russia:** World Trade Centre, Hotel Mezhdunarodnaya-2, office 921, Krasnapresnenskaya naberezhnaya 12, 123610 Moscow, tel: 253-2921, fax: 253-0084.

Passports and visas

A valid (full) passport is required for tourist visits to Hungary, but visas are not required for tourists who are citizens of the USA, Canada, the UK or any other EU country. Citizens of other countries as well as business or other non-tourist travellers should check in advance with their nearest Hungarian embassy or via a travel agent.

Currency

The Hungarian currency is the **forint** (Ft). This is divided into 100 **fillérs**, but these are so small in real value as to be virtually worthless. At the time of writing forints cannot be purchased outside Hungary in advance, although this might change in the near future. However, currency can be obtained easily at the airport on arrival and at border crossings, as well as at numerous points on the way to Budapest and throughout the city; you should always obtain an official receipt of conversion. There is no obligation to exchange any minimum amount per day.

International credit cards are accepted by an increasing number of places, particularly large hotels, top restaurants and shops, but by and large Hungary still has a cash economy, therefore obtaining forints is advisable, particularly for petrol, everyday shopping and ordinary restaurants.

Tourists can reconvert forints into hard currency at the point of departure, up to 50 per cent of the total amount bought. For this you will need to produce your official receipts.

Foreigners are still accosted on the streets by unofficial money-changers seeking hard currency. This practice is both illegal and unwise—you may end up with a fistful of counterfeit notes, or worthless notes of some other country's currency, and the rates obtainable on the illegal market hardly differ from the official rate.

Climate

Hungary has a continental climate which varies greatly through the seasons. The hottest months are June, July and August, when the daytime temperature can reach into the 30s (Celsius). The heat and the crowds can make central Budapest unbearable in August, but you can escape to the open-air swimming pools, the parks or to the cooler Buda Hills, not far from the centre.

The coldest month is January, with an average temperature of just below 0°C. Warm clothing is obviously needed, but all buildings and public transport are well heated. Some museums may close for part of the winter, and other attractions, such as the fun fair and the zoo, are only semi-operational.

The most comfortable times of year for sightseeing are usually April–May and September–October.

Public holidays and annual events

New Year's Day. A public holiday.

'Farsang'. The name of the season traditionally marking the end of winter. Recent years have seen a revival of public events in Budapest, including a carnival, fancy-dress street parade and open-air music. This takes place at the weekend, usually the last Saturday in February.

15 March. A national holiday marking the anniversary of the Hungarian Uprising against Austria in 1848. Often labelled a youth day (because the youth of Pest and the youthful poet Sándor Petőfi led the way in 1848), it is usually marked by rather serious political content. Nevertheless there are always several spectacles, particularly in Kossuth tér beside parliament (very formal); the Petőfi statue in Március 15 tér by the Pest end of Elizabeth Bridge (speeches, wreaths, decoration with paper flags); and the steps of the National Museum, where, apart from speeches, there is often some open-air happening involving song, dance and performance. The Hungarian tricolour appears all over town, on both public and private buildings, and many people wear little rosettes with the national colours.

Budapest Spring Festival. A well-established annual cultural event involving top-class Hungarian and foreign artists. It takes place over several days in March, particularly in the second half of the month. The varied programme includes ballet, music, opera, theatre and folk dance performances as well as special exhibitions. Budapest's large, annual Art Expo, which exhibits works by contemporary Hungarian and foreign painters, also usually takes place during the spring festival.

22 April—Earth Day. Not a public holiday, but slowly assuming importance as 'green' issues catch on. Drivers are asked to leave their cars at home and there are several 'bicycle events' organised around the city as well as other activities in parks and public places.

Easter. On Easter Saturday many churches throughout Budapest organise local processions. Traditional costumes are worn and the old church flags and emblems are brought out. Traditional village Easter activities—egg painting, dances, etc.—

survive to an extent in the city and can mainly be found in the network of community centres (see p 41) and in some museums.

Easter Monday is a public holiday, when city dwellers carry on the tradition of 'watering'. In the villages the young men used to drag the young women to the well and shower them with a bucket of water. In the city this old fertility rite has survived in the degenerated form of men and boys spraying perfume or water on the heads of women and girls and muttering the appropriate verse (in return for a kiss, a painted egg and/or glass of *pálinka*).

1 May. A public holiday. The traditional May Day celebrations used to involve a big parade of trade union and workers' organisations along Dózsa György út by the City Park. It was a festive occasion involving a carnival atmosphere with balloons, banners and floats which finished up with further activities in the park.

Today the May Day festive atmosphere continues, though without the big parade. Unions still organise a large event in the City Park involving not only speeches but also acrobats, clowns, games, contests, rides, balloons, music, food and beer tents. Similar events on a smaller scale can usually be found in other parts of the city such as the People's Park (Népliget), the 'Nagy-rét' meadow near Hűvösvölgy or, nearer the centre, in the Tabán, the green space between Gellért Hill and Castle Hill, where open-air pop concerts are sometimes organised.

Children's Day (*Gyermek Nap*). Not a fixed date, but usually the last Sunday in May. As the name implies this is a special day of events for children. Anything could be involved, but the type and location(s) of activities can change each year. Check with Tourinform (see p 23).

Whit Monday. A public holiday.

30 June. The date which officially marked the final withdrawal of the last Soviet troops from Hungary in 1991. Since then the municipality has sponsored on this date (or on the last weekend in June) public festivities throughout the city—music, dance, performances, etc.

Summer Opera and Ballet Festival. This usually takes place every August.

20 August. A national holiday—St Stephen's Day, marking the foundation of the Hungarian state (Stephen was the first king) and, traditionally, the 'day of new bread'. Recent years have seen the revival of the church procession through the city behind the holy relic of Stephen's right hand.

In addition, many summertime holiday activities take place—Margaret Island usually has a lot going on. A main attraction is the traditional big evening firework display on Gellért Hill, which is visible from many vantage points.

Budapest Wine Festival. Wine-tasting opportunities take place in September in the streets and squares of the city.

Architectural Heritage Days. The third or fourth weekend in September. For two days in the year the only chance to see inside some of the city's most sumptuous buildings such as the National Bank and the Ministry of Finance. Organised by the Ödön Lechner Foundation.

Budapest Music Weeks. Usually the first two weeks in October, but may begin in late September. An attempt to create an autumn equivalent of the Spring Festival. In fact mini-festivals are increasingly being organised throughout the year, such that music lovers should find plenty of attractions at whatever time they visit.

23 October. A national holiday—the anniversary of the outbreak of the 1956 Uprising and the proclamation in 1989 of Hungary's new constitutional status. Officially very much a 'political' day (speeches, etc.), but there may be some parades worth watching and some special concerts.

Christmas. 25 and 26 December are public holidays, though it is actually Christmas Eve when the traditional family Christmas dinner takes place. (Public transport closes down about 16.00 on the 24th!).

There is (as yet) no sense of overkill in terms of early Christmas shopping or Christmas decorations in Budapest, but there is often a large Christmas tree erected in Vörösmarty tér. Here and elsewhere in the centre street stalls appear, accompanied occasionally by live music and other performances.

As at Easter, some community centres may organise traditional, folk-culture activities, such as children dressed up performing the Bethlehem story.

New Year. As the end of the year approaches the streets of Budapest begin to fill with stalls selling trinkets, masks and, in particular, noisy paper trumpets, which many delight in blowing at all times, though they are intended for 31 December celebrations. On New Year's Eve the city centre takes on a carnival atmosphere, particularly around the Great Boulevard (Nagykörút).

Getting to Budapest

By air

Up to four scheduled direct flights a day from **London** Heathrow to Budapest are operated by British Airways and Malév, the Hungarian national carrier. The flight takes about 2hrs 20min. Information about ticket prices and times should be available from any travel agent. Flights are more expensive in the high summer season, and special offers may be available during the winter months. Obtaining relatively cheap tickets from 'bucket shops' is increasingly possible, through newspaper and magazine advertisements and shopping around. Care should be taken with cheap flights offered jointly with cheap accommodation. It has been known for non-existent hotels to be advertised.

Flights to Budapest from Manchester and other airports in the UK are available with other airlines, but these involve transferring at Brussels, Frankfurt or elsewhere.

Malév and Delta Airlines operate daily non-stop flights from **New York** (JFK) to Budapest. The flight takes approximately 7½hrs. Other, possibly cheaper, flights and combinations of flights are available from the USA, but all involve transfer or touch down, and take much longer.

There are no direct flights to Budapest from **Canada**. All routes involve transfer.

Budapest Ferihegy Airport has three terminals. Ferihegy 1 was built in the early 1950s and still has a certain 'behind the Iron Curtain' atmosphere. Ferihegy

2 is modern and could be anywhere. The third terminal is brand new and is due to open some time after publication of this guidebook.

Arrival at the airport presents no particular problems: passport control is usually swift and passengers are likely to spend more time waiting for their luggage to appear. Conventional red and green channels operate for customs control. There are duty free shops in the arrivals section, prior to passport control.

The airport is situated just over 20km to the south-east of the centre. There is no direct rail link but a variety of transfer services operate.

Travellers should be wary of private taxi operators touting for business at the airport; there have been many complaints of overcharging. The alternatives, which are both cheaper and reliable, are the **Airport-Taxi** service, taxis (with blue logo) which operate at fixed, banded rates in accordance with the distance to the general area of destination, and the **LRI** (Airport Administration) **minibus service**. This efficient and popular service takes several passengers together to their individual destinations in the city. A per capita flat rate from each terminal applies whatever the distance. The extra time involved is balanced by the fact that for up to three people, the cost is less than that of a taxi. For the return journey, the minibus will collect you from anywhere in the city for the same fee (tel: 157–8555). These LRI services are regular and available with relatively little delay. Contact the well-advertised information desk in the arrivals lounge. English spoken.

Public transport services also operate from the airport. A **bus service** runs every 30 minutes non-stop to the central bus station in Deák tér. The fare, payable on the bus, is fixed, and being to one destination only is lower than that of the LRI service.

The cheapest way to get from the airport to anywhere in the city is by normal service **bus red 93** to its terminus, which in turn is the Kőbánya-Kispest terminus of metro line 3. Trains run from here every few minutes to the centre.

The Vienna option. Vienna is only 250km from Budapest. Given the fact that cheap return flights from London to Vienna are often only half the cost of an Apex return to Budapest, it may be worth considering flying to Vienna. Of course, financial savings have to be weighed against greater total journey time.

Vienna airport is on the Budapest side of the city and the Vienna–Budapest coaches call at the airport. There are only three scheduled coach services daily, but an alternative is to travel into central Vienna and get the train. There is an express bus service and a train service from the airport to the centre. Several trains daily, mostly from Westbanhof, some from Südbanhof, leave Vienna for Budapest on a journey which takes under 3½hrs.

A third, though more expensive way, is to travel from Vienna to Budapest on the river Danube. From May to September a hydrofoil service operates up to three times a day. However, it is not quite as romantic as river travel can often be. There is little to see until the beautiful Danube Bend area north of Budapest, and in any case these fast-moving vessels are enclosed and visibility is limited.

Information about current timetables of the above Vienna–Budapest services should be available by post from the Hungarian Tourist Board, A-1010 Vienna 1, Parkring 12. III Stiege, 6 Stock.

By rail
There are daily departures from London's Victoria station of a number of trains to Budapest. The total journey takes about 30hrs and the basic option is between a long crossing via Ostend and then a change of trains in Vienna, and a shorter

crossing via Calais and a change of stations in Paris. Trains arrive at the Keleti (Eastern) Railway Station, which is on red metro line 2.

There is a faster option via Ostend which reduces the journey by about 4hrs, though this involves changes at Cologne, Frankfurt and Vienna.

In terms of price, the rail journey compares unfavourably with flying. The basic return ticket (not including extras like a sleeping compartment), while less than the full air fare, costs more than is usually paid for a return Apex air ticket. Exceptions include the cost of a child's ticket and, on the slower Ostend route, the price for a Euro Youth ticket holder. The latter may work out cheaper than an air fare.

Rail travel does have the advantage of being able to break the journey in Paris, Vienna or elsewhere.

For detailed information on timetabling and pricing structure, contact International Rail Centre, Hudsons Place, Victoria, London SW1V 1JY, tel: 0171–834 2345.

There are no delays for passport and customs control; these are carried out on the train as it makes its way across the Hungarian frontier.

By coach

There are five departures a week from Victoria Coach Station in London. Two are direct, via Vienna, and take about 26hrs (less than the train!) and three are connecting services, which take longer and involve a wait in Frankfurt. In the summer there are daily services, but only three of these are direct, via Vienna.

Travelling by coach for such a length of time may not be very comfortable, but it is certainly competitive on price. A return ticket costs just over half the price of the Apex air fare.

Coaches stop at the Hungarian border for passport and customs control, but usually this involves only a small delay. They arrive at Erzsébet tér in central Budapest, next to the Deák tér metro interchange.

For further information contact Eurolines, 52 Grosvenor Gardens, London SW1, tel: 0171–730 8235 or 01582-404511 or any National Express agent throughout the country.

By car

Budapest is approximately 1600km (1000 miles) from the Channel. The most direct motorway route involves heading for Cologne (Köln) and then Frankfurt, followed by Würzburg, Nürnburg, Regensburg and Passau, then across Austria past Linz and, after taking the southern ring A21 motorway, which is clearly marked for Budapest, through Vienna (via a relatively easy urban motorway network). From there it is motorway all the way to Budapest, via the main border crossing at Hegyeshalom.

An alternative is to leave the A21 before Vienna at Alland and head for Baden and then the (well-signposted) border crossing at Klingenbach, a few kilometres beyond which is the large Hungarian town of Sopron. From here roads 84 and 85 lead to the Hegyeshalom–Budapest M1 motorway just before Győr.

This alternative route adds no great distance, but it does take longer since most of it is non-motorway. The advantages, in addition to a break from tedious motorway driving, are that you avoid the danger of delays at the busy Hegyeshalom crossing and you can stop to see Sopron, one of Hungary's attractive historic towns.

Just before the M1 reaches Budapest, at the Budaörs service area, there is a Budapest Tourist Information office where maps of the city and other information can be obtained.

Although officially a British registration plate is enough proof of third-party insurance, a Green Card is advisable. Motorists should also take their driving licence *and* registration document, as border checks sometimes include demands for proof of ownership.

In general, however, even at Hegyeshalom, crossing into Hungary by car is problem-free and usually takes little time.

Speed limits are 120km/hr on motorways, 80km/hr on other roads, and strictly 50km/hr in all built-up areas (villages, towns and the capital) even though usually there are no signs to this effect.

Outside built-up areas, the use of headlights is compulsory **at all times of the day**. Use of front seat belts is compulsory at all times; use of rear seat belts is compulsory outside built-up areas. Children less than 150cm tall may not travel in the front seat. There is a total ban on alcohol for drivers in Hungary.

Petrol stations are abundant in Hungary, and lead-free fuel and diesel are readily available. Service agents of all Western car manufacturers can be found in Budapest, though it may be wise to bring essential spares in case of breakdown.

The Hungarian Automobile Club (Autóklub) has a reciprocal arrangement with foreign automobile associations. Members of the latter can avail themselves of the former's emergency breakdown service, which for minor matters is likely to be free (emergency telephone number in Budapest—252–8000; elsewhere—freephone 088). In the case of more serious problems, letters of credit will be required or a fee will be charged, but the Autóklub is reliable and its rates are reasonable. Its paying services can be used by anyone, whether a member of a foreign association or not.

In the case of an accident involving another vehicle, it is wise to wait for the arrival of the police. A declaration from them may be necessary and/or useful in subsequent insurance proceedings.

Where to stay

The standard of top-grade hotels in Budapest is high, on a par with international norms. At the same time, accommodation is not cheap. For a double room in a top-grade, 4–5 star hotel you can expect to pay anything between £125 and £200 per night. The range of medium-priced, 3-star hotels is somewhat limited, but prices are lower. A double room costs a minimum of £60, but could be twice that amount.

The relative lack of good quality, cheaper hotels has been balanced in recent years by the appearance of small, privately-run family hotels and guest houses (*panziók*). Facilities are limited but standards are good and prices relatively low at £40–£60 for a double room. Few are centrally located, but many are found in pleasant areas of the Buda Hills. Some 2-star and other hotels are more central and can be cheaper even than guest houses.

The cheapest forms of accommodation are rented rooms in a private flat or house, youth hostels and camp sites.

Booking accommodation in advance is advisable, particularly in the high season. Independent travellers can write to or fax the hotels for a brochure and quotationand/or booking. It may be worth comparing the prices by this method with those charged by agents who are able to book accommodation for individuals. One company in the US which can do this, and handle Canadian enquiries, is Tradesco Tours, 6033 West Century Boulevard 670, Los Angeles, CA 90045, tel: (310) 649–5808; toll free: (800) 833-3402 (US), (800) 488–4321 (US and Canada); fax: (310) 649–5852.

In Budapest itself there is as yet no established central room reservation bureau. Individuals arriving without booked accommodation can phone or simply turn up at a hotel (in the high season phoning first is best).

Some Budapest travel agents offer a room booking service, though this may involve paying more than organising it yourself. One where you are not likely to pay more, and which is open on Saturday and Sunday, is To-Ma Tour, V. Október 6 u. 22, tel: 153–0819.

The system for booking a private room is better organised and a number of agents offer this service (see below).

A selection of hotels

Top-grade hotels
Atrium Hyatt Hotel, 1051 Budapest, Roosevelt tér 2, tel: 266–1234, fax: 266–8271. By the Pest end of the Chain Bridge.

Budapest Marriott, 1052 Budapest, Apáczai Csere János u. 4, tel: 266–7000, fax: 266-5000. Near Elizabeth Bridge, facing the river, all rooms with a view. Budapest's first large modern hotel, completely revamped in the mid 1990s.

Forum Hotel, 1052 Budapest, Apáczai Csere János u. 12–14, tel: 117–8088, fax: 117–9808. On the Pest embankment, near the Chain Bridge.

Gellért Hotel, 1111 Budapest, Szent Gellért tér, tel: 185-2200, fax: 166–6631. Celebrated old hotel adjoining famous Art Nouveau baths and spa complex of same name. Buda end of Liberty (Szabadság) Bridge.

Grand Hotel Corvinus Kempinski, 1051 Budapest, Erzsébet tér 7–8, tel: 266–1000, fax: 266–2000. One of the city's newest hotels. A large, post-modern design in the heart of Pest, though with no river view.

Grand Hotel Hungaria, 1074 Budapest, Rákóczi út 90, tel: 322–9050, fax: 268–1999. A large hotel very near the Eastern Railway Station.

Helia Hotel, 1133 Budapest, Kárpát u. 62–64, tel: 270–3277, fax: 270–2262. Facing Margaret Island on the Pest side. A modern thermal, spa hotel with facilities for people with disabilities.

Hilton Hotel, 1014 Budapest, Hess András tér 1–3, tel: 175–1000, fax: 156–0285. Next to the Matthias Church in the Castle District, overlooking the Danube with superb views.

Korona Hotel, 1053 Budapest, Kecskeméti u. 14, tel: 117–4111, fax: 118–3867. A newish hotel conveniently situated by Kálvin tér.

Radisson Béke Hotel, 1067 Budapest, Teréz krt 43, tel: 132–3300, fax: 153–3380. Turn-of-the-century, but modernised. On the busy ring boulevard.

Ramada Grand Hotel, 1138 Budapest, Margitsziget, tel: 132–1100, fax: 153–3029. Peaceful, elegant former late-19C sanatorium at north end of Margaret Island.

3-star and medium-price hotels

Agro Hotel, 1121 Budapest, Normafa út 54, tel: 175–4011, fax: 175–6164. Largish hotel some distance from the centre, but in the very attractive Normafa region of the Buda Hills, with fine views.

Astoria Hotel, 1053 Budapest, Kossuth Lajos u. 19, tel: 117–3411, fax: 118–6798. Historic city-centre hotel retaining its pre First World War charm.

Central Hotel, 1063 Budapest, Munkácsy Mihály u. 5–7, tel: 321–2000, fax: 322–9445. Experience something of the old days. This is a former government guest house for visiting dignitaries.

Dunapart Hotel, 1011 Budapest, Szilágyi Dezső tér, Alsó rakpart, tel: 155–9244, fax: 155–3770. A small floating hotel on the river, with fine views of parliament and the passing river traffic.

Hotel Carmen, 1145 Budapest, Amerikai út 23, tel:/fax: 252–4976. Small, new hotel on the Pest side with good transport links to the centre.

Nemzeti Hotel, 1088 Budapest, József krt 4, tel: 269–9310, fax: 114–0019. 1890s family hotel, restored some years ago.

Panorama Hotel, 1121 Budapest, Rege út 21, tel: 175–0522, fax: 175–9727. Built hunting-lodge style in 1938. In the Buda Hills at the upper terminus of the cog-wheel railway.

Petneházy Country Club, 1029 Adyliget, Feketefey u. 2–4, tel: 176–5992, fax: 176–5738. Modern chalet complex in green setting on the city boundary. Riding, swimming and tennis opportunities.

Taverna Hotel, 1052 Budapest, Váci u. 20, tel: 138–4999, fax: 118–7188. Modernish hotel on the city's most fashionable shopping street.

Victoria Hotel, 1011 Budapest, Bem rakpart 11, tel: 201–8644, fax: 201–5816. Modern private hotel on the Buda embankment.

Walzer Hotel, 1124 Budapest, Németvölgyi út 110, tel: 267–1300, fax: 267–1297. New, attractive, small hotel on the Buda side.

Low-price and 2-star hotels

Budai Sport Centrum, 1121 Budapest, Jánoshegyi út. Postal address: 1536 Budapest 114. Pf. 272, tel: 202–4397, fax: 156–7167. In the woods between Normafa and János Hill. Modern hotel high above the city with grand views.

Griff Hotel, 1113 Budapest, Bartók Béla út 152, tel/fax: 166-7276. This is the centre of the Eravis chain of low-priced, mainly 2-star hotels, which have been converted and modernised from former workers' hostels.

Hotel Garden, 1021 Budapest, Tárogató út 2–4, tel/fax: 274–2008. Occupies part of what was formerly a trade union school accommodation. On the Buda side.

Lejtő úti Pihenő, 1124 Budapest, Lejtő út 28, tel/fax: 166–5848. Guest house of the Ministry of Agriculture, now open to the public. Comfortable rooms; swimming pool and tennis courts in pleasant grounds.

MEDOSZ Hotel, 1061 Budapest, Jókai tér 9, tel: 153–1700, fax: 132–4316. Another former trade union accommodation, centrally located in Pest.

Professzorok Háza, 1146 Budapest, Ajtósi Dürer sor 19–21, tel: 251–3563, fax: 251–5332. Former high school and accommodation of the old (communist) Party. A fair number of services. Near the City Park.

'Motorway' hotels

The following are conveniently located for motorists approaching Budapest from the west on the M1 motorway.

Etap Hotel, 2045 Törökbálint, Tó u. 1, tel/fax: (23) 337–736. Basic but clean. Standard, low price for room sleeping up to three. About 14km from the centre. Take the Törökbálint exit on the M1.

Forte Agip Hotel, 2040 Budaörs, Agip u. 2, tel: (06–23) 313–500, fax: (06–23) 313–505. New, 3-star hotel and conference centre at the Budaörs service area, just before the M1 reaches the city boundary (after the M1/M7 junction). Tourist information office nearby.

Private hotels and guest houses

Beatrix Panzió1021 Budapest, Széher út 3, tel/fax: 176–3730. Award-winning guest house, near Buda's main artery of Szilágyi Erzsébet fasor.

Budai Hotel, 1121 Budapest, Rácz Aladár u. 45–47, tel: 209–1721, fax: 186–8987. Unlike most of the *panziók* this has its own restaurant. Magnificent view from the terrace.

Buda Villa Panzió, 1125 Budapest, Kiss Áron u. 6, tel/fax: 176–2679. Family atmosphere.

Hotel Villa Korda, 1025 Budapest, Szikla u. 9, tel: 269–7270, fax: 168–4001. 'Neo-Classical' villa—built in 1992.

Molnár Panzió, 1124 Budapest, Fodor u. 143, tel/fax: 209–2974. Most rooms with balcony and good view.

UhU Villa, 1025 Budapest, Keselyű u. 1/a, tel/fax: 176–3876. Set in very pleasant, quiet, wooded surroundings.

Vadvirág Panzió, 1025 Budapest, Nagybányai út 18, tel: 275–0200. Quiet location not far from Pasaréti tér.

The Association of *Panziók* in Budapest issues a coloured brochure listing about 30 private guest houses. This should be available from Hungarian Tourist Offices abroad and from Tourinform in Budapest.

Panzió Centrum, 1125 Budapest, Szarvas u. 24 (tel: 176–0057, fax: 201–9186) has an overlapping list and also undertakes bookings.

Youth hostels

A number of organisations run networks of youth hostels in the summer, which are often used as student residences at other times. Backpackers arriving by train, however, should be wary of people touting for business at the stations. Standards vary enormously. It is better to make your way to Tourinform (see p 23) for wider information about hostels.

Information and a catalogue can be obtained in advance from the Hungarian Youth Hostel Federation, 1065 Budapest, Bajcsy-Zsilinsky út 31.II.3. PO Box 483 Budapest 1396, tel/fax: 131–9705.

Private rooms

One of the cheapest forms of accommodation and often a way of meeting Hungarians involves renting a room in a private flat—what in Hungary is called the 'paying guest service' (*Fizetővendég Szolgálat*). Bookings can be made at a number of places, including: Budapest Tourist, Baross tér 3, near the Eastern Railway Station; Cooptourist, in the underpass by the Western Railway Station; IBUSZ, Petőfi tér 3 (Ferenciek tere stop on the blue metro), open 24hrs a day.

Camping sites

By west European standards, camping sites in Budapest are pretty poor and you are hard pressed to find anything resembling, for example, a good French site. Nevertheless, some sites have particular attractions.

All sites listed below have hot water and electricity connections. Seasonal opening times may vary, depending on the weather. 'Facilities' refers to toilets, showers, washing and washing-up provisions. (Road distances are from Deák tér in central Pest.)

Római Camping, 1031 Budapest, Szentendrei út 189 (9.5km), tel: 168–6260, fax: 250–0426. Open all year. The largest site (over 2000 people). Flat, well-worn grassy areas, lots of shade under the trees. Restaurant and shop on site, plenty of facilities but on the unclean side, suffering from age and over-use. Main advantages are easy access on the HÉV railway, and free use of the site's swimming pool.

Mini Camping, 1039 Budapest, Királyok útja 257 (13.5km). Open May–Sept. A small (120 people), grassy, well cared for, flat site near the Danube. Minimal shade. Few, but clean facilities. Attractive local restaurant attached.

Hárs-Hegyi Camping, 1138 Budapest, Hárs-hegyi út 7 (8km), tel: 115–1482, fax: 176–1912. Open Easter to mid-October. Medium-sized (over 400 people). In the Buda Hills, very shaded, grassy, terraced. Shop, restaurant on site. Facilities plentiful and clean, though suffering from old-age, like the whole site.

Zugligeti 'Niche' Camping, 1121 Budapest, Zugligeti út 101 (7.5km), tel: 156–8641. Open March to mid-November. A small (250 people), very pretty site, tucked into a niche in the Buda Hills by the foot of the Libegő (Chair Lift). Friendly reception. Facilities few, but very clean and well-tended, as is the whole site. Stony ground-level for caravans, with (rather cramped) tent spaces formed in terraces up the steep hillside. The restaurant is in a very attractively restored former tram terminus.

Csillebérci Camping, 1121 Budapest, Konkoly-Thege Miklós u. 21 (10km), tel: 156–5772, fax: 175-9327. Open mid-April to October. A small, flat, grassy area (24 pitches) set aside in the massive former Pioneers' (youth) camp at the top of Széchenyi-hegy in the Buda Hills. Reasonably clean, if rather old facilities. Camping area quiet, with some shade, though the rest of the complex can be quite lively with visiting youths and schoolchildren. Access to all services, including shop, restaurant and well-kept, open-air pool.

Rosengarten Camping, 1106 Budapest, Pilisi u. 7 (8km). Open all year. A small (150 people), flat, well-tended, grassy site, with limited shade. Bar but no restaurant or shop. Facilities few, but clean. Friendly reception.

Metró-Tenisz Camping, 1162 Budapest, Csömöri út 158 (10km), tel: 163–5584. Open Apr–Oct. Flat, with 50 pitches and some shade. Restaurant and bar on site, plus popular local restaurant next door. Several tennis courts and pool tables available. Adequate, clean facilities.

Getting Around

Orientation

Orientation in Budapest is relatively easy. The river Danube splits the city in two—Buda is the hilly side to the west of the Danube, Pest is the flat side to the east. A good starting point for any first-time visitor is the Fishermen's Bastion on Castle Hill, from where the general layout of the city can be seen.

Budapest is divided into 23 districts. District I is the Castle and neighbouring Water Town areas of Buda. The inner city on the Pest side is District V. This is surrounded by districts XIII, VI, VII, VIII and IX, running from north to south roughly along the line of the Great Boulevard. The middle figures of the four-figure post code of addresses indicates the district (thus 1107 is District X, 1056 is district V, etc.).

Even street numbers invariably ascend on the left-hand side, odd numbers on the right. The lower numbers usually begin either from the Danube end, or, in Pest, from the end nearest the Kossuth Lajos utca/Rákóczi út axis. Street name plates give the district (*kerület*) with a Roman numeral and usually indicate the street numbers in the block to which they are attached. The numbers generally refer to a whole building and do not differentiate between shops which might occupy the ground floor and have separate entrances.

Familiarity with the location of certain key places is useful for orientation purposes—Moszkva tér and Batthyány tér in Buda; Deák tér, Ferenciek tere and the Great Boulevard in Pest.

There is a map of the city in most metro stations. Free, small, city-centre maps are available at Tourinform and often at hotel reception desks. More detailed maps of Budapest are available from many booksellers and at specialist map shops at VI. Bajcsy-Zsilinszky út 37 and VII. Nyár u. 1. Two recommended map-books are Cartographia's *Budapest Atlas* and Officina Nova's *Euro-city Budapest*. Both are handily spiral-bound and have good indexes. The former shows street numbers. The latter has an easier-to-see scale, but is larger and a bit more unwieldy.

Public transport

Public transport in Budapest is excellent by international standards. Buses, trams, trolleybuses, three metro lines and four suburban electric railway lines (HÉV) criss-cross the city providing an efficient and fairly swift way of getting about. Services are frequent and still relatively cheap compared to other major capital cities.

On public transport a ticket (*jegy*) is required for each journey or part of journey (i.e. when changing from bus to bus, or to tram, or from one metro line to another, a new ticket is required). There is only one type of single-journey ticket used for all means of transport.

Tickets, purchased in advance from metro stations and some newsagents and tobacconists, have to be validated in the punching machines on buses, trams, trolleys and on the yellow (No. 1) underground. With the red (No. 2) and blue (No. 3) metro lines, the punching machines are at the top of the escalator or before entering the platform.

Cost-saving day (*napi*), 3-day, week (*heti*), 2-week and monthly (*havi*) passes are available, and the bloc purchase of single tickets is also relatively cheaper. Photos are required for the weekly tickets and all passes of longer duration. Children up to six travel free if accompanied, but other concessions for young people are officially not available for foreigners.

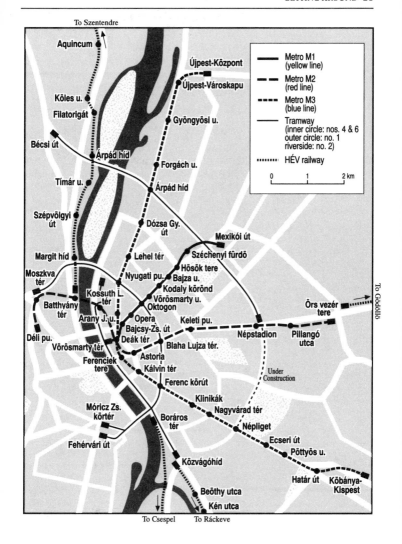

To Szentendre

Aquincum

Újpest-Központ

Újpest-Városkapu

Köles u.

Filatorigát

Gyöngyösi u.

Bécsi út

Árpád híd

Forgách u.

Tímár u.

Árpád híd

Szépvölgyi út

Dózsa Gy. út

Mexikói út

Margit híd

Lehel tér

Széchenyi fürdő

Moszkva tér

Nyugati pu.

Hősök tere

Bajza u.

Kossuth L. tér

Kodaly körönd

Batthyány tér

Vörösmarty u.

Oktogon

Örs vezér tere

Arany J. u.

Opera

Keleti pu.

Déli pu.

Bajcsy-Zs. út

Deák tér

Népstadion

Pillangó utca

Vörösmarty tér

Blaha Lujza tér.

Ferenciek tere

Astoria

Kálvin tér

Under Construction

Ferenc körút

Klinikák

Nagyvárad tér

Móricz Zs. körtér

Boráros tér

Népliget

Fehérvári út

Ecseri út

Pöttyös u.

Közvágóhíd

Határ út

Kőbánya-Kispest

Beöthy utca

Kén utca

To Csepel   To Ráckeve

To Gödöllő

| Metro M1 (yellow line) |
| Metro M2 (red line) |
| Metro M3 (blue line) |
| Tramway (inner circle: nos. 4 & 6 outer circle: no. 1 riverside: no. 2) |
| HÉV railway |

0   1   2 km

Services start around 04.30 and finish around 23.30. Some all-night bus and tram services operate, but not many. Trams and metro trains stop automatically at every stop, but on buses and trolleys you have to press the button near the door when you want to get off. If faced with a choice between a bus and a tram, choose the latter as trams rarely get held up by city-centre traffic.

The three metro lines meet only at one place—Deák tér.

Maps showing the transport network (*tömegközlekedési hálózat*) are available at some metro stations, but many ordinary city maps also show transport routes. In addition, most metro stations have large maps of the city showing the transport network. Bus and tram stops often have a plate listing the stops on the route.

Smoking is forbidden on all means of public transport.

Taxis

As overcharging of foreigners is not uncommon it is advisable only to use taxis with a recognisable taxi company logo, and which display the company's rates both on the dashboard and on one of the rear windows. Taxis which lurk near hotels waiting for business are best avoided unless money is no object. The usual percentage for tipping applies and most drivers are happy to give an official receipt (*számla*) which includes the tip.

Taxis are plentiful in Budapest and can usually be hailed on the steet or picked up at one of the many taxi ranks without problem. Taxis usually arrive within 5–10 minutes of a telephone call.

Four well-established companies are: **Budataxi** 129–4000; **City Taxi** 211–1111; **Fő taxi** 222–2222; **Volántaxi** 166–6666.

Driving

Visitors arriving by car are strongly advised to leave their vehicles where they are staying and to use the excellent public transport system. There are a number of 'park and ride' facilities around the centre, but these are generally small and are full after the morning rush hour.

Driving in Budapest is not easy (lane discipline, for example, often appears non-existent) and parking is a major problem in the centre. Crossing from Buda to Pest and vice-versa involves using one of the road bridges. These act as traffic funnels on each side, and delays and congestion are endemic.

Unless otherwise stated the speed limit for motorists in the city is 50km/hr. There are some clearly marked roads where the limit is 70km/hr.

Cars may only approach Margaret Island from Árpád Bridge at the northern end, and then only as far as the car park at the tip of the island. Cars are only allowed through the Castle District with a permit.

There are several car-hire companies in Budapest, including: **Avis**, V. Szervita tér 8, tel: 118–4685; **Budget**, Hotel Mercure Buda, I. Krisztina krt 41–43, tel: 156–6333; **Hertz/Fő Taxi**, VII. Kertész u. 24–28, tel: 322–4636; **Budapest Rent A Car**, V. Roosevelt tér 5, tel: 117–2129. These and other firms also have vehicles which can be hired at the airport.

Cycling

Cycling is becoming increasingly popular in Budapest, but in the centre it is still a dangerous activity due to pollution, volume of traffic and driving habits. In recent years the number of designated cycle lanes in the city has increased noticeably, but these still only represent a tiny proportion of the total road network. Maps of the cycle network are available in bookshops.

Margaret Island is one place in the centre where cycling is pleasurable and relatively safe—private vehicles are not allowed on the island. Bicycles, tandems and four-wheel pedal carriages are available for hire in the summer towards both ends of the island.

Finding things out

Tourinform

This is the central tourist information office of the Hungarian Tourist Board. Situated in the centre of Pest, 50m from Deák tér, at V. Sütő u. 2 (tel: 117–9800, fax: 117–9578, telex: 223086; postal address: 1364 Budapest, PO Box 185), it is open every day 08.00–20.00 (Oct–Mar early closing Sat and Sun at 15.00).

Tourinform deals with all tourist enquiries concerning both Budapest and the rest of Hungary. Staff members speak several languages, including English, and are invariably helpful and efficient. Their services are highly recommended for any visitor seeking information. Enquiries can be made in person, or by phone, fax, telex or even by post from abroad.

Budapest Tourist Information

This is the overall name of the tourist information offices (two at the time of writing) of the Budapest municipality, which handle enquiries related to Budaest only. English is spoken. There are plans for further offices, to be linked by computer to a central accommodation booking service. The present locations are: at the Budaörs service area, by the Agip–Hugaria complex on the M1 motorway (which approaches Budapest from the west), just before it reaches the city limits, tel/fax: (23) 313–518 and inside the Western Railway Station at Nyugati tér (to the left as you enter from the street), tel: 132–0597. Both offices are open 09.00–18.00.

English-language publications

Budapest has three locally published, English-language weekly newspapers—*Budapest Week*, *The Budapest Sun* and *Budapest Business Journal*. The first two contain, apart from general news, extensive listings of current events, exhibitions, performances, films in English, restaurants, night-spots, clubs, etc. Both are available in city-centre newsagents and in hotel shops.

The Hungarian Tourist Board issues two, free, monthly listings publications. *Budapest Panorama* has listings of concerts, opera, ballet, theatre and music performances, visual arts, museums and exhibitions, as well as a guide to restaurants, casinos, etc. in the city. Published in English, German, Italian and French, it is available in hotels and tourist offices. *Programme in Hungary* is similar, though it covers the whole country and includes information about sports events. Published free, in English and German.

Where Budapest is a free monthly entertainment, shopping and restaurant guide with an accent on upmarket locations. It also contains feature articles about the city and its culture. Distributed widely in hotels throughout Budapest.

Budapest Pocket Guide is a quarterly pocket-size guide containing consise practical information for tourists and business travellers on a wide range of topics. It is distributed free on Malév flights, at Ferihegy airport, at airline offices, hotels and travel agencies.

Insider's Hungary, ed. Peterjon Cresswell (Budapest Week/Citimédia) is packed with practical information and insights into everyday life. A very useful work for both short and long stay visitors.

Readers of Hungarian can turn to *Pesti Müsor*, a comprehensive weekly listings magazine covering Budapest and provincial towns, on sale at newsagents, and *Pesti Est*, a free, weekly listings brochure for events in Budapest, available at Tourinform, various night spots and other locations.

Useful addresses

Embassies
Australian Embassy, VI. Délibáb u. 30, tel: 153–4233. **British Embassy**, V. Harmincad u. 6, tel: 266–2888. **Canadian Embassy**, XII. Budakeszi út 32, tel: 275–1200. **US Embassy**, V. Szabadság tér 12, tel: 112–6450/1/2/3/4).

Airlines
Air Canada, XI. Lovas u. 1, tel: 175–4618. **Air France**, V. Kristóf tér 6, tel: 118–0411. **Alitalia**, V. Ferenciek tere 2, tel: 118–6882. **Austrian Airlines**, V. Régiposta u. 5, tel: 117–1550. **British Airways**, VIII. Rákóczi út 1–3, tel: 118–3299. **Delta Airlines**, V. Apáczai Csere János u. 4, tel: 266–1400. **KLM**, VIII. Rákóczi út 1–3, tel: 117–4742. **Lufthansa**, V. Váci u. 19–21, tel: 266–4511. **Malév**, V. Dorottya u. 2, tel: 266–5616. **SAS**, V. Váci u. 1–3, tel: 118–5377. **Swissair**, V. Kristóf tér 7–8, tel: 267-2500.

Travel enquiries
Ferihegy airport terminal 1: Flight information: 157–7155; Lost luggage: 157–7690. **Ferihegy airport terminal 2:** Flight information departures: 157–7000; Flight information arrivals: 157–8000; Lost luggage: 157–8108.

MÁV Hungarian Railways: International enquiries 06.00–20.00: 142–9150, 20.00–06.00: Southern Station 175–6293; Eastern Station 113–6835; Western Station 149–0115. **MÁV ticket office:** VI. Andrássy út 35 (open Mon–Fri 09.00–18.00; Oct–Mar early closing at 17.00), or any station.

Long-distance bus enquiries: Central bus station, V. Erzsébet tér, tel: 117–2562 (Mon–Fri 06.00–19.00).

Travel agents
The following offer a variety of general sightseeing tours in English around the city and its environs. Their services are widely advertised in hotels, travel offices and public places. **Budapest Tourist**, V. Roosevelt tér 5, tel: 117–3555. **Budatours**, VI. Andrássy út 2, tel: 131–1585. **Budavár Tours**, I. Batthyány tér 3, tel: 155–4299. **Cityrama**, V. Báthory u. 22, tel: 112–5424. **IBUSZ**, V. Ferenciek tere 10, tel: 117–7767.

The following offer some special services. **Express Travel** deals with discounts, etc. for people travelling with student, youth or teacher cards: V. Semmelweis u. 4, tel: 117–8600; also at the Eastern Railway Station. **Vista Air Travel** specialises in cheap air tickets from Budapest: VII. Károly krt 21, tel: 269–6032.

Specialist tours
Jewish heritage. Walking and coach tours in English of the old Jewish quarter and other locations with Jewish connections. Contact Chosen Tours, tel: 166–5165 or just turn up for the walking tour at 10.30 any Tues or Fri (Mar–Oct) in front of the Dohány u. Synagogue.

Opera House, VI. Andrássy út 22. Guided tour in English and other languages around this sumptuously decorated building, daily at 15.00 and 16.00, from the door to the side of the main entrance.

Parliament, V. Kossuth Lajos tér. Visitors can only see the rich, neo-Gothic interior in organised groups when MPs are not in session. A number of travel agents organise tours, but you can also turn up individually at those organised (more cheaply) by Parliament itself. Parliamentary schedules permitting, tours in English take place Wed–Sun at 10.00 (in the summer—roughly June–Sept—there are also tours at 14.00). Tours start at entrance XII. Booking is not possible, and it is advisable to turn up early as there is a limit of 50 people per tour (tickets from entrance X).

Vintage train tours. In the summer months at weekends from the city to the Danube Bend. Contact MÁV Nostalgia Tours, V. Belgrád rakpart 26, tel: 117–1665. They also have an office in the Western Railway Station.

General information

Boat trips

A variety of services operate on the Danube in the summer months (generally May–Sept, and even outside this period, depending on the route and operator).

Cruises operated by **MAHART** start from the Pest embankment near Vigadó tér. The standard route is around Margaret Island and up and down the city-centre stretch of the river. There are also scheduled, day and half-day boat trips to the beautiful Danube Bend, calling at various places.

BKV (City Transport Authority) cruises start from the embankment near Petőfi tér and are similar to the standard route described above. BKV also operates longer cruises to Szentendre and back.

Note: cruises are being operated increasingly on a 'commercial' basis by private operators; prices can vary enormously. It is worth comparing the prices, as there is no need to pay 'Western prices', possibly in hard currency, for something which could be much cheaper in forints. Information is usually displayed at the embarkation points. Where possible it is usually cheaper to go for scheduled services.

One of the scheduled services is the BKV-operated river bus (*Hajó vonaljárat*) service. Boats continuously ply the river from Boráros tér in the south to Pünkösdfürdő in the north. Pick-up and set-down points in the city centre are at Gellért tér, Petőfi tér, Batthyány tér and Jászai Mari tér at the Pest end of Margaret Bridge (from here they go northwards calling at Margaret Island, Óbuda Island and other places). Tickets are bought on the spot.

Using this service you can devise your own cruise at a fraction of the normal cost, e.g. take a boat to 'Római-part', walk northwards along this beautiful stretch of the river (where in summer it is always lively with holidaymakers and watersports activities) and return by boat from Pünkösdfürdő.

Bookshops

Bestsellers (V. Október 6 u. 11, tel: 112–1295) is an English-language general bookshop. It has a wide selection, including fiction and a special section on travel writing and guidebooks. Staff are invariably helpful and books can be ordered.

Four other city-centre bookshops which have a range of English-language books, including locally published works about Budapest and Hungary, are listed below. The first three are in central Pest, the fourth is in the Castle District in Buda.

Corvina Bookshop, V. Kossuth Lajos u. 4. **Foreign Language Bookshop**, V. Párisi udvar (the passage between Ferenciek tere and Petőfi Sándor u.). **Libri Bookshop**, V. Váci u. 32. **Litea**, I. Hess András tér 4 (in the courtyard through the passage).

Our Budapest is a series of small books (50–100pp each) published by the city council to popularise knowledge of Budapest, its urban history and architecture. Apart from Hungarian, most are available in English, German and Italian. Individually and collectively they represent one of the best sources of information about the city for foreign visitors. Titles published so far include: Bridges of the Danube; Budapest for Children; The Caves of Buda; Coffee-Houses; Courtyards; Healing Budapest; Industrial Monuments; Neo-Classical Pest; Night Lights; Ornamentation; Palaces of Money; Parks and Forests; Shop Fronts; Springs and Fountains; A Tour of Our Locals; The Turn of the Century; Urban Transportation.

Second-hand bookshops. These often contain a section of books in English, including books about Hungary. Three that do are: **Bibliotéka Antikvárium**, VI. Andrássy út 2; **Központi Antikvárium**, V. Múzeum krt 13–15; **Legenda Antikvárium**, V. Ferenciek tere 3

English-language libraries. **British Council Library**, VI. Benczúr u. 26 (open Mon–Thur 11.00–18.00, Fri 11.00–17.00); **National Foreign Language Library** (*Országos Idegennyelvű Könyvtár*), V. Molnár u. 11. (At the time of writing closed for extensive renovations; due to reopen in the second half of the 1990s.)

Children

This guidebook is not specifically aimed at children or adults with children, but using the index the main places of interest to children can be found. They include: the *Libegő* (chair-lift) to János Hill and the look-out tower there; swimming pools, particularly the Gellért and Palatinus open-air baths, which have wave machines (the latter also has long water chutes as do the Római and Dagály open-air baths); the zoo, circus and fun-fair in the City Park; boat rides on the Danube; Budakeszi Game Park; and Margaret Island for its cycle and pedal vehicle hire, and its small game reserve.

Hungarian museums are not noted for being very child-friendly in their displays, but two small museums offering some hands-on activities are the Postal Museum in Pest and the Telephone Museum in the Castle District. The Palace of Wonders (*Csodák Palotája*) aims to be a genuine, child-friendly, hands-on science museum, but at the time of writing is only at the planning stage (check with Tourinform).

The longest playground slides in Budapest are on Óbuda Island and on the south side of Gellért Hill, above Kelenhegyi út, which is at the side of the Gellért Hotel.

Churches

Outside service times, access to churches is often restricted to the porch by the main entrance. This does not apply, however, to large churches which are major monuments. These are usually open throughout the day.

The following church services in English are held in Budapest: **Scottish Mission Church**, VI. Vörösmarty u. 51. Anglican service on 1st and 3rd Sundays of the month at 11.00; Presbyterian service on 2nd and 4th Sundays at 11.00. **International Baptist Church**, Móricz Zsigmond Gimnázium, II. Törökvész út 48–54. Sundays 10.30. **RC Church of Christ the King**, VIII. Reviczky u. 9. Mass at 11.15 on the last Sunday of the month. **St Elizabeth's RC Church**, VII. Rózsák tere. Mass at 17.00 on the 2nd Sunday. **Jesus Heart Jesuit Church**, VIII. Mária u. 25. Mass every Saturday at 17.00.

Cinemas

Many English-language films are screened in Budapest, often recent releases. Comprehensive listings can be found in the English language newspapers (see 'Finding Things Out' page 23).

Electric current

The voltage in Hungary is 220 volts. British appliances made for 240 volts function normally in Hungary. Sockets are for 2-round-pin plugs and many are not earthed. A standard continental adaptor allows the use of British 13 amp, square-pin plugs. Shavers can be used in either standard shaving sockets or ordinary wall sockets. It may be necessary to file down the inside edge of the shaving plug's pins. This should not affect the use of the appliance on your return home.

Emergencies

Ambulance—tel: 04
Fire Brigade—tel: 05
Police—tel: 07

Theft. In recent years the number of thefts has been rising dramatically, particularly in the crowded tourist areas of central Budapest. Visitors should take special care of their personal possessions when on the street, shopping, etc. Cases of theft and attack can be reported to the Budapest Central Police Station (*Budapest Rendőrfőkapitányság*), V. Deák Ferenc u. 16–18 (by Deák tér metro station).

Lost Property. For property lost on public transport in Budapest: **BKV** (Budapest Transport Authority) VII. Akácfa u. 18, tel: 322–6613; on a flight: **Ferihegy 1** (tel: 157–7690); **Ferihegy 2** (tel: 157–8108).

Health and Medicine. Foreigners in Hungary can receive first-aid treatment and transport to hospital free of charge; generally all other treatment will be charged. With some countries (e.g. the UK), an agreement also allows foreign visitors to receive free emergency health care and emergency dental treatment.

Even if private transport to a hospital is available, it may be wise to ring the emergency ambulance number to ascertain which hospitals are receiving emergency patients that day. Bear in mind, also, that most ambulances in Budapest will have a doctor 'on board'.

Pharmacies (*Gyógyszertár* or *Patika*) can be found throughout the city. The usual system is to queue to place your order, then queue at the cash till to pay, then queue again to collect your items. It can therefore take some time.

The chemists at the following locations are open throughout the night and at weekends with a limited service for emergencies: II. Széna tér 1 (near Moszkva tér); II. Frankel Leó út. 22 (by the Buda end of Margaret Bridge); IX. Boráros tér 3 (Pest end of Petőfi Bridge); IX. Üllői út 121 (Nagyvárad tér metro station); XII. Alkotás u. 3 (by the Southern Railway Station).

Galleries

Recent years have seen the opening of a large number of private art galleries. These are not concentrated in any one area, but are spread throughout the city. Potential purchasers should be aware that in general a work of art more than 50 years old will probably need special export permission—this may not be granted if the work is 'protected', which generally means more than 70–75 years old. Members of the Hungarian Art Dealers' Association should be able to give advice and help with these and related matters. In addition they are pledged to adhere to accepted international art gallery guidelines. Members of the association in Budapest include **Ambiance Galéria**, II. Csalogány u. 13–19; **Artel**, XIII. Pannónia u. 11; **Éri Galéria**, 1250 Bp. I PoB 39; **Kieselbach Galéria**, V. Falk Miksa u. 13; **Körmendi Galéria**, V. Deák Ference u. 15; **Műgyűjtők Galériája**, V. Kossuth Lajos u. 12. Small auctions every Friday afternoon. Large ones every six months. **Műterem Galéria**, II. Kelemen László u. 13; **Nagyházi Galéria**, V. Balaton u. 8; **Piktura Galéria**, XIII. Pannónia u. 22; **Qualitás Galéria**, V. Haris köz 17; **Rózsa Galéria**, I. Szentháromság u. 13. Contemporary Hungarian naive art. **Studio 1900**, XIII. Hegedus Gyula u. 24/b; **TM Galéria**, V. Feherhajó u. 10; **Várfok 14 Mühelygaléria**, I. Várfok u. 14.

Other galleries include **Darvas Galéria**, II. Fillér u. 17–19. Posters; **Dovin Galéria**, V. Haris köz 1; **Éva Bod Studio**, II. Bimbó út 72, ceramic figurines, vases and mosaics; **Erlin Galéria**, IX. Ráday u. 49; **Fiatal Iparmüvészek Stúdiója**, V. Kálmán Imre u. 16, applied arts of young Hungarian artists; **Immo Art Galéria**, V. Deák Ferenc u. 15; **Vár Galéria**, I. Táncsics Mihály u. 17.

Museums

Very few museums are open every day—**most close on Monday**. Most museums operate shorter hours in the low/winter season (roughly Oct–Mar). This can involve closing one or even two hours earlier than in the high/summer season.

Opening times given in the main text are for **summer season** only. Last entrance is usually 30 or even 45 minutes before final closing.

Exhibition texts are occasionally written in English; booklets in English about the displays, however, are often available, but usually have to be requested. (*Van valami a múzeumról angolul?*—Is there something about the museum in English?). Major museums can usually provide an English-speaking guide for a fee, given prior notice.

There is little provision for people with mobility difficulties. Remarks about wheelchair access (w/a) in the text are relative—the general standard is low. However, most major museums and many smaller ones can provide access via various side entrances and/or lifts. It takes organising and may require a helper, but it is worth asking. For transport and other details see **Museums checklist**, p 190.

Post office services

Post offices are normally open on weekdays from 08.00 to 18.00 and on Saturdays from 08.00 to 14.00. Two post offices in Budapest are open 24 hours a day including Sunday—at Teréz krt 51 (near the Western Railway Station) and at Baross tér (on the left-hand side of the Eastern Railway Station). Stamps can often be purchased at tobacconists' shops.

Public phone boxes in Budapest take Ft10 and Ft20 coins, though many are equipped to take phone cards only. These can be purchased in many retail outlets, but the cheapest card at Ft500 is rather expensive and has too many units for the average short-stay visitor (unless you intend to phone abroad for some length of time).

For local telephone calls in Budapest simply dial the number. For calls to anywhere else in Hungary dial 06, wait for the tone, then dial the district code and subscriber's number (though many mobile phone subscribers in Budapest also require 06 first).

To make an international call first dial 00 and wait for the high-pitched steady tone, then dial the country code (44 for Britain, 1 for the USA and Canada, 353 for the Irish Republic, 61 for Australia), the area code and the subscriber's number.

(For dialling Britain the initial zero of the area code is not required.) International calls can also be made through an (English-speaking) operator on 09.

For directory enquiries the ordinary number is 117-0170. An English speaker can usually be found (267-7111 is also for enquiries with an English speaker.)

There are public telefax services at the post offices at VI. Teréz krt 51 and V. Petőfi Sándor u. 17.

airmail	légiposta	stamp	bélyeg
postcard	levelezőlap	telegram	távirat
post office	posta	telephone number	telefonszám

(See pp 182–186 for pronunciation guide and more useful words.)

Public toilets
Public toilets in Hungary are not easily found and, when they are, are not often in a clean condition. It is better to use the toilet facilites in a café, bar or, best of all, in a hotel. A payment of up to 20 forints is usually expected and there is often a saucer or plate by the entrance for this.

Shopping
In general food shops open early, around 06.00 or 07.00 in the morning and stay open until 19.00 or 20.00 in the evening, though there are many small, 24-hour shops (*éjjel-nappal*) throughout the city where food and drink are available.

Other shops tend to open only at 10.00 in the morning and close around 18.00, except on Thursdays when many shops stay open until 20.00. Most shops are closed on Sundays and **on Saturday afternoon after 13.00 or 14.00.** Some food shops, tobacconists and sweetshops are open on Saturday afternoon and Sunday, but not many.

Two major markets in Budapest are the large covered market on Vámház krt, at the Pest end of Liberty Bridge, and the Lehel tér open-air market in the XIIIth district just north of the centre in Pest. The latter is open on Sunday mornings.

There are well-established Hungarian folk-art shops, which sell a variety of gifts and souvenirs, at the following addresses: V. Váci u. 14 (open every day), V. Kálvin tér 5, XIII. Szent István krt 26, and VIII. József krt 78. The Castle District also has a number of shops selling folk items, and in the summer, many street sellers.

Useful words. See pp 182–186 for a pronunciation guide and more useful words.

bookshop	könyvesbolt
butchers	hentesáru/hús bolt
delicatessen	csemege
department store	áruház
food shop	élelmiszer
fruit	gyümölcs
jewellery	ékszer
record shop	lemezbolt
sweetshop	édességbolt
supermarket	közért
tobacconists	trafik/dohánybolt
toiletries and cosmetics	illatszer
vegetables	zöldség

Useful phrases

How much is this please?	Mennyibe kerül?
Can you show me that one?	Megmutatná azt?
I'll take this.	Megveszem.
Is there anything similar?	Van valami hasonló?
Have you got any.....?	Van....?
It's too big/small.	Túl nagy/túl kicsi.

Theatre and concert tickets

Theatre tickets can be obtained in advance from the **Central Theatre Ticket Offices** at VI. Andrássy út 18 (tel: 112–0000) and II. Moszkva tér 3 (tel: 135–9136). Concert tickets for most classical and some pop concerts are available at the **National Philharmonia Central Ticket Office**, V. Vörösmarty tér 1, which is through the glass doors and to the right on the ground floor of the modern building facing the Vörösmarty statue (tel: 117–6222).

Both theatre and concert tickets are also available at **Publika Jegyiroda** in the main IBUSZ office in Ferenciek tere (tel: 118–2430).

Music Mix, V. Váci u. 33 (tel: 117–7736) is a 'one-stop' ticket agency, not only for music events, but for all types of performance and production.

Time

Budapest is on Central European Time, six hours ahead of New York and Ottawa, nine hours ahead of Los Angeles, one hour ahead of London, but at the same time as the rest of western Europe. The clocks change one hour forward on the last weekend in March and one hour back on the last weekend in September.

Tipping

Conventions regarding tipping are similar to those in other countries, i.e. taxi drivers, porters, waiters and waitresses etc. (though see page 35 for tipping in restaurants). The standard amount is 10–15 per cent.

VAT

There is value added tax (ÁFA) on many items in Hungary. The standard rate is 25 per cent. Foreign citizens purchasing items for personal export may be able to reclaim the VAT, but the minimum retail price for a single item must be Ft25,000, and the tax cannot be reclaimed for works of art or antiques.

The simplest way to reclaim VAT involves shopping in an outlet displaying a tax free shopping sign. Such shops should be able to supply a leaflet in English explaining the process. This involves filling in a form in the shop (passport will be required), and getting the form stamped at the airport or border on leaving, where the goods in question will have to be shown to the customs.

Cash can be refunded on the spot, which in most cases would then involve immediate conversion into hard currency, as the forint is not convertible abroad and there are low limits concerning the amount of forints which can be taken out of the country! VAT refunds on purchases made by credit card can be made by crediting the card account.

Wheelchair access

Hungary is not at the forefront of countries making provision for people with disabilities. Although ramps do exist at certain places where there are steps, by and large public buildings and facilities in Budapest are poor for wheelchair access (abbreviated as w/a in the text).

Hungarian food

By Katalin Rácz

The most common misconception about Hungarian cuisine is that most dishes look red due to the enormous quantity of paprika used in cooking, and that you can hardly stand up after a meal because it has been heavy due to the use of lard. Neither describes the true nature of Hungarian food. Lard has been almost completely driven out of the kitchen as a result of health-conscious thinking and the realisation that pure sunflower oil, something which Hungary is so rich in, replaces lard very well.

When properly used, paprika is the finest and most delicious of spices. It gives colour and aroma to reputed dishes such as goulash and paprika chicken, and to various other stews. Paprika, in Hungary, covers a whole range of sweet and hot peppers in fresh vegetable, dried and powder form. The spice is said to have been introduced as a seasoning among the poor by the Turks. According to a 1684 dictionary, its first Hungarian name was Turkish pepper, *török bors*. Paprika seems to be a rare example of a food making its way up rather than down the social ladder.

It was around the mid-19C that paprika found a place in refined cookery. What helped was an invention by the Pálffy brothers of Szeged—the centre of paprika milling today in the south of Hungary—of a machine that stripped paprika fruits of their hot seeds and ribs. These could then be ground separately from the milder dried fleshy part. By mixing the two, different strengths of the spice could be obtained.

Incidentally, a curious fact about paprika, as discovered by Nobel prize-winner Professor Albert Szent-Györgyi (1893–1986), then of Szeged University, is that paprika has five times as much vitamin C as any other fruit.

In addition to the Turkish influence, many national cuisines have left their mark in refining and changing Hungarian specialities; or rather, Hungarians have transformed those dishes and made them into Hungarian specialities. Throughout its history Hungarian cuisine was influenced by the Italians, Turks, Germans, Austrians, Czechs, Slovaks, Serbs and Croats. Italians, for example, in King Matthias's Renaissance court, introduced gnocchi, albeit transformed into several types of large and small dumplings to be served with stew or cooked in soups.

Other quintessential ingredients, in addition to paprika, are onions, sour cream and smoked bacon. It is the way a stew, *pörkölt*, or some soups are made from these otherwise basic ingredients that gives them their distinctive and so characteristic taste in Hungarian cooking. The chopped onion is fried in oil or lard and, when lightly brown, paprika is stirred in. Sour cream is either cooked with the food or added at serving.

Hungarians consume an enormous quantity of meat, mainly pork and beef. However, these days many restaurants serve game, which is plentiful in the country—venison, wild boar and wild duck being the most popular.

Poultry is also popular, as is freshwater fish. Hungary is rich in rivers and lakes so carp, *ponty*, pike-perch, *fogas*, cat-fish, *harcsa*, and trout, *pisztráng*, are widely eaten. As for poultry, goose liver immediately comes to mind. It is best roasted or grilled, cold or hot.

Meat dishes are usually served with potatoes prepared in different ways or rice, and hardly any vegetables unless a side salad is served. Salads differ according to season: in the summer fresh green salads and in the winter a variety of pickles are eaten.

Hungarian meat specialities include stews prepared of veal, pork or beef, *pörkölt*, pan-fried beef served in various ways, *rostélyos*, pork slices in a mushroom and sour cream sauce, *Bakonyi sertéshús*, served with gnocchi, *nokedli*. Among poultry dishes, most popular is chicken paprika, *paprikás csirke*, similar in the way it is prepared to a *pörkölt*, with sour cream and gnocchi. And of course, there is the internationally reputed goulash. *Gulyás*, as it is written in Hungarian, is not a stew as known abroad, but a thick soup of beef and vegetables, which can be a meal in itself.

The origins of *gulyás* go back centuries. It is said that when the Magyars were still nomads, they prepared several meals once they had slaughtered an animal. They cut up the meat and cooked it in a heavy cauldron, which was set up on three sticks over an open fire, until all the juices evaporated. Then they dried the cubes of meat in the sun and stored them. When they wanted to eat they simply added water and other ingredients. This explains why *gulyás* is often served in little cauldrons (*bogrács*) in restaurants, where it is often called *bogrács gulyás*.

Hungarian cooking is a seasonal affair. In the harsh winters, heavier more filling dishes are made, with lots of smoked meat. One of the most popular winter dishes, included in most restaurant menus in the winter, is stuffed cabbage, *töltött káposzta*, made of sauerkraut, dumplings of minced pork and smoked sausage and other smoked meat. Some Hungarian families live on it for days, since it is one of those rare dishes that gets better with time. Hence the Hungarian saying: 'Love is not like stuffed cabbage, once cold you cannot reheat it.'

A typical summer dish makes use of tomatoes and fresh paprika in the form of a special type of yellow pepper. It is called *lecsó*, a Hungarian ratatouille, eaten as it is or added to meat.

Vegetarians can have a hard time in Hungary's meat-eating culture. However, there are plenty of items among traditional Hungarian dishes that are exculsively made of vegetables, such as *főzelékek* (braised vegetables), mushrooms made in different ways, such as *rántott gomba* (mushrooms coated with breadcrumbs and deep fried), *gombapörkölt* (mushroom stew) and r*ántott sajt* (cheese coated in bread-crumbs and deep fried). *Főzelék*, which has always been popular in home cooking and has recently made its way back to fine restaurant tables, is a Hungarian way of making vegetables, whereby chopped, shredded vegetables or pulses are cooked and thickened with roux and/or sour cream.

Lángos, a deep fried yeast dough, which can be found at such places as markets and open-air swimming pools, is eaten at any time.

When it comes to desserts, pride of place goes to the strudel, *rétes*. The idea of building up thin layers of dough is so basic in Middle Eastern cookery that it is assumed it came to Hungary with the Turks. As they say, the filo pastry must be made so transparently thin, that you can read a love letter or a newspaper through it. Late in the spring and in the summer it is filled with sweet or morello cherries, at other times, with apples, cabbage, curd-cheese or ground poppy seed. In restaurants you do not find lavish gateaux on the menu, but strudel, pancakes filled with walnuts, curd-cheese or jam, and curd-cheese dumplings with sour cream.

Hungarians eat lavish creamy gateaux, tortes, tarts and pies in a patisserie, called a *cukrászda*. One such cake is *Dobos torta*, which bears the name of József Dobos, who invented these thin layers of buttery cake, sandwiched between mocha cream, decorated with chopped hazelnuts and covered with a hard caramel glaze.

A meal usually finishes with coffee, which is drunk not only after a meal but on any occasion between meals. Budapest used to be a café society, a tradition being revived today. The beverage was introduced by the Turks, but later the style of making it became similar to that of the Italian espresso. It can be served on its own, *fekete*, or with milk or whipped cream.

Menu, including some Hungarian specialities
Levesek (Soups)

Gulyásleves, Goulash soup—a thick soup made from cubes of beef, carrots, parsnips, celeriac, onions, potatoes and small dumplings. It can replace the main course

Újházi tyúkhúsleves, Hen soup

Gombaleves, Mushroom soup

Jókai bableves, Bean soup à la Jókai, a thick soup made of beans, vegetables such as carrots and parsnips, smoked pork and small dumplings

Hideg meggyleves, Cold morello cherry soup (morello cherries with sour or single cream) is a summer speciality. It is eaten cold, and is light and refreshing

Halászlé, Fish soup—can be eaten as a main course. It is made from an assortment of fresh river fish, carp being the main ingredient

Hideg előételek (Cold appetisers)
Libamáj zsirjában, Roast goose liver

Meleg előételek (Warm starters)
Hortobágyi palacsinta, Pancakes Hortobágy-style are filled with minced pork stew and covered with a sauce made from the stew, mushrooms and sour cream

Gombafejek rántva, Mushrooms coated with breadcrumbs, deep fried and served with rice and tartar sauce

Rántott sajt, Cheese made in the same way as above

Halak (Fish)
Rántott ponty, Fillet of carp fried in breadcrumbs

Süllő roston, Young pike-perch grilled

Fogas szeletek Kalocsa módra, Pike-perch Kalocsa-style is prepared with a sauce of lecsó

Mandulás pisztráng, Trout with almonds

Szárnyasok (Poultry)
Paprikás csirke, Chicken paprika

Rántott csirke, Chicken pieces fried in breadcrumbs

Kacsasült, Roast duck

Pulykamell roston, Grilled breast of turkey

Frissensültek (Freshly made meat dishes)
Rántott borjúszelet, Veal fried in breadcrumbs

Rántott sertésszelet, Pork fried in breadcrumbs

Libamáj roston, Goose liver grilled
Brassói aprópecsenye, Braised pork Brassó-style is thinly chopped pork with spices
Csülök Pékné módra, Roast pork knuckle
Cigánypecsenye, Pan-fried slice of pork with spices
Hagymás rostélyos Pan-fried beef with fried onion rings

Készételek (Ready-made dishes)

Töltött paprika, Stuffed peppers—fresh green peppers stuffed with mince pork and rice, served with freshly made tomato sauce
Töltöttkáposzta, Stuffed cabbage—sauerkraut with meat balls, smoked ham and sausage. Sour cream is added at serving
Marhapörkölt, Beef stew—the cubes of meat are cooked with onion and paprika
Borjúpörkölt, Veal stew
Bakonyi sertéshús, Pork slices Bakonyi-style in a mushroom and sour cream sauce served with gnocchi

Főzelékek (Braised vegetables thickened with roux and/or sour cream)

Karalábéfőzelék, Kholrabi
Parajfőzelék, Spinach
Lencsefőzelék, Lentils

Köretek (Side dishes)

Főttburgonya, Boiled potatoes
Sültburgonya, Roast potatoes
Hasábburgonya, Chips
Rizs, Rice
Rizibizi, Boiled rice with green peas

Saláták (Salads)

Paradicsomsaláta, Tomato salad
Csemegeuborka, Gherkins
Uborkasaláta, Cucumber salad
Ecetes paprika, Pickled hot paprika
Céklasaláta, Beetroot salad

Édességek (Desserts)

Almás rétes, Apple strudel
Cseresznyés rétes, Cherry strudel
Túrós rétes, Strudel with curd cheese and raisin
Gundel palacsinta, Pancakes Gundel-style. Bearing the name of a famous chef and restaurateur, they are filled with walnuts and topped with chocolate sauce. Brandy is poured on and lit when served at the table
Somlói galuska, Cake with walnuts and raisins topped with chocolate sauce and whipped cream

Brief vocabulary

menu	*étlap*	wine	*bor*
waiter	*pincer*	beer	*sor*
tea	*tea*	lunch	*ebéd*
coffee	*kávé*	dinner	*vacsora*
restaurant	*étterem/vendéglő*	the bill, please!	*fizetni!*
		child's portion	*gyermek adag*

Restaurants

There are hundreds of restaurants in Budapest and many types of international cuisine can be found. In addition, there is a plethora of fast-food, pizza and other outlets, including the well-known American chains. Finding something to eat in Budapest is not a problem, even on a limited budget.

The following is a selected list of places, most of which specialise in Hungarian cuisine. Almost all enjoy good reputations for the quality of their food, but it has to be said that opinions can differ greatly on any one restaurant, even in the highest categories.

As the names imply, the categories employed here—exclusive, elegant, medium-price, inexpensive and cheap—reflect both price levels and ambience, though inevitably there is some overlap. At the time of writing it is still true that Western visitors find average restaurant prices in Hungary to be much lower than in the equivalent categories at home.

For eating out in Budapest it is always wise to book in advance, since, despite the great number of restaurants, finding a table on the spot can often be difficult.

The usual rates of tipping (10–15 per cent) apply, but the normal system in Hungary involves giving the tip when paying the bill, rather than leaving it on the table. This is done either by rounding the bill up to include the tip and then saying what you want to pay or asking for change such that the tip is included in the payment. Taking a pencil and paper can be handy for communicating this.

Gypsy music is common in many restaurants, particularly those freqented by tourists. Some people like it, others are not so keen. If you are one of the latter it is wise to check in advance whether there is music or not, or at least to book a table away from the music. The musicians tend to approach tables looking for requests and/or tips. After definite appreciation, and certainly requests, a Ft500–1000 payment is customary. To avoid this, simply maintain a stony appearance.

Unfortunately foreign visitors (and Hungarians) too often complain of being cheated in restaurants ('mistakes' can happen in every category of restaurant). Ways to avoid this include:

—studying the menu carefully and noting the prices;

—checking if garnishes (potatoes, rice, vegetables, etc.) are included in the price of the main meal or not;

—being wary of accepting 'special' recommendations from waiters without knowing the price;

—asking for the drinks menu (*itallap*) in advance (it is often the drinks that boost the bill beyond expectations);

—requesting an itemised bill if there are doubts about the total.

Always take the bill away with you when you leave. Complaints made later after reflecting on the cost are difficult to sustain without proof of what has been paid.

Further information about restaurants, particularly up-market places, can be found in *Where Budapest*, distributed free in hotels, and in the annual *Good Living Guide to Hungary* by gourmet British ex-pat and former restauranteur Sam Worthington—available in bookshops, subjective (like all such listings, including the one below), but a good read with lots of laughs. Readers of Hungarian can turn to *Foglaljon Helyet!*, perhaps the most comprehensive listing available, also obtainable in bookshops.

Exclusive restaurants

Bank Klub Étterem, V. Arany János u. 35, tel: 269–4037. As the name implies a businessperson's venue, with fax and other services on hand.

Fortuna, I. Hess András tér 1, tel: 175–6857. In the 'tourist' Castle District. Gypsy music.

Garvics, II. Ürömi köz 2, tel: 168–3254. 'Organic architecture' in a restaurant.

Gourmet Restaurant, I. Ybl Miklós tér. In the nicely restored Várkert Casino. Dine while watching the punters lose their fortunes.

Gundel, XIV. Állatkerti út 2, tel: 121–3550. Hungary's most famous top-class restaurant. In the City Park, behind the Fine Arts Museum.

Robinson Étterem, XIV. Városligeti tó, tel: 343–0955. On a small island in the City Park lake.

Százéves, V. Pesti Barnabás u. 2, tel: 118–3608. In Budapest's oldest secular Baroque building. Gypsy music.

Vadrózsa, II. Pentelei Molnár u. 15, tel: 135–1118. Dine amidst neo-Baroque surroundings. Garden.

Elegant restaurants

Aranyszarvas, I. Szarvas tér 1, tel: 175–6451. In the Tabán. Game specialities. Gypsy music.

Fészek Klub, VII. Kertész u. 36, tel: 322–6043. Shaded garden courtyard with neo-Renaissance arcades.

Kacsa, I. Fő u. 75, tel: 201–9992. The name means 'duck' and that is the speciality you find.

Kárpátia, V. Ferenciek tere 7–8, tel: 267–0247. In the centre of Pest. Impressive neo-Gothic interior.

Kéhli, III. Mókus u. 22, tel. 188–6938. Several rooms in an old Óbuda house. Bone marrow on toast (*velőscsont*) is a popular speciality.

Kisbuda Gyöngye, III. Kenyeres u. 34, tel: 168–6402. Cosy, homely furnishings. Fine reputation.

Kispesti Halásztanya, XIX.Városház tér 6, tel: 282–9873. Built in 1928 in mock-peasant style. Large garden. Folklore show.

Margitkert, II. Margit u. 15, tel: 212–3157. Courtyards. Gypsy music.

Mátyás Pince, V. Marcius 15 tér 7, tel: 118–1650. Loud gypsy music and loud groups of foreigners in this rather 'touristy' cellar restaurant. Nevertheless, atmospheric, with 'medieval' stained glass and frescoes on historical themes.

Múzeum Kávéház, VIII. Múzeum krt 12, tel: 138–4221. By the National Museum. Originally an old coffee-house. Piano music.

Remiz, II. Budakeszi út 5, tel: 176–1896. Garden and piano music.

Udvarház. On the top of Hármashatár Hill, tel: 188–8780. Terrace and good view.

Verbunkos, XIII. Victor Hugo u. 35, tel: 149–5351. Folklore show.

Medium-price restaurants

Apostolok, V. Kígyó u. 4, tel: 267–0290. Old-established restaurant with attractive interior. Very central.

Borkatakomba, XXII. Nagytétényi út 64, tel: 226–0997. Former wine cellar in the far south of Buda.

Duna Palota, V. Zrínyi u. 5, tel: 117–2790. Large, elegant dining hall, formerly for the exclusive use of the Interior Ministry. Live music shows.

Fenyőgyöngye, II. Szépvölgyi út 155, tel: 168–8144. In a green area at the foot of Hármashatár Hill. Well located to combine with a walk.

Kaltenberg Bajor Söröző, IX. Kinizsi u. 30, tel: 215–9792. Cellar, beer-hall atmosphere. Bavarian specialities, beer brewed on the premises.

Karavella Serfőzde, IX. Ülloi út 95, tel: 215–9283. Bright cellar. Special beer brewed on the premises.

Kerék Kisvendéglő, III. Bécsi út 103, tel: 250–4261. Traditional, old-established, small Óbuda restaurant with good reputation. Excellent violinist. Small courtyard.

Kikelet, II. Fillér u. 85, tel: 212–5444. Garden with fine view.

Király Vendéglő, II. Pusztaszeri út 43/b, tel: 212–1285. Small terrace with some view.

Kulacs, VII. Osvát u. 11, tel: 122–3082. Traditional old Pest restaurant. Former haunt of local resident and self-taught pianist Rezső Seress (1889–1968), whose melody *Gloomy Sunday* became famous in the West and featured countless times in Hollywood films. Today, gypsy band, with occasional female *primás* (lead violinist)—a rarity in Hungary.

Margitszigeti Európa Ház, Margaret Island, tel: 112–9472. Small restaurant on the east side of Margaret Island with attractive terrace view overlooking the Danube.

Margitszigeti Vendégház, Margaret Island, tel: 132–8740. Next to the above, with similar terrace.

Náncsi Néni, II. Ördögárok út 80, tel: 176–5809. Traditional Hungarian cooking with atmosphere to match. Large garden. Very popular and highly reputed. On the outskirts of Buda, but worth the journey.

Tabáni Kakas, I. Attila út 27, tel: 175–7165. Small atmospheric restaurant below the rear of the Royal Palace. Poultry specialities.

Inexpensive restaurants

Ádám Söröző, VI. Andrássy út 41, tel: 142–0358. Popular beer-hall with Prague-style atmoshphere.

Aranyhal, XIV. Thököly út 121, tel: 163–6053. Fish specialities.

Beugró, VI. Szív út 30, tel: 112–2077. Corner bar/restaurant in old Pest neighbourhood.

Bohémtanya, VI. Paulay Ede út 6, tel: 322–1453. Near Deák tér. Very popular. Booking difficult. Just turn up and queue.

Calgary, II. Frankel Leó út. 24, tel: 115–9087. Cosy atmosphere.

Csarnok Vendéglő, V. Hold u. 11, tel: 269–4906. Small, popular, with some outside seating in summer. Behind the US embassy.

Kánaán, XIII. Csanády u. 18, tel: 129–9833. Small but pleasant.

Kis Tölgyfa, II. Budakeszi út 75, tel: 275–1332. On the way to the hills. Garden.

Márkus Vendéglő, II. Lövőház u. 17, tel: 115–1024. By the market near Moszkva tér.

Makk Hetes, XII. Németvölgyi út 56, tel: 155–7330. Small, popular, local family-run restaurant.

Marxim Söröző, II. Kisrókus u. 23, tel: 115–5036. Cellar in an industrial side-street (though central). The theme is a take-off of the old Stalinist days, with posters and slogans to match. Popular with young Hungarians. Mainly pizzas.

Slovak Söröző, V. Bihari János u. 17, tel: 269–3108. Slovak specialities.

Söröző a Szent Jupáthoz, II. Retek u. 16, tel: 212–2929/33. Hot, beer-hall-type cellar by the market near Moszkva tér. Open 24hrs round the clock!

Sport Vendéglő, XVI. Csömöri út 156, tel: 183–3364. Popular local restaurant with good reputation. Some outside seating. A distance from the centre—make sure you find the XVI District's 'Csömöri út'.

Szerb Vendéglő, V. Nagy Ignác u. 16, tel: 111–1858. Serbian specialities. Invariably rather hot and crowded, but with appropriate atmosphere.

Tüköry Söröző, V. Hold u. 15, tel: 269–5027. Basic Hungarian fare. Near the 'Csarnok' listed above.

58-os, 'Niche' Camping, Zugligeti út 101, tel: 156–8641. Attractive, unusual location in a former tram terminal in the city's prettiest camp site, at the bottom of the *Libegő* (Chair-lift). Open-air section.

Cheap eating places

Gresham Borozó, V. Mérleg u. 2. Central, popular lunchtime spot. Closed weekends.

Kádár Étkezde, VII. Klauzál tér 9, tel: 121–3622.

Kisharang Étkezde, V. Október 6 u. 17. Open till 20.00. Weekends lunchtime only.

Lóvasút Étkezde, XII. Alkótás u. 9. By the Southern Railway Station. Open 24hrs.

Mérleg Vendéglő, V. Mérleg u. 6. This and the Kisharang above are between Roosevelt tér and Erzsébet tér.

Minerva Étterem, 7th-floor cafeteria of the Hungarian Chamber of Commerce, V. Kossuth Lajos tér 6–8. By Parliament.

Pince Csárda, II. Török u. 1. Atmospheric cellar. A Hungarian down-market 'Yates's Wine Lodge' with eating section at rear.

Vendéglátóipari Főiskola (College of Catering), V. Alkotmány u. 9–11, tel: 111–4827. Near Parliament. Three pleasant restaurants in the basement open to the public. One self-service, another à la carte, the third with three-course set menu (with choices) at fixed, low price. Eat food prepared by Hungary's future chefs and be served by the country's budding head waiters and waitresses. Excellent value and an experience in itself. Lunchtimes only and only during term times.

Cafés

Pre-1945 Budapest was noted for its coffee-house culture. Hundreds of cafés served as meeting places for writers, artists, poets and journalists. Café society, which was an essential ingredient of Budapest life in the first half of the 20C, virtually disappeared after the Second World War, but in a few places the ambience of old times can still be felt. Such places include the following (further information in the main text):

The New York, VII. Erzsébet krt 9–11. By far the most opulent of the remaining pre-war cafés. Sumptuously decorated interior dating from the 1890s.

Gerbaud, V. Vörösmarty tér 7. Here since 1870, still with turn-of-the-century furnishings inside. Noted for its cakes. Outside seating in the summer on this central square.

Astoria, V. Kossuth Lajos u. 19. Impressive Art Nouveau ground-floor coffee lounge in the pre-1914 hotel of the same name.
Művész, VI. Andrássy út 29. Here since about 1910. A small café, traditionally popular with Budapest's gentlefolk.
Ruszwurm, I. Szentháromság u. 7. The city's oldest café, from the 1820s. Tiny but with original furnishings. Near the Matthias Church in the Castle District.
Angelika, I. Batthyány tér 7. Relatively modern, but the (genuinely old) low-vaulted ceilings and the Baroque-style furnishings provide the atmosphere.

Two popular modern cafés in large hotels generate a certain old-time atmosphere:
Bécsi Kávéház, Forum Hotel, by the Danube near the Chain Bridge. The name means Viennese Coffee-house and the interior has been made to resemble one.
Zsolnay Café, Béke Hotel, VI. Teréz krt 43. Decoration and painted crockery from the famous Zsolnay porcelain factory in the south Hungarian town of Pécs.

The mixing of literary and coffee-house cultures is maintained by some bookshops today which have 'coffee corners'. They include:
The Writers Bookshop, VI. Andrássy út 45. This actually used to be a famous coffee-house called 'The Japan', and was a favourite meeting place of writers and artists. The 'coffee shop' is tiny today, but there are archive photos on the wall of the old days.
Litea Bookshop, I. Hess András tér 4 (through the gateway to the courtyard at the back).
Fővárosi Könyvesbolt, VI. Király u. 50.
Századvég Könyvesbolt, V. Veres Pálné u. 4–6.

Some modern or modernised cafés are contributing to a revival of café society:
Anna Café, V. Váci u. 5.
Café Mozart, VII. Erzsébet krt 36.
Pierrot, I. Fortuna u. 14.
Bécsi Kávéház, V. Váci u. 50.
Talk Talk, V. Magyar u. 12–14.

Cukrászda

This term is sometimes applied to a large café, but usually it refers to a small patisserie, cake shop or confectioner's, where coffee and other drinks are also available. Some have tables where you can sit, others simply a 'stand-up' bar. There are many throughout the city, some with a high reputation. A good sign is if you can see through to a back room where cakes and other delicacies are being made. Then you know that what you see on sale is 'home made' and probably fresh. A common practice is to order cakes to take away and eat at home. Highly recommended are:
Auguszt Cukrászda, II. Fény u. 8. By the market near Moszkva tér. One of the city's oldest such firms, established in 1870. It also has an outlet in Pest at V. Kossuth Lajos u. 14–16.
Daubner Cukrászda, II. Szépvölgyi út 50. Another old-established firm. Some way from the centre, but very popular for its 'take-away' cakes, particularly its 'ice-cream' cakes.
Szalai Cukrászda, V. Balassi Bálint u. 7. Near the north side of Parliament. A family business of many years and a typical Pest *cukrászda*.

Wine and beer bars

Hungary has been a wine-producing and wine-consuming country for centuries. Despite these long traditions, however, there are few genuine wine cellars in Budapest, even though vines were cultivated in the Budapest region right up to the late 19C. The many *borozók* that do exist are rather wine bars, many with a slightly seedy atmosphere.

An exception is the *Borkatakomba* in southern Buda (XXII. Nagytétényi u. 64, tel: 226–0997). This is part of a cellar complex of an old vineyard, though today it functions more as a restaurant.

The Castle District used to have a number of genuine wine cellars, but most of these have been converted into 'tourist-trap' restaurants. Mention can be made, however, of the Hilton Hotel's *Faust Wine Cellar*, which has been fashioned out of the original cellar of a former Dominican monastery.

Beer drinking is a relatively recent phenomenon in Hungarian culture and, unlike Prague for example, Budapest cannot boast of any traditional, atmospheric beer-halls. As with the wine bars, one *söröző* (beer bar) is very much like another.

Recent years have witnessed the appearance of many 'English pubs' in Budapest, but beer drinkers familiar with the genuine article can expect not to be impressed.

Night life

The past few years have seen many clubs, discos and other night spots open in Budapest. It is difficult to guess which will survive in the longer run, but below is a brief, selected list of places which appear to be well established. Almost all of them are in central Pest.

For further information check the listings in the English-language newspapers and other publications mentioned in the section 'Finding Things Out'.

Benczúr Klub, VI. Benczúr u. 28. In the impressive building of the postal workers' social centre. Wide-ranging, regular music events.

Black & White Pizzeria, VII. Akácfa u. 13. Large, bistro-type cellar with blues/jazz.

Crazy Café, VI. Jókai u. 30. Modernised cellar. Several bars with live performances in one of them.

Incognito, VI. Liszt Ferenc tér 3. Popular bar with music.

Fiatal Muvészek Klubja, VI. Andrássy út 112. Rock and pop.

Gyökér Klub, VI. Eötvös u. 46, entrance from Szobi u. International folk and blues. Dancing.

Jazz Café, V. Balassi Bálint u. 25. Live music.

Közgáz D.C., IX. Fővám tér 8. Student disco with regular live performances.

Merlin Jazz Club, V. Gerlóczy u. 4. Live music. Dinner available.

Miniatür, II. Buday László u. 10. Tiny, old piano bar which survived the 'communist' era.

Petőfi Csarnok, in the City Park (Városliget). Old-established large hall for rock and other concerts.

Picasso Point, VI. Hajós u. 31. Bistro/drink bar above, disco below.

Stella Garden, Margaret Island, to the left from the approach link from Margaret Bridge. Open-air concerts. Summer only.

Trocadero Café, V. Szent István krt 15. Latin live and disco music.

Community centres

Budapest has a network of cultural centres (*művelődési házak*) which, apart from a variety of community activities, regularly feature evening concerts and other performances.

They are noted in particular as centres of the 'Dance House' (*Táncház*) movement. This movement has involved a revival over the past 20 years of traditional folk music and dancing. A Dance House is usually completely informal and involves live music, drinking and dancing for all. No skill is required, though some tuition is often available for those who so desire.

Foreign visitors rarely go to such events, but they would find themselves more than welcome and would be able to participate in an authentic experience of popular culture.

Major community centres which regularly feature Dance House and other events are:

Almássy tér Leisure Centre, VII. Almássy tér 6 (in Pest, near Erzsébet krt).

Marcibányi tér Cultural Centre, II Marczibányi tér 5/a (not far from Moszkva tér).

First District Cultural House, I Bem rakpart 6 (near the Buda end of the Chain Bridge).

Folklore Centre, XI. Fehérvári út 47 (in Buda, to the south of Móricz Zsigmond körtér).

Inner City Cultural Centre, V. Molnár u. 9 (in central Pest).

Spa City—swimming pools and baths

Budapest has long been famous for its hot thermal waters and its numerous springs, rich in salts and minerals. Today the city has many pools and baths providing a wide choice, particularly in the summer months (May to mid-September) when the open-air pools are open. These can get very crowded, particularly in high season if the weather is hot, but can be near empty up to mid-June and in early September, before and after the school summer holidays.

The usual system involves leaving your clothes in either a cabin or locker. An attendant locks the door, and gives you a tag. Remember the number on the door for when you return! Swimming caps are compulsory in some baths. Towels, swimming costumes, etc. can be hired at most of the baths.

Swimming in the Danube is not allowed within the city limits.

Gellért Baths (Gellért fürdő)

Probably the most famous of all Budapest's baths and the one that most visitors have heard of. Consequently, during the tourist season it can sometimes get very crowded. The management, sensibly, restricts the inflow, but this can mean queuing for some time just to get in. Nevertheless, worth a visit, if only to view the architectural splendours—the baths is part of the Gellért Hotel spa complex, which was built in Art Nouveau style around the time of the First World War.

Inside there is a 33m pool and a small thermal pool (open all year). Outside there is a large main pool and a small thermal pool (open only in the summer months). Both are suitable for children—the shallow end of the main pool is barely 10cm deep. A popular attraction is the outdoor pool's wave machine. Waves appear on the hour every hour for ten minutes or so.

The sun-bathing areas are part concrete, part grass, though it is not the best place for peace and quiet. There is a terrace restaurant and a buffet, and a small snack bar in the entrance hall.

The ordinary 'swimming' ticket also includes entrance to the Gellért's impressive Art Nouveau and atmospheric Turkish-type thermal pools and steam rooms (segregated areas for men and women, access from the main indoor pool). These can also be visited separately with a cheaper ticket.

The Gellért is also a major treatment centre and has salt baths, mud baths and inhalation rooms, which utilise the rich mineral waters of Gellért Hill's 13 thermal springs. These services are available to visitors and locals alike.

The spa complex is at the Buda end of Liberty (Szabadság) Bridge. Trams 47 and 49 run there from Deák tér, as do tram 19 from Batthyány tér and tram 18 from Moszkva tér. Entrance is to the right of the hotel, from Kelenhegyi út. The labyrinth of steps and corridors makes wheelchair access to the swimming areas impossible.

Palatinus Open-Air Baths (Palatinus stranfürdő)

This complex is situated half-way along the west side of Margaret Island in a beautiful setting of greenery and tall trees. The whole area is massive and can accommodate thousands of people at a time. The main pool, one of the largest in Europe, is huge (over 110m in length) and is as broad as most pools are long! A sight in itself because of its size, it is also relatively safe for children as it is entered all around by a very gentle slope.

In addition there is a separate children's pool, two thermal pools and a pool with a wave machine, which operates on the hour. A further attraction are four enormous spiral slides and one long, straight slide going into a separate pool towards the south end. There are playgrounds at either end of the complex.

Palatinus is a place where you can stay all day, with large, grassy sun-bathing areas (and nude sun-bathing on a roof-top) and lots of buffets and food kiosks, but it does get extremely crowded in the high season. From the terrace of one of the buffets there is a view of the Danube and the Buda Hills.

Swimming caps are not necessary. Wheelchair access is not too bad—once inside, the whole area is flat. Open May to mid-September. Bus 26 from Nyugati tér takes you right there.

Alfréd Hajós Swimming Baths (Hajós uszoda)

Also on the west side of Margaret Island, though nearer the southern tip, so easily reached on foot from Margaret Bridge or again by bus 26.

Open all year, this complex combines indoor and outdoor pools, one of which remains open to the public even in the winter. There are two main outdoor pools and children's pools both inside and out. The grounds are by no means as extensive as at Palatinus and not so attractive, so it is more of a 'swimming' and less of a 'family' place, though it is very popular with young people.

There is an exterior buffet with small terrace and another inside by the entrance. Swimming caps are compulsory 'for long hair'. Free access to a sauna inside.

Széchenyi Baths (Széchenyi gyógyfürdő)

Situated in the City Park (Városliget) in a large, currently dilapidated though undergoing reconstruction, neo-Baroque building (Széchenyi-fürdő stop on the yellow underground).

The unusual attraction here is that the water is so warm that, although the pools are open-air, they are open all year round. This is the place where they take those photographs of people playing chess in the pool during the winter with the steam rising all around.

There are three pools: one for swimming, a thermal pool (38°C) and a large children's pool (34°C). Buffet and a separate restaurant in the building overlooking one of the pools. Sauna service with complete facilities.

Dagály Baths (Dagály strandfürdő)

This is a huge open-air complex, not far from the Pest end of Árpád Bridge. It is not quite so crowded as Palatinus, since it is not generally known by tourists.

Set in pleasant, extensive grounds with grass and trees, there are two main pools (50m and 25m—the latter covered), two thermal pools (one for children) and a large, shallow children's pool with a big slide. The main pools are open all year as the water is warm.

Caps are compulsory in the main pools. There are kiosks for drinks and snacks scattered throughout the grounds, and there is a sauna and fitness centre. Wheelchair access is reasonably good. Entrance is on Népfürdő u.—bus 84 from Lehel tér. In the summer you can get here by boat along the river from the Pest end of Margaret Bridge.

Csillaghegy Open-Air Baths (Csillaghegyi strandfürdő)

This is one of the most attractive open-air pools in Budapest, set on a hillside with much grassy area and many pine trees. Being some way out it is not often frequented by tourists, though it is very easy to reach on the HÉV railway from Batthyány tér (Csillaghegy station, then a 300m walk).

There are two main pools, one with lanes for 'serious' swimming only (caps compulsory in this one). Although Csillaghegy is mainly a summer spot, this pool is covered over in winter to make it 'indoor'. The water at Csillaghegy is well known for being on the cold side, but on a hot day this is hardly noticeable.

The grounds stretch up the side of the hill leading to two levels of grassy, sunbathing areas. The upper level has a small, shallow children's pool. There are snack bars on both levels and drinks, etc. can also be obtained from the hotel bar which backs onto the pool area.

Wheelchair access is good, the main pools being on the same level as the entrance. Non-swimming spectators are allowed in and there are some seats by the main pools.

Római Open-air Baths (Római strandfürdő)

This complex, on the site of ancient Roman baths, hence the name, is situated to the north of the centre right by the city's biggest camp site, and therefore is not the quietest spot in the summer. Nevertheless it covers a large, flat area (wheelchair access OK) with lots of grass for sunbathing.

There are three pools in all, one for children only and one for swimming only. A special attraction is the pair of huge spiral water slides. There are playgrounds and several food and drink kiosks.

Pünkösdfürdő

This open-air baths is even farther out, almost on the northern boundary of the city. However it is right by the Danube (Buda side) and a fun way to get there is by boat from Margaret Bridge. Allow up to an hour for the journey. (Alternatively, HÉV to Békásmegyer, then bus 146, though it is the 145 when returning.)

Smaller than Római baths, but there is a fairly large grassy area with some shade. Three pools in all, one for children. Wheelchair access good. A couple of kiosks for drinks, etc. There are some small swings and a seesaw. The water is on the cold side, though unnoticeable in hot weather.

Lejtő út Recreation Centre (Lejtő úti Pihenő).

This is a former guest house of the Ministry of Agriculture, all facilities of which are now open to the public. These include a 25m open-air swimming pool set in pleasant grounds. Lejtő út is off Hegyalja út not far from the Farkasrét Cemetery in Buda. It can be reached on bus 8 from Március 15 tér in Pest, or on tram 59 from Moszkva tér in Buda.

The following two indoor pools, although far from the centre are easily reached. They are rarely visited by tourists, but are two of the best 'ordinary' swimming baths in the city.

Kispest Swimming Pool

One of the nicest indoor swimming pools in Budapest incorporating, in modern design, traditional Hungarian wooden architectural styles. It is set in small grounds, which in the summer serve as a sun-bathing area. There is a 33m main pool (with saunas by the pool) and a fairly large, separate childen's pool.

The address is Simonyi Zsigmond u. 31, which is way out in the east of Pest, but actually very easy to reach being only a few minutes' walk from the Kőbánya-Kispest terminus of the blue metro line (to the left from the exit).

Kondorosi út Sports Centre

A very pleasant, modern, indoor swimming baths situated to the south of the centre on the Buda side at Kondorosi út 14. (Tram 47 from Deák tér or 18 from Moszkva tér.)

There is a 33m, 8-lane main pool, a 16m children's pool, buffet, sauna and solarium. The grounds outside are used for sunbathing in the summer (café here) and there are tennis courts for hire.

The following three hotels all have indoor pools open to the public. The first two are fairly new hotels and the facilities are very modern. Although relatively expensive, all three, being 'thermal' hotels, have special facilities for people with disabilities.

Acquincum Hotel. Árpád fejedelem útja, facing the Danube at the Buda end of Árpád Bridge. One large swimming pool and two fairly shallow thermal pools, jacuzzi.

Helia Hotel. On the Pest side of the Danube opposite the middle of Margaret Island. Entrance from Kárpát u. (trolleybus 79). 20m main pool, two 'sitting' pools, one of which is thermal, plus jacuzzi. Access to sun terrace in the summer.

Thermal Hotel. At the northern end of Margaret Island (bus 26 from Nyugati tér). One swimming, two thermal pools, sauna.

The 'Turkish experience'

For nearly 150 years, from 1541 to 1686, Buda and Pest belonged to the Ottoman empire, yet virtually the only remaining architecural relics of that period are the baths which the Turks constructed. These baths, which are not for swimming but rather relaxing, chatting and socialising, provide a unique experience in Europe.

Nothing is required, just walk in off the street. Towels and 'modesty' loin cloths are provided. When busy, a queuing system operates.

Rudas Baths, I. Döbrentei tér 9, by the Buda end of Elizabeth Bridge. The octagonal pool and its dome are a 400-year-old Turkish momument. The small, dark, vaulted interior, with its several warm pools of varying temperatures, generates an authentic Turkish atmosphere. Steam room, massage and rest room. There is also a separate, ordinary swimming pool, plus special medicinal services. The 'Turkish' section is for men only.

Király Baths, II. Fő u. 84. Also dating from the 16C, though with a 'new' wing added in the 19C. Four pools open to women only Tues, Thurs and Sat, other days men only. Closed Sun.

Rác Baths, I. Hadnagy u. 8–10, standing alone in the Tabán area at the foot of Gellért Hill. The exterior is 19C, but the octagonal pool and dome inside are Turkish original. The 40°C water comes from springs under the building. Mon, Wed and Fri women only; Tues, Thurs and Sat men only; closed Sun.

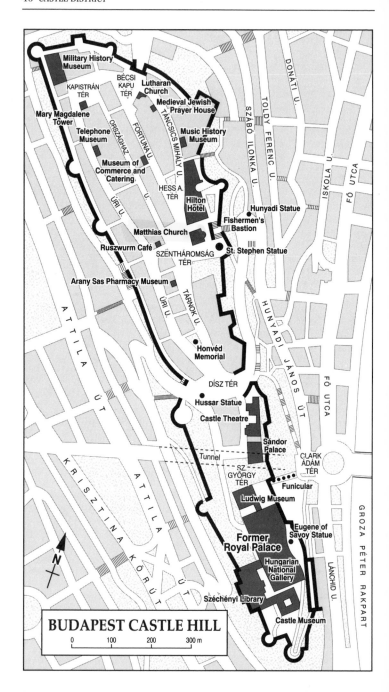

BUDAPEST CASTLE HILL

0   100   200   300 m

BUDAPEST

1 · The Castle District

The **Castle District** (*Várnegyed*) is the area of predominantly former dwelling houses in the northern part of Castle Hill. It stretches from Dísz tér in the south to Bécsi Kapu tér and Kapisztrán tér in the north, a distance of approximately 800m. This walk, however, weaves around the various streets of the Castle District covering some 3km. It includes the Coronation or Matthias Church, one of the symbols of Budapest, and the Fishermen's Bastion, from where there is a marvellous view of the city.

CASTLE HILL (Várhegy) rises to 60m above the Danube and is topped by an 11m-thick layer of limestone. A network of caves and passages, extending for more than 10km through the limestone, was developed mainly in the Middle Ages for defensive purposes, by connecting cavities fashioned by thermal springs. About 80 wells were also dug to ensure the water supply. Later the caves were partitioned and used as cellars by occupants of the houses above. In World War II they served as an air-raid shelter and an army hospital was also established underground.

History

Above ground, it was not until the mid 13C that there was any major settlement. Then, after the Mongol invasion of 1241–42, King Béla IV had a fortress built on the hill, and a civilian population gathered around the royal quarters. Buda only became the permanent royal seat, however, after the so-called New Palace was built during the 1387–1437 reign of Sigismund of Luxemburg.

In the 15C King Matthias Corvinus (ruled 1458–90) had the Gothic palace enlarged and enriched with Renaissance elements. A humanist court developed around Matthias, representing one of the major centres of Renaissance culture in Europe and a golden era in Hungarian history. Decline set in following Matthias's death and the Turkish occupation of Buda in 1541 initiated a period of plunder and destruction. The churches were turned into mosques, most of the wealthy population fled and the houses were left to ruin.

Buda Castle was recaptured in 1686 by a united Christian army set up with the support of Pope Innocent XI. The victory over the Turks was proclaimed and celebrated all over the Christian world. But the long years of Ottoman rule, the destruction caused by the siege and the ravaging of the victorious armies had left the castle district with only about 600 inhabitants as against 8000 in the time of Matthias. Reconstruction began slowly and continued into the following century. Former Gothic dwelling houses were rebuilt in Baroque style. This can clearly be seen today in the many houses which have Gothic sedilia in their gateways but Baroque upper floors.

Buda became a royal free borough in 1703 but the former splendour did not return as the Habsburgs maintained their rule from Vienna. Important government offices were situated in Pozsony (today Bratislava, capital of Slovakia).

During the 1848–49 War of Independence, Buda Castle was occupied by the Hungarians and later recaptured by Austrian troops. Many dwellings again suffered serious damage and the Royal Palace, which had been partially reconstructed in the previous century, was burnt down. Following the unification of Buda, Pest and Óbuda in 1873 the Castle District started to develop once again. New government and ministerial offices were built, the Matthias Church was reconstructed and the Palace enlarged.

World War II brought a further wave of destruction when, in the winter of 1944–45, German troops entrenched on Castle Hill attempted to hold out in face of the encroaching Red Army. By the time Budapest was finally liberated on 13 February not a single habitable house remained in the Castle District. Painstaking reconstruction of the area took place over the following 40 years. Today almost every building in the Castle District is a listed monument.

The walk begins in DÍSZ TÉR at the southern end of the Castle District. To get there from Pest, take bus 16 from the south-east corner of Erzsébet tér. Alternatively, the so-called Castle minibuses (*Vár-busz*) run from Moszkva tér in Buda through the Castle District and back. They depart from Várfok u., at the top of the steps opposite the exit of the Moszkva tér metro station.

Dísz tér (Parade Square) recalls the military parades held here in the 19C. A **statue of a hussar** in the uniform of the time of Maria Theresa stands in the south-west corner of the square (Zsigmond Kisfaludi Strobl, 1932).

The first hussars were South Slav light cavalry organised by King Matthias into a regiment in 1480. The hussars' fighting ability was based on speed as they carried no heavy armour. They excelled in close combat, surprise attacks and unexpected manoeuvres. Their arms were the curved sabre (later a broadsword), the pike and the pointed dagger, and they were noted throughout Europe for their heroic deeds and striking uniform.

In the northern part of Dísz tér is György Zala's 1893 **Honvéd Memorial** depicting a *honvéd* (soldier) and angel, and commemorating the recapture of the castle on 21 May 1849 during the War of Independence against Austria. Veterans of the attack collected money to pay for this memorial to their fallen comrades.

The Baroque **No. 3** on the south side is the former Batthyány Mansion (Márton Sigl, 1745–48). **No. 5** next door has a wall plaque recording that the Apostolic Nuncio, Angelo Rotta, was based here from 1930 to 1945. Archbishop Rotta (1872–1965) was one of a number of foreign diplomats who made efforts to protect Jews in 1944.

The neo-Classical **No. 13** opposite dates from 1815. Reliefs above the first-floor windows depict Diana, Rhea Sylvia and Pallas Athene. **No. 6** on the south side is today the Algerian Embassy. The intricate wrought-iron work above the door is actually 20C, the work of Sándor Sima.

TÁRNOK UTCA runs northwards from Dísz tér and derives its name from the *tárnokmester* (treasurer), a court dignitary who dealt with the royal revenues. The street was a centre of commerce in the Middle Ages.

No. 1 on the right dates from the 15C but was rebuilt c 1700. The stone doorframe was added in 1795. **No. 5** was built in Baroque style around 1725 using the walls of three former medieval houses. **No. 14** on the left was constructed in stages in the 14–15C. On the protruding first floor there used to be a 'palatinum', a hall characteristic of buildings in the Castle District. The paintwork on the façade was originally 16C though it was restored after the Second World War in the early

1950s. **No. 16**, today a restaurant and beer-hall, dates from the 14–15C and has been rebuilt several times.

The **Arany Sas** (Golden Eagle) **Pharmacy Museum** is at Tárnok u. 18 (open 10.30–18.00 except Mon; children/students free; w/a possible). The pharmacy was established in 1688 by Ferenc Ignác Bősinger, a former mayor. It was the first pharmacy in Buda Castle after the expulsion of the Turks, and moved here in the mid 18C. The building was formerly a merchant's house and dates from the early 15C. The present neo-Classical façade is from 1820, though the Madonna statue in a niche is the work of the noted 20C ceramicist Margit Kovács. Inside, pharmaceutical items of the Renaissance and the Baroque age are on display.

Pál Pátzay's **female-figure fountain** stands just beyond the museum at the end of Balta köz. The artist modelled it in 1930 while on a scholarship in Rome, but curiously it was only erected in 1975, a few years before his death.

Tárnok u. ends in SZENTHÁROMSÁG TÉR (Holy Trinity Square) in the middle of which stands the 16m limestone **Holy Trinity Column**, which was commissioned by the Buda Council following a plague and made between 1710 and 1713 by Anton Hörger and Philip Ungleich. Seriously damaged in 1944–45 it was resculpted in the 1960s. Reliefs on the plinth depict biblical King David praying for the passing of the plague, a scene from the Black Death, and the construction of the column itself. Above are various saints and at the top the Holy Trinity.

The building at the south-west corner of the square, running the length of Szentháromság u., is the **former Buda Town Hall**, which was designed at the beginning of the 18C by the Italian architect Venerio Ceresola. The building's original Baroque design is barely noticeable today, following reconstruction after the Second World War. It functioned as a municipal headquarters until the unification of Buda, Pest and Óbuda in 1873, and today houses a number of academic institutes.

The Castle District's Holy Trinity Column, like many in central Europe, was erected following a plague

On the corner of this building there is an attractive **statue of Pallas Athene**, the Greek goddess of wisdom and protector of cities. The Buda coat of arms can be seen on her shield, and in her left hand she holds a spear. The statue is actually a copy. The 1784 original by Carlo Adami, which used to stand near here, is today just inside the southern gateway of the Budapest City Council on Városház u. in Pest. The spear has often been vandalised, and even stolen. For this reason the image of the statue has become well known—thanks to one Mihály Ráday. Many years ago Ráday was a young employee of Hungarian TV. In 1980 he used the statue and its disappearing spear as the centrepiece of a programme about the decline of the city's architectural heritage. Ever since he has regularly presented a popular TV series called *Unokáink sem fogják látni* (Our grandchildren won't see it). This helped spur the movement for the protection of the city's built environment, which uses the Pallas Athene statue as its symbol.

The tiny but ever popular **Ruszwurm Cukrászda** is at Szentháromság u. 7. There used to be a gingerbread shop here in the Middle Ages, and there has been a pastry shop and café here since 1827, which makes the Ruszwurm one of the oldest in the city. The present name comes from a former owner, Vilmos Ruszwurm, who ran the café from 1884 for nearly 40 years. The Empire-style interior with its glass-fronted cupboards is very much as it was in the old days.

A bronze **statue of Mercury** stands in front of Szentháromság tér 7–8. The work of Greek-born sculptor Agamemnon Makrisz (1981), it depicts the Roman counterpart of Hermes, the messenger of the gods in Greek mythology. The building behind functioned for many years as an international press centre. Post-war reconstruction of the building to its right, at **No. 2** Országház u., revealed several medieval details. Traceried niches can be seen in the gateway as well as some arches of a 15C arcade in the courtyard. The wine cellar of the restaurant here has been fashioned out of a cave cut into the rock.

The **former Ministry of Finance** stands on the north side of Szentháromság tér. It was designed by Sándor Fellner in late-Eclectic style with Hungarian Secessionist ornamentation. Today it appears simpler than when first built in 1906; some spires, for example, were destroyed in the Second World War. In the 1960s the building functioned as a student hostel; today it houses a variety of institutes and offices.

MATTHIAS CHURCH

The Church of Our Lady (Nagyboldogasszony-templom), commonly known as the **Matthias Church (Mátyás-templom)**, stands on the east side of Szentháromság tér. It has become a symbol of Buda and a popular tourist attraction, though it is still a functioning church with regular masses.

History

Tradition has it that in 1015 King Stephen built a small church to Mary here, but that was destroyed during the Mongol invasion of 1241–42. The present church was originally founded by Béla IV following that invasion—a 1255 charter mentions it being under construction. It was a basilica comparable in style with the northern French Gothic architecture of the period. It became the parish church of the Germans who had recently settled in Buda and whose numbers were growing due to the expanding trade of the town. The poorer Hungarians, who were mostly farmers, vinegrowers and craftsmen, had to make do with the less grandiose Church of Mary Magdalene at the northern end of the Castle District.

In 1302, after the death of András III, the last of the Árpád dynasty, the church was the scene of an extraordinary event. The citizens and clergy of Buda 'excommunicated' Pope Boniface VIII for supporting Charles Robert of Anjou's claim to the throne in opposition to their favoured candidate, King Wenceslas of Bohemia. However, resistance crumbled after a few years and Charles Robert was crowned in the church in 1309. Apart from this occasion the church was not used as a coronation church in the Middle Ages; Hungarian kings were usually crowned in Székesfehérvár, a town 70km south-west of Budapest.

At the turn of the 14C the church was remodelled into a hall-church in high Gothic style by Louis the Great and Sigismund of Luxemburg. A royal

THE MATTHIAS CHURCH

1. Mary portal
2. Main portal
3. Loreto Chapel below the South Tower
4. Coat of arms of King Matthias
5. High altar
6. St Ladislas Chapel
7. Oratory of the Knights of Malta (above)
8. Royal Oratory (above)
9. St Stephen Chapel
10. Tomb of Béla III
11. St Imre Chapel
12. Baptismal font below the Béla Tower
13. Pulpit
14. Entrance to the crypt
15. Medieval figural capitals

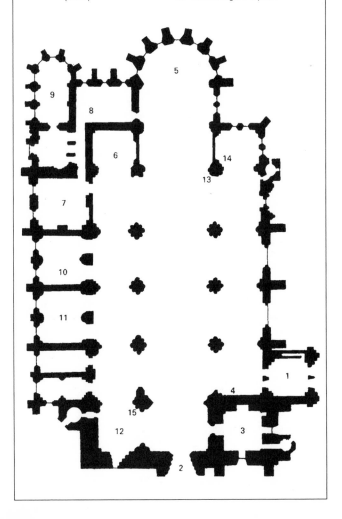

oratory was built during the reign of King Matthias Corvinus and the tower which had collapsed in 1384 was rebuilt. The church became the scene of ceremonies and political events. Matthias's two marriage ceremonies (with Catherine Podebrad and Beatrice of Aragon) both took place here amidst great splendour.

Following the Turkish victory over the Hungarians at the battle of Mohács in 1526, the ecclesiastical treasures of the church were transferred to Pozsony (today Bratislava). The Turks occupied Buda in 1541 and converted the church into the city's main mosque. The medieval furnishings were destroyed as were the wall decorations. Two ornamental chandeliers above the high altar were taken to Constantinople where they still hang in St Sophia's. Buda was finally recaptured from the Turks in 1686, following which the church was given first to the Franciscans and later to the Jesuits, who restored the building, decorating its interior in a rich Baroque style.

The church regained some of its former importance in the second half of the 19C. In 1867, following the founding of the Dual Monarchy, the splendid coronation of Emperor Franz Josef as king of Hungary took place here to the music of Liszt's Coronation Mass, which had been specially composed for the occasion.

Deterioration, however, necessitated reconstruction of the church, and this took place under the direction of the architect Frigyes Schulek between 1873 and 1896. Where possible original structural and decorative elements were preserved, but Schulek designed new elements of his own with the result that only parts of the main walls, the square bottom part of the southern tower, the interior pillars and some parts of the Mary Portal on the south façade, are genuinely medieval.

The last king of Hungary, Charles IV, was crowned here in 1916 during the First World War. During the siege of Budapest in the winter of 1944–45 the church was badly damaged and post-war restoration work was not completed until 1970.

The acoustics of the church have always been excellent. As early as the 15C, in the reign of King Matthias, a choir of 70 was singing chorales here. The tradition continues, and many concerts are held throughout the year.

Exterior. On the tympanum of the main (west) portal facing Szentháromság tér there is a relief of the Madonna enthroned with angels. The work of Lajos Lantai (c 1890), it is made from coloured pyrogranite from the Zsolnay factory in Pécs. To the left is a large rose window and to its left is the north tower, named Béla tower after Béla IV, the founder of the church. The decorative south tower has two square lower sections, which are medieval, below three octagonal upper parts, which are more or less a faithful copy of the tower built in Matthias's time. In the middle one there is a copy of the Hungarian coat of arms together with the Corvinus coat of arms showing Matthias's symbol, the raven. The attractive open-work structure and the stone spire decorated with crockets and gargoyles above is Schulek's design from the late 19C.

The **Mary Portal** on the south façade dates from the reign of King Louis the Great (ruled 1342–1382). On the exterior of the porch, in niches on either side of the gate, are statues of the 11C Hungarian kings SS Stephen and Ladislas. Inside, above the entrance, there is a multifigural scene of the Death of the Virgin. In the lower part Mary is seen kneeling with the disciples and in the upper part Christ, surrounded by the four seated Evangelists, is receiving His mother's soul. The work is largely 14C. The parts that have been added later are painted brown.

Interior. Through the portal, on the inside wall of the south tower to the left, the original coat of arms of King Matthias can be seen. To its left, above the Mary Portal, are five circular paintings by Károly Lotz showing the birth and childhood of Christ. The decorative painting on the walls and pillars, designed by Bertalan Székely at the end of the 19C, consists of floral and geometrical motifs, partly medieval and partly Art Nouveau in character. The overall effect gives the church a rather Byzantine feel.

The **Loreto Chapel** is on the ground floor below the south tower. Above its wrought-iron gate is a wall painting of the Virgin and inside is a Baroque Madonna of Italian style from c 1700.

There are two figural capitals from the Middle Ages in the bay beneath the Béla tower. One represents a monster fighting with dragons, the other a hooded and a bearded man with an open book. The west wall of the tower has a recessed round window with the figure of a lamb symbolising the Good Shepherd. The north wall is decorated with a painting by Károly Lotz showing Pope Calixtus III ordering the church bells to be tolled at noon every day in memory of János Hunyadi's victory over the Turks at Nándorfehérvár (Belgrade) in 1456, which halted the Ottoman advance for nearly a century. In the centre of the bay is a neo-Romanesque baptismal font.

The **St Imre Chapel** is the first chapel on the north side of the church. It has a wall painting by Bertalan Székely depicting scenes from the life of St Francis of Assisi. The cabinets of the neo-Gothic triptych contain wooden sculptures of St Stephen, the first king of Hungary, St Imre, Stephen's son who died at the age of 24 in 1031, and St Gellért, Imre's tutor. The pictures on the wings by Mihály Zichy represent four scenes from Imre's life: the prince's birth; visiting the Benedictine Abbey at Pannonhalma in western Hungary; being taught by Bishop Gellért; and on his death bed.

In the next chapel is the double sarcophagus of King Béla III and his wife, Anne of Châtillon. They were originally buried in the cathedral at Székesfehérvár. Their graves were discovered during excavations in 1848 and they were then brought here. The richly carved sepulchral ornament above the sarcophagus (the work of Ferenc Mikula and István Hausen) is an imitation of a portal of a 12C French cathedral and dates from the time of Schulek's restoration.

The side chapel to the left of the chancel is covered with wall paintings by Károly Lotz depicting the life and funeral of St Ladislas, king of Hungary 1077–95. The **chancel** has a fine wrought-iron gate and around the apse is a series of sedilia which had figural wall paintings in the Middle Ages. The medieval-style stained glass windows above are by Ede Kratzmann to the designs of Bertalan Székely and Károly Lotz. On the left and above, the stone balcony with lions on either side indicates the position of the royal oratory, which was added in Matthias's time. The high altar, composed of early-Gothic elements, is the work of Schulek and replaced the former Baroque altar. The neo-Gothic stone pulpit shows the four Evangelists and the four Fathers of the Church. The stained glass windows on the southern wall of the church represent the Virgin, St Elizabeth of Hungary and St Margaret of Hungary.

Access to the **crypt** is on the right of the chancel. Fragments of the original church are displayed here and a red marble sarcophagus contains the bones found in the royal tombs of Székesfehérvár. Stairs lead up from the crypt to the **St Stephen Chapel**, which Schulek designed. On the walls are scenes from Stephen's life (Bertalan Székely) and on the columns are statues of King Stephen and his wife Queen Gizella. The stained glass windows depict Hungarian saints and holy people and below the windows are sedilia with rich tracery. Ecclesiastical items are displayed in the glass cabinet.

A neo-Gothic staircase leads to the **Royal Oratory** (on the left), which overlooks the chancel. Here is a small display of vestments including priests' coronation robes and the coronation thrones of Franz Josef and Charles IV. There is also a replica of the Hungarian Crown Jewels. Along the passage to the west is the Oratory of the Maltese Knights (Schulek's design). The west wall is decorated with coats of arms of the Knights of Malta. There is a copy here of the first Hungarian bible of 1626.

The stairs lead to a **Collection of Ecclesiastical Art** (open daily 09.00–19.00) in a gallery stretching along the northern wall of the church. Monstrances, chalices and various other ecclesiastical items are on display here.

A large, bronze, equestrian **statue of King (St) Stephen** stands in the cobbled area by the south-east corner of the Matthias Church. It was designed by Alajos Stróbl and completed in 1906 after ten years' work. Stephen (István) was Hungary's first monarch, ruling in the early part of the 11C. His significance is twofold—he unified the country, thus establishing the Hungarian state, and he was instrumental in the conversion of the Magyars to Christianity.

Stephen is depicted here wearing the Hungarian crown and the coronation mantle. The statue's altar-like, neo-Romanesque limestone plinth was designed by Frigyes Schulek. The relief at the rear modestly shows Schulek as a bearded figure kneeling before King Stephen holding a model of the Matthias Church. This historical mix-up is complemented by the fact that research shows that the crown on Stephen's head, depicting a real crown which can be seen in the National Museum, could not have existed in Stephen's time.

The neo-Romanesque **Fishermen's Bastion** (Halászbástya) beyond the statue was also designed by Frigyes Schulek and built at the turn of the century as part of the reconstruction of the Matthias Church and its surroundings. Tradition has it that this stretch of the medieval ramparts used to be defended by the fishermen's guild, though the name might also derive from a nearby former fish market.

The function of the present bastion was both decorative and to serve as a lookout terrace over the Danube—the view and both the natural and architectural setting are superb: Margaret Island, Margaret Bridge and the Parliament are to the left, the Chain Bridge, the riverside hotels, Inner City Parish Church, Elizabeth Bridge and Gellért Hill to the right. International recognition of this unique environment was attained in 1988, when the entire panorama of the Danube embankment in central Budapest was added to UNESCO's World Heritage List.

Below the Fishermen's Bastion, in Hunyadi János út which weaves up the hill, stands a bronze **statue of János Hunyadi** (c 1407–56), the father of Matthias Corvinus and the commander who defeated the Turks at the important battle of Nándorfehérvár in 1456 (István Tóth, 1903).

Nearby is a replica of **St George and the Dragon** by the 14C Hungarian sculptors Márton and György Kolozsvári. The small-bodied round horse of the statue and the saddle are typical of those traditionally used by the Magyars after their great migration from the East in the 9C, as are the garments and the equipment of St George. The original, which today is in Prague, was made in 1387 and is one of the oldest surviving Hungarian statues. It is regarded as a superb work of Gothic sculpture and so it is somewhat curious that this copy, commissioned by the

Ministry of Religion and Education in 1904, is rather hidden, below the Bastion, and not on full display at the top.

Not only for the English

Although the patron saint of England, St George was not English at all. He originated from south-east Europe and died a soldier-martyr's death c 303 in Palestine. He came to personify the ideals of Christian chivalry and was a patron of Byzantine armies long before his cult was established in England during the time of the Crusades. The image of St George fighting the dragon can be found throughout eastern Europe.

At the far north end of the Fishermen's Bastion, up the steps and through the gate, in the ruins of a former 13C Dominican church, stands Károly Antal's 1937 **statue of Julianus and Gellért**.

A quest for roots

Julianus and Gellért were two Dominican friars who travelled to the East in 1235 to find descendants of the Magyars who had remained behind when the majority migrated in the second half of the first millennium AD. Only Julianus, seen here pointing, was able to reach his goal, finding groups of pagan Magyars, who spoke a version of Hungarian, on the banks of the Volga. But he returned with dire warnings, bringing King Béla IV news of the approaching Mongol invasion, which was to wreak havoc on the entire country and much of Europe. Two years later Julianus set out again with the mission of persuading the eastern Hungarians to move to the Carpathian Basin. He was too late—the Mongols had already overrun and dispersed these long-lost relatives.

The Budapest **Hilton Hotel** stands on the north side of the Matthias Church. As seen from Pest across the Danube, it blends well with the Buda skyline—a remarkable achievement by architect Béla Pintér. The blending is even physically present in the structure itself. A Dominican church and monastery stood here in the Middle Ages, the ruins of which have been incorporated into the hotel's Dominican Courtyard, where concerts sometimes take place. Similarly, the hotel's Faust Wine Cellar is a reconstruction from remains of the original monastery wine cellar. This mixing of the old and the new has not pleased everyone and the Hilton has been controversial ever since it was built in 1976.

The hotel's main entrance is on its western side, in HESS ANDRÁS TÉR. The façade here integrates the remains of an 18C Jesuit college. On the wall of the St Nicholas Tower, to the left of the entrance, there is a copy of the 1486 **Matthias Relief**, from Bautzen in Germany. This is regarded as the only authentic representation of Hungary's great Renaissance ruler, King Matthias.

Hess András tér is named after Hungary's William Caxton. Hess, who was probably of German origin, learned the printing trade in Rome before being invited to Buda in 1473 by Vice Chancellor László Karai to establish the country's first printing press. It is believed he had his workshop here (on the site of today's Fortuna Restaurant opposite the hotel). Hess was responsible for the first printed book in Hungary, the *Buda Chronicle*, which was published in Latin.

Interestingly, although commemorating a 15C innovator, the square has had its present name only since 1954. Previously it was named after Pope Innocent XI (1611–89), who organised and helped finance the Christian armies who came to drive the Turks out of Hungary in the 1680s. A **statue of Pope Innocent,** by József Damkó, still stands in the square. It was placed here in 1936, the 250th anniversary of the recapture of Buda Castle from the Turks. The reliefs on the plinth commemorate the Polish King Jan Sobieski, the Doge of Venice and Leopold of Habsburg, who all also supported the anti-Turkish struggle.

Hess András tér 3 behind the statue is the **former Red Hedgehog Inn,** mentioned in a census as early as 1686. In the 18C theatrical performances were held here. The building was formed c 1700 by joining three medieval houses and in the early 19C it was rebuilt in neo-Classical style. The first-floor window frame on the Fortuna u. façade to the left and the 15C door in the gateway are Gothic, while the main façade, with the hedgehog relief above the door, is neo-Classical.

The neo-Classical **No. 4**, on the western side of the square, was also formed from three originally medieval houses. In the gateway of the building, which is now a restaurant, sedilia characteristic of the Castle District's medieval houses can still be seen. The passageway here leads to a pleasant courtyard with several shops, including a bookshop with English-language works and a tea/coffee area.

The streets in the northern part of the Castle District are often quiet and devoid of visitors. Nevertheless, they contain a number of interesting buildings and several museums, and the route thus continues north from Hess András tér along TÁNCSICS MIHÁLY U.

Mihály Táncsics—radical land reformer
Mihály Táncsics (1799–1884) was a champion of the peasants and national independence. Until the age of 20 he had worked as a serf, then he became a weaver; self-taught, he travelled all over Europe. In 1846 he was the first to demand the emancipation of the serfs without compensation. Set free from prison by young revolutionaries on 15 March 1848, the first day of the national uprising, his radical demand the following year that any land over 2000 hold (863ha) in the possession of landlords be distributed amongst the needy was rejected by the leaders of the independent Hungarian government.

After the defeat of the War of Independence he went underground for eight years under a death sentence, but reappeared in political life for a short time after the Compromise of 1867.

The **National Inspectorate for Historical Monuments** is based at Táncsics Mihály u. 1 on the right, in an originally Baroque house built c 1775. On the wall facing the Hilton there is a relief of Imre Henszlmann (1813–88), an architect and architectural historian, and a leading advocate of monument preservation in the late 19C. Inside there is a specialist architecture reference library, open to the public. The foyer of the building often has temporary exhibitions on architectural themes.

The **Music History Museum** (Zenetörténeti Múzeum) occupies the former Erdődy Mansion at Táncsics Mihály u. 7 (tel: 175–9011; open Mon 16.00–20.00, Wed–Sun 10.00–18.00; labelling in English; good w/a). The Baroque mansion was designed by the Viennese architect Máté Nepauer and constructed in 1750–69. On the ground floor the small display includes an instrument-making bench, old violins, hurdy-gurdies, zithers, bagpipes (a traditional Hungarian folk instrument), horns and cimbaloms. The upstairs 'Bartók Workshop' is very specialised with collections of scores showing the development of Béla Bartók's works. Regular concerts are held in the museum (usually on Mondays) and in the summer these take place in the courtyard outside.

No. 9 is the site of the Royal Mint which stood here in the Middle Ages. The present three-storey building, the former Joseph Barracks, was built c 1810 for military purposes and later served as a prison. Memorial plaques recall that Mihály Táncsics was imprisoned here in 1847–48 and again from 1860 to 1867, and that Lajos Kossuth was also imprisoned here for three years in the late 1830s, during which time he learnt English. Many other Hungarian patriots also spent time within these walls during the 19C.

No. 16 on the left was built c 1700 on medieval foundations and received its present Baroque façade in the second half of the 18C. The fresco on the first floor shows Christ and the Virgin Mary surrounded by saints. The plaque at No. 13 records that the poet and translator Árpád Tóth (1886–1928) spent the last ten years of his life here.

The **medieval Jewish Prayer House** (Középkori Zsidó Imaház) at Táncsics Mihály u. 26 dates from the late 14C, though the present building is 18C Baroque, (open Tues–Fri 10.00–14.00, Sat, Sun 10.00–18.00, closed Nov–Apr). This street was the centre of Jewish life in the late 14C when it was called 'Jewish Street' for a while, and religious inscriptions and frescoes have been found here. There are some Jewish tombstones, unearthed nearby, as well as religious objects and documents relating to the history of the Castle District's Jewish population. The remains of a 15C synagogue have been found in the garden of the house opposite (No. 23), but at the time of writing excavations have not been fully carried out and nothing can be viewed.

Táncsics Mihály u. ends in BÉCSI KAPU TÉR (Vienna Gate Square), which gets its name from that of a medieval town-gate. The small, single-steepled **Lutheran Church** here was designed by Mór Kollina and built in 1895–96; concerts are occasionally held inside in the summer. The bronze plaque on the south wall commemorates pastor Gábor Sztehlo (1909–74), who saved the lives of some 2000 children, including many Jewish children, during World War II.

The present stone **gateway** opposite the church was built in 1936 on the 250th anniversary of the recapture of Buda Castle from the Turks. Children (and adults) may enjoy climbing up the gate. The statue of the angel holding a cross in front of the gate is a **monument to the recapture of Buda** (Béla Ohmann, 1936).

Across the road is a memorial plaque in Latin commemorating the Swabian, Hessian, Würtemburgian, Bavarian, Austrian, Flemish, Walloon, Spanish, Italian and Hungarian soldiers who formed the united Christian army which liberated Buda in 1686.

Through the gate and to the right is the **Europa Grove**, which has a collection of various types of trees planted by European mayors in 1972 on the centenary of the unification of Buda, Óbuda and Pest. To the left stands a rather severe **statue of Mihály Táncsics** (Imre Varga, 1969). Beyond this, Lovas u., which curves to the left under the castle walls, is an 'open-air museum', containing Budapest street lamps from 1844 to 1944.

Returning to Bécsi kapu tér, the **Ferenc Kazinczy memorial** here is in the form of a female figure (holding a lamp symbolising eternal art) above a well (János Pásztor, 1936). Kazinczy (1759–1831) was a leading figure in the development of Hungarian literature and of language reform.

The huge neo-Romanesque building of the **National Archives** (Samu Pecz, 1913–20) stands on the north side of the square, and houses charters and other historic documents. The archives themselves date back to 1756 when they were founded in Pozsony (Bratislava). Note the coloured patterned roof, which was restored as original in 1988.

The National Archives and the Lutheran Church. One of many appealing views in and around the Castle District

The houses in a row on the west side of the square are of medieval origin but were reconstructed in the 18C following damage which occurred during the siege of 1686. **No. 5** on the right, with the balustrades and stucco ornaments, was built c 1780 in Rococo style. It shares a roof with **No. 6**, which has a statue of St John of Nepomuk in a niche on the façade. The reliefs on the façade of **No. 7** were added in the early 19C. At the top Pallas Athene is surrounded by symbolic figures of the arts and sciences. Between the first-floor windows are portraits of Virgil, Cicero, Socrates and Livy, with Quintilian and Seneca in the middle. Baron Lajos Hatvany (1880–1961) a writer, literary historian and one of the founders of the *Nyugat* journal, lived here in the mid 1930s, during which time Thomas Mann stayed here on his three visits to Hungary. **No. 8** has been rebuilt several times; the corner bay window dates from 1929–30.

The route now continues south along FORTUNA UTCA, which in the Middle Ages was called French Street (Francia utca) after the French craftsmen who lived here. The present name dates from the late 18C and refers to the Fortuna Inn which used to be situated here (see below). In the direction of the route the street numbers are in descending order.

Like many buildings in the Castle District the houses in this street had to be rebuilt after the sieges of 1686, 1849 and 1945. Nevertheless many original elements remain such as the Gothic frames of the door and windows at **No. 14** on the right. **No. 10**, two doors away, dates back to the 13C. It has been rebuilt several times and now stands in its late 18C Louis XVI style, but medieval details can be seen on the façade. The building belonged to the Order of Malta before World War II, hence the Maltese cross over the door. The doorframe with its keystone with a mask at **No. 13** on the other side of the road is Baroque (c 1730).

No. 6 on the right was built on medieval foundations in the early 18C, though the façade is early 19C. Above the double door is a relief of Cupid. **No. 4** next door was built in Louis XVI style from the remains of three medieval houses. The Fortuna Inn was situated here from 1784 to 1868, during which time it was regarded as Buda's most elegant place for entertainment and lodging. Today it houses the **Museum of Hungarian Commerce and Catering** (Magyar Kereskedelmi és Vendéglátóipari Múzeum) which, when it opened in 1966, was the world's first catering museum (tel: 175–4031; open 10.00–18.00 except Mon; free on Fri/free for children at all times; w/a reasonable). Albeit small, this is an attractive museum, of interest to all ages. On the left the exhibition covers the history of confectionery and pastry shops, with models of cake-making equipment and model shops. On the right is presented the Hungarian retail trade in the first half of the 20C—posters, model shops, goods, working advertisement models, etc. A recorded message about the content and background of the museum is available in English in the coin-operated box.

The house opposite the museum at **No. 9** has a relief of the goddess Fortuna on the first floor (Ferenc Medgyessy, 1921).

The route now continues west along the short Fortuna köz at the side of the museum to ORSZÁGHÁZ UTCA, the main thoroughfare of the Castle District in the Middle Ages. **No. 18**, facing Fortuna köz, was rebuilt in its original 15C form after World War II. **No. 20** on its right is 14C and has survived fairly well. Above the ground floor is a trefoil-arched cornice. The initials J.N. and the date 1771 on the keystone of the Baroque gate refer to Johann Nickl, a butcher and former owner of the house.

No. 22 was originally 15C, but was rebuilt in the 16C and again in the 18C. There is Renaissance graffiti on the bottom of the bay window and mid 18C Baroque stucco ornamentation on the balcony.

Proceeding northwards, **No. 9** on the right has 14C traceried sedilia in the gateway. The large building at **No. 28** on the left is the former Cloister of the Poor Clares and was built in the late 18C to the design of Franz Anton Hillebrandt. The wing facing Országház u. was for a time in the 1790s used by the Diet (Parliament) which is the origin of the present name of the street ('Országház' means Parliament). Both the Lower and the Upper House used to meet here. Today the building belongs to the Hungarian Academy of Sciences. The large plaque by the entrance recalls that in 1945 the Gestapo imprisoned about 350 people here, both Hungarians and foreigners, a quarter of whom were executed.

The Baroque **No. 17** across the street (today a restaurant) was erected c 1700 from two medieval houses. The gate's keystone has a relief showing a croissant, indicating the trade of a former owner. In front of No. 21, across Kard u., there is a **statue of Márton Lendvay** (1807–58), an actor and prominent member of the National Theatre (László Dunaisky, 1860).

Országház u. ends in KAPISZTRÁN TÉR at the northern end of the Castle District. Here stands the **Mary Magdelene Tower.** The church to which it belonged was badly damaged in World War II and had to be pulled down, though the outline of the foundations can still be seen. The tower itself was reconstructed after the war, copying the original 18C Baroque spire. The church was originally built in the 13C and was used by the Hungarian population of the district (Germans worshipped in what is today the Matthias Church). A parish school was added in the 15C. For a while under the Turkish occupation it was the only Christian church in Buda; Catholics used the chancel, Protestants the nave. Then in 1605 it was turned into a mosque. Following the expulsion of the Turks in 1686 it was given to the Franciscans. The Habsburg Franz I was crowned here as Ferenc I of Hungary in 1792, and from 1817 it served as a garrison church for troops stationed nearby.

In the north-west corner of Kapisztrán tér is József Dámkó's 1922 **statue of St John Capistranus** (1386–1456), an Italian Franciscan friar and zealous proselytiser who raised an army of Crusaders to help János Hunyadi in his campaign against the Turks. The two were prominent participants in the famous victory of the Hungarians at Nándorfehérvár (Belgrade) in July 1456, though, due to the neglect of unburied corpses, within two weeks Hunyadi was dead from the plague, and by the autumn Capistranus had also died. The latter is depicted here in Franciscan garb exhorting his followers above a fallen Turkish soldier.

The complex of buildings behind the statue stands on the site of a former municipal barracks, which were redesigned by Márton Dankó in 1847. After various names it assumed the title of Nándor Barracks. The north wing was transformed in 1892 by Guido Hoepfner, then after 1926 the wing accommodating troops was converted into a military museum which opened in 1937. Restored after World War II, the building today houses the **Museum of Military History** (Hadtörténeti Múzeum); the entrance is on the west side of the building at Tóth Árpád sétány 40 (tel: 156–9522; open Tues–Sat 09.00–17.00, Sun/holidays 09.00–18.00; children free; snack bar; w/a difficult). The exhibits cover military history connected with the 1848 Revolution and the following War of Independence, the Austro–Hungarian Monarchy and the First World War, the Hungarian army in the 1920s and 1930s, and the 1956 Uprising. There is also a special collection of small weapons. The museum usually has several temporary exhibitions running simultaneously.

TÓTH ÁRPÁD SÉTÁNY is a pleasant walkway running along the western ramparts of Castle Hill, and affording an excellent view of the Buda Hills and the area to the west of the castle. In front of the entrance to the Military History Museum canons from different ages are exhibited. At the north-west corner of Castle Hill is the so-called **Esztergom Round Bastion**, 48m in diameter. Nearby, along the northern rampart round the corner of the museum, is the **Abdurrahman memorial**, a symbolic gravestone in memory of the last Pasha of Buda. The inscription, in Hungarian and Turkish, reads: 'Abdurrahman Abdi Arnaut Pasha, the last governor of Buda during 143 years of Turkish occupation, fell close to this spot in his 70th year on the afternoon of 2 September 1686. A valiant foe, may he rest in peace.' The monument was erected in 1932 and the tablet in front records that its costs were covered by the descendants of György Szabó, a Hungarian soldier who fell on this spot on the same day as the Pasha.

The route now continues from Kapisztrán tér, south along ÚRI UTCA, which runs the length of the Castle District all the way to Dísz tér. The street numbers are in descending order.

No. 51 on the left is a former Franciscan monastery, built between 1701 and 1753. Here the 'Hungarian Jacobins' and their leader, Ignác Martinovics, were imprisoned and sentenced to death in 1795. In front of the building there is a cast-iron **statue of Artemis**. The work of an unknown 19C sculptor, it copies Classical Greek representations of the goddess. The fountain, originally placed nearby, was not just for decoration but also a source of drinking water.

No. 62 on the right bears the inscription 'Primate's Palace'. The building dates from the 1790s, but in 1874 it became the property of János Szcitovszky, Archbishop of Esztergom and Primate of Hungary.

No. 49 opposite is the Úri u. wing of the late 18C Cloister of the Poor Clares; note the Gothic elements at the end of the building. On the ground floor is the **Telephone Museum** (Telefónia Múzeum), which prior to its opening in 1991 had for many years been a functioning telephone sub-station (tel: 201–8188; open 10.00–18.00 except Mon; free on Wed; w/a good). This is a rare example in Hungary of a museum giving some 'hands-on' opportunities for playing and learning. You can call up your own English-speaking guide, dial a song or a story, talk to, or send faxes to each other.

The attractive Baroque building at **No. 58** on the right is today a registry office.

Dating from c 1720, its façade was renovated in 1904 by Zsigmond Quittner. The Baroque-style statues in the first floor niches of **No. 54–56** next door represent the four seasons. The house itself was completely rebuilt in 1902.

No. 45 opposite dates from the end of the 17C, though the present façade is from the 1790s. In the 1930s it belonged to the Zwack family, producers of the distinctive digestive drink 'Unicum'. Today it houses the Turkish Embassy. Wags point out that the Turks were expelled in 1686 after ruling Hungary for 150 years, but here they are back in the prime Castle District, an area accommodating few other embassies.

No. 48–50 was built in the 18C from two medieval houses; there are Gothic sedilia in the gateway. **No. 40** was also formed from two medieval dwelling houses, the neo-Classical façade dating from c 1830. The cross-vaulted gateway has Gothic sedilia. The name of the little street here, Nőegylet u., means 'Women's Association Street'. It refers to a women's charity organisation of aristocratic 19C origins which was based here in the 1930s.

The striking façade of **No. 31**, on the left, is almost entirely Gothic. Despite the various wars and sieges enough survived to be able to reconstruct the mansion in detail. In the 14C a two-storey house was built here, to which another floor was added in 1440. Several remodellings followed until 1686 and the recapture of Buda from the Turks, when the building was severely damaged. It was rebuilt at the beginning of the 18C and the original façade was kept. Then in 1862 the façade was redesigned in Romantic style. During the siege of 1944–45 the Romantic decorations fell off revealing the original walls. Extensive archaeological research enabled the medieval façade to be restored. Similar restoration of original Gothic elements can be clearly seen in the gateways of the buildings opposite at **Nos. 38, 36, 34** and **32**.

At the junction of Úri u. and Szentháromság u. there is an equestrian **statue of András Hadik** (György Vastagh Jr, 1937). Hadik (1711–90) rose from being a rank-and-file hussar to become a field-marshal under Maria Theresa in whose service he commanded a Hungarian unit alongside the Austrians in the Seven Years War, holding Berlin to ransom for a time. From 1764 to 1768 he was governor of Transylvania, and from 1773 with the title of count he was head of the Vienna military council—the first and last Hungarian to hold this post. He was also an early advocate of the abolition of serfdom in Hungary.

The entrance to the **Buda Castle Waxworks** (Budavári Labirinthus) is situated a short way along Úri u. at No. 9 on the left (tel: 175–6858; open 10.00–18.00; no w/a). The sometimes gruesome exhibition of Hungarian historical characters is actually underground in one of the caves which constitute a system of galleries running under the Castle District (see introduction to this route).

Úri u. leads south back into Dísz tér, the start of the route.

2 · The Royal Palace

Set at the southern end of Castle Hill, the former Royal Palace (Budavári Palota), with its central dome, dominates the Buda skyline as seen from the city-centre Pest embankment. Today it houses a major national library and a complex of museums including the Hungarian National Gallery, the country's main collection of Hungarian works of art.

The building

The first royal residence was established on Castle Hill in the 13C by Béla IV following the Mongol invasion, but today nothing remains of either the residence or the accompanying fortress.

During the time of the Angevin kings Charles Robert (ruled 1307–42) and Louis the Great (ruled 1342–82), a new castle was built. Then a large Gothic palace arose under Holy Roman Emperor Sigismund of Luxemburg, who was king of Hungary from 1387 to 1437. A system of fortifications was also built to defend the palace.

The age of King Matthias (ruled 1458–90) is regarded as the golden age of the palace and of Buda generally. He had most of the Gothic buildings rebuilt in Italian Renaissance style and had new buildings added. There were marble baptismal fonts, spacious banqueting halls and bed chambers with gilded ceilings. Outside there were lawns, gravel paths, fish ponds and fountains. The Royal Palace became a significant European centre of politics, culture and art. A large library was assembled, and scholars and writers flocked to the court.

During the period of Ottoman rule the palace suffered little structural damage, although many of the interior furnishings and the precious library were dispersed. The building was destroyed, however, during the three-month siege of 1686 when the united Christian armies finally expelled the Turks from Buda.

In the early 18C under Charles III the ruins of the medieval palace were pulled down and a new, smaller palace was built. During the reign of Maria Theresa in the second half of the 18C a large palace comprising 203 rooms was constructed. The university was based here between 1777 and 1784 after it had been moved from Nagyszombat (Trnava, Slovakia). Later the Viennese court assigned the palace to the Palatine, the Austrian ruler's representative in Hungary.

Following establishment of the Austro–Hungarian Dual Monarchy in 1867, large-scale extensions were planned under the direction of the architect Miklós Ybl. He added a new building looking westwards (today the National Széchényi Library). After Ybl's death, work was resumed by Alajos Hauszmann in 1893. He more than doubled the length of the buildings overlooking the Danube by adding a replica of the Maria Theresa wing to the north and connecting the two wings by a central block topped by a dome. This symmetrical neo-Baroque palace was completed in 1905.

The palace was completely burnt out during the 1944–45 siege of Budapest. During the course of reconstruction, which started in 1950, excavations revealed remnants of the former medieval palace. Hauszmann's large block was rebuilt, though with a simpler roof and a neo-Classical dome. The interior was reconstructed for the museums, work being finally completed only in the 1980s.

Statues and monuments

The reliefs and statues which can be seen on and around the Royal Palace all date from the turn of the century. By the north-east corner, at the top of the funicular railway, is Gyula Donáth's 1905 bronze representation of the Magyar mythical **Turul bird.** According to legend a 'Turul' bird begat Álmos, the son of Emese. It was the former's son, Árpád, who led the Magyars in the conquest of c 896.

The neo-Baroque, wrought-iron gateway and fence behind the bird is a product of the noted 19C workshop of Gyula Jungfer. In front of the Danube façade of Building A is Károly Senyei's fountain statue, **Angling Children** (1912).

Nearby, in front of C wing by the entrance to the National Gallery, stands an equestrian **statue of Prince Eugene of Savoy** (1663–1736). The sculptor, József Róna, was a self-made man from a poor background. Although he only had three years of schooling, he managed to obtain a scholarship to study at the Academy in Vienna and later received many commissions for public statues erected in the late 19C. His neo-Baroque Eugene of Savoy is considered his finest work.

The town authorities of Zenta (today in Serbia) wanted to commemorate the 200th anniversary of the battle of Zenta in 1697, where Eugene of Savoy's victory sealed the fate of Turkish rule in Hungary. They commissioned the statue from Róna at short notice and set about raising the money with a lottery. The sculpture was completed within a year, but not enough money had been raised. The architect wrote to Emperor Franz Josef who bought the statue and ordered that it be placed in the Castle. Róna is reported as saying it 'was placed in one of the most beautiful spots in the world.' Two reliefs on the base show scenes from the 1697 battle.

On either side to the rear are Miklós Ligeti's 1903 bronze statues of **Csongor** and **Tünde**, the two lovers in Mihály Vörösmarty's 19C drama which bears their name.

The statue in the middle of the courtyard on the west (rear) side of the palace and bounded by wings A, B and C is entitled **Horseman** (György Vastagh Jr, 1901). It depicts a traditional Hungarian *csikós* with his mount.

On the wall nearby is the large, eye-catching **Matthias Fountain** (Alajos Stróbl, 1904), which recalls one of the romantic tales associated with the popular 15C King Matthias. He is presented here in hunting garb, holding a crossbow; a stag lies at his feet. The seated figure on the left below is Galeotto Marzio, the Italian humanist scholar who was a chronicler at the king's court. On the right is Szép Ilonka (Ilonka the Beautiful), immortalised in a romantic ballad of 19C poet Mihály Vörösmarty. Ilonka falls in love with the king after she met him by chance when he was hunting in the forest. But later, discovering who he was, she dies of a broken heart believing her love to be hopeless.

The rear **Lion Court** to the south derives its name from the lion statues by the archway leading into it (János Fadrusz, 1901–02). The two statues flanking the entrance to the Castle Museum on the south side of the courtyard represent **War** and **Peace** and are the work of Károly Senyei (1900).

HUNGARIAN NATIONAL GALLERY

The **Hungarian National Gallery** (Magyar Nemzeti Galéria), the country's main collection of Hungarian works of art, occupies the central wings (B, C and D) of the former Royal Palace. The main entrance is on the Danube side, by the statue of Eugene of Savoy (tel: 175–7533 ext 423; open 10.00–18.00 except Mon; free on Sat; all titles in English; pleasant café area; bookshop; lift for w/a).

History

The content of the National Gallery owes much to the nature of its origins, which stem from the national reform movements of the first half of the 19C. The Founding Society of the National Picture Gallery was set up in 1845 to embrace the cause of Hungarian artists. Its first exhibition opened at the National Museum in March 1846. The National Picture Gallery was established in 1851 and this can be regarded as the precursor of today's Hungarian National Gallery.

When it opened in 1906 the Museum of Fine Arts took over the holdings, which had been greatly enhanced by the acquisition of the Esterházy collection in 1870. Later, a separate New Hungarian Picture Gallery opened in

1928 in the building which is today the Academy of Fine Arts on Andrássy út. In 1953, works belonging to the municipality of Budapest were incorporated and the resulting collection constituted the core of the National Gallery.

In 1957 the Hungarian National Gallery was established as an independent museum in the building of what is today the Ethnographical Museum in Pest. It moved to the reconstructed Royal Palace in 1975.

On the landing at the top of the first flight of stairs, visitors are confronted by Peter Krafft's huge **Zrínyi's Sortie** (1825), portraying Miklós Zrínyi's attack against Turkish forces at Szigetvár in 1566. As a historical painting depicting a major national event from Hungary's past, it sets the tone for a large element of one of the museum's major permanent exhibitions, that of **19C painting and sculpture**, on the first floor.

Gyula Benczúr's **Recapture of Buda Castle** (1896) in the central cupola hall at the top of the next flight is another work based on a national theme, the end of 150 years of Ottoman rule. The portrayal here of Karl of Lotharingia and Eugene of Savoy indicate, however, that the end of one empire meant the start of another, that of the Habsburgs. Thus the picture pointedly highlights one of the many triumphs-cum-tragedies in the twists and turns of Hungary's history.

There are further examples of 'national' historical painting in both directions. To the right, in D wing, hangs **The Mourning of László Hunyadi** by Viktor Madarász (1859). Hunyadi was beheaded by the Habsburg Ladislas V in 1457, but the allusion to the execution of many Hungarians following the failed 1848–49 War of Independence against Austria was clear to all. Hungary's tragic fate, depicted here, is reflected in many of the paintings in this section.

To the left, in B wing, is another of Gyula Benczúr's works, **The Baptism of Vajk** (1875). Vajk was the pagan name of King (St) Stephen, Hungary's first monarch (ruled 1000–38). His conversion to Christianity, and that of the Magyars, signified a major step in the integration of Hungary into European culture and politics.

At the far end of B wing there is a special room containing works of **Mihály Munkácsy** and **László Paál**. Munkácsy (1844–1900) was one of the very few 19C Hungarian painters to gain international recognition, partly because he spent most of his time in Munich and later Paris. He is noted for his genre paintings and rather romantic representation of ordinary characters, as exemplified here by his Condemned Cell (1870) immediately on the left. But he could also produce 'Turneresque' landscapes (Dusty Country Road II, c 1883). Paál's work, however, is almost entirely landscape.

19C trends which moved away from the national theme are represented by a number of artists including **Pál Szinyei Merse**, the 'founder of Hungarian Impressionism'. His Picnic in May (1873) and other works hang together in B wing.

The permanent exhibition of **20C Hungarian painting, sculpture and medals** can be found on the second and third floors. All the schools of 20C Hungarian painting up to 1945 are represented here, including the plein-air painters of the influential Nagybánya colony (Simon Hollósy, Károly Ferenczy, et al.). Although most of the artists are unknown outside Hungary, it can be seen that the trends which unfolded throughout Europe (Post-Impressionism, Art Nouveau, Fauvism, Cubism, Constructivism, etc.) are reflected in many of the works exhibited here.

One who did not neatly fit any trends, but whose work caught the attention of

NATIONAL GALLERY

1. Lapidarium. Medieval and Renaissance stone carvings
2. Gothic wood sculpture and panel paintings
3. Late Gothic winged atlars, wood carvings and panel paintings
4. Late Renaissance and Baroque art
5a. 19C neo-Classical, Romantic and Historicist painting
5b. 19C 'National Historical' painting
5c. Mihály Munkácsy and László Paál
5d. Pál Szinyei Merse
5e. Late 19C new trends
6. 20C paintings, sculpture and medals (up to 1945)
7. Contemporary art
8. Temporary exhibitions
9. Bookshop
10. Café
11. Habsburg crypt entrance

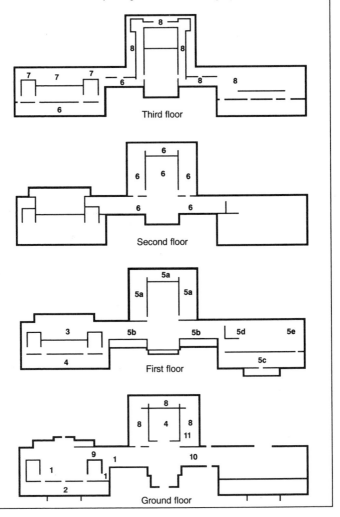

Third floor

Second floor

First floor

Ground floor

even Picasso, was **Tivadar Csontváry Kosztka**. His strange fusion of Expressionism and Symbolism is shown in his large Ruins of the Greek Theatre at Taormina (1905), hanging on the landing between the first and second floors.

Among the other exhibitions in the National Gallery one deserves particular mention—the **Late 15C and 16C Winged Altarpieces** in the former grand throne room of the Royal Palace on the first floor in D wing. This striking collection is unique in Central Europe. The majority of altarpieces and panel pictures on display come from churches in the former Upper Hungary (today Slovakia). Hungarian late Gothic painting reached its climax at the beginning of the 16C in the art of Master MS, whose work is represented here by The Visitation.

The small **Habsburg Crypt** in the basement of the Palace can be visited at set times with a guide (details from the information desk by the entrance). Here are several tombs of members of the Habsburg family associated with Hungary, notably Palatine Archduke Joseph (1776–1847). His statue here is by Görgy Zala. The Habsburg palatines (imperial representatives) resided in the Royal Palace from the late 18C to 1849.

The **Ludwig Museum** (Ludwig Múzeum) occupies Building A, the northernmost wing of the former Royal Palace (tel: 212–2534; entrance from the rear courtyard; open 10.00–18.00 except Mon; free on Tue; snack bar). The basis of the collection was donated in 1989 by art collector Peter Ludwig and the Aachen-based Ludwig Foundation. The permanent exhibition of **International Contemporary Art** includes both foreign and Hungarian works from the late 1950s.

The Budapest History Museum's **Castle Museum** (Vármúzeum) is situated in Building E, the southernmost wing of the former Royal Palace (tel: 175–7533; entrance via the Lion Courtyard; open 10.00–18.00 except Tues; free on Wed; auto-guides; snack bar; w/a poor).

The permanent exhibition, **Budapest in the Middle Ages**, is on the ground floor. Although rather short of actual items (Hungarian medieval culture having been almost literally swept away during the 150 years of Turkish rule), there are many fragments accompanied by numerous drawings, maps and diagrams, all with extensive texts in both Hungarian and English.

Also on the ground floor is the exhibition of **Gothic Statues from the Royal Palace**. These were found unexpectedly in 1974 during excavations undertaken in parallel with the long-term reconstruction of the Palace following the damage of 1944–45. These late 14C and early 15C statues are mainly of secular figures and are believed to be the product of a Buda workshop where French influence was strong.

Entrance to the reconstructed parts of the **Royal Palace of Medieval Buda** is downstairs in the basement. The exhibition, which was made possible by the above-mentioned archaeological excavations, weaves through a series of underground passages, galleries and reconstructed halls.

The passages lead to a tiny prison cell, a late-Gothic cross-vaulted hall and a 14C tower chapel. Items displayed include a reconstructed oven, tiles, kitchen utensils and prison memorabilia, as well as fragments of fireplaces and red-marble Renaissance carvings from the time of King Matthias. There are texts in English throughout.

A new permanent exhibition, **Budapest in Modern Times** (from 1686) opened on the first floor in December 1995.

The **National Széchényi Library** (Országos Széchényi Könyvtár) occupies Building F, on the west side of the Lion Courtyard at the rear of the former Royal Palace complex. The library is a public reference library, open to all. A day ticket is available on request at the desk (reading rooms open Mon 13.00–21.00; Tues–Sat 09.00–21.00). The central collection of this national deposit library consists mostly of 'Hungarica', i.e. publications printed in Hungary or abroad if written in Hungarian, or by a Hungarian, or relating to Hungary. In addition there are collections of newspapers and journals, ancient books, manuscripts, graphics and small prints, a map collection, a music collection and a theatre history collection.

History
The library was founded in 1802 on the initiative of Count Ferenc Széchényi (1754–1820) the father of István, the noted 19C Hungarian reformer. Széchényi searched the entire country and, at his own expense, amassed a collection of books which he donated to the nation. The National Museum in Pest, which opened in 1846, was the home of the library for many years. In 1949 the Széchényi Library was officially declared the National Library, becoming at the same time an independent state institution.

From the rear of the Royal Palace there is a view across to Nap-hegy (Sun Hill). The prominent, glass-walled building there, with mast and satellite dishes, is the new building of **MTI** (Hungarian News Agency). This is one of the few examples of Late Modern, or 'high-tech' architecture in the city (Csaba Virág, 1990). For a closer look, take bus 78 from Ferenciek tere to its terminus. The bus can also be picked up below the rear of the Palace in Dózsa György tér (accessible by lift from F wing).

The area immediately to the north of the Royal Palace, at the top of the funicular railway, is called SZENT GYÖRGY TÉR. Today it is bare, or occupied by derelict buildings, both as a result of war damage dating from 1944–45. Before that, government offices used to stand here, and there has been much argument as to whether the area should be designated an official quarter once again.

The **Sándor Palace** (Sándor palota), the former official residence of Hungary's prime ministers, stands by the top of the funicular. Although severely damaged in 1944–45, it has been restored. It was here that Hungarian premier Count Pál Teleki shot himself on 2 April 1941 in protest at Hungary's joining the German invasion of Yugoslavia only months after a treaty of 'eternal friendship' had been signed between the two countries. Albeit a futile gesture, Winston Churchill believed it had rescued some of Hungary's honour.

The **Castle Theatre** (Várszínház) stands just to the north of the Sándor Palace. This, the oldest extant theatre building in Budapest, was originally a church built for the Carmelites in 1736. The interior was redesigned in 1787, three years after the order had been dissolved by Joseph II. It was originally used by the German Theatre Company, then in 1790 the first professional group of Hungarian actors, László Kelemen's Hungarian Theatre, gave its first presentation here. German and Hungarian companies alternated throughout the 19C. Following serious damage in World War II and slow reconstruction, the theatre was only able to reopen in 1978.

3 · Gellért Hill and the Tabán

Gellért Hill (Gellért-hegy) stands over 230m above sea level and, topped by the Liberation Monument, is one of the dominating elements of the Danube panorama. It is named after the 11C Gellért (Gerard), the Benedictine Abbot of San Giorgio Maggiore in Venice, who, on his way to Palestine on a pilgrimage, was invited by Hungary's King Stephen to participate in the conversion of the Magyars to Christianity and to be the tutor of his son, Imre.

The **Tabán** is the name of the low-lying area between Gellért Hill and Castle Hill.

This route (about 1.5km) begins in SZENT GELLÉRT TÉR at the Buda end of Liberty Bridge (see p 104), climbs to the top of the hill, descends to Elizabeth Bridge and then explores some of the sights of the Tabán. Szent Gellért tér can be reached from Deák tér on trams 47 and 49. Trams 18 from Moszkva tér, and 19 from Batthyány tér, also go there.

The Art Nouveau **Gellért Hotel** at Szent Gellért tér 1 is one of the few remaining hotels in the city which enjoys an international reputation dating from the pre-1945 era.

History
The hotel was built between 1912 and 1918 to the designs of Artúr Sebestyén, Ármin Hegedüs and Izidor Sterk. A year

The elegant Szabadság (Liberty) Bridge, seen here from Gellért tér, was an engineering achievement of its time

after opening, during Béla Kun's communist regime, the hotel was commandeered for military purposes. Following the fall of the Council Republic it was taken over by the Romanian army and later it became the headquarters of Miklós Horthy, who had ostentatiously led the counter-revolutionary forces into Budapest, riding a white horse and proclaiming his intention of cleansing the 'sinful city'.

In the 1920s the Gellért became one of the centres of well-to-do social life. In 1927 the open-air pool behind the hotel was constructed and seven years later the indoor thermal and 'champagne-bubble' pools were built. These facilities were an important factor in the promotion of Budapest as an international 'spa city' in the 1930s. Members of Europe's royal families, foreign politicians, poets, artists and millionaires all flocked to the Gellért.

In January 1945 the hotel suffered severe war damage such that only its walls were left standing. The exterior was restored, but the present interior furnishings are not original. Nevertheless, a visit to the Gellért, particularly to its public swimming pools, can still recall the glamour of times past.

The impressive stained glass windows on the landings of the main staircase depict the Hungarian Magic Stag legend, recorded by poet János Arany. Although concerning an ancient theme, they are very modern (Gyula Bozó, 1994–95).

The entrance to the **Gellért Baths** is on the right side of the hotel in Kelenhegyi út. The ornate Secessionist interior can be viewed from just inside the entrance here. Apart from medicinal steam, mud and salt baths where treatment is available, there are also public indoor and outdoor thermal and swimming pools (see p 41).

The **Chapel in the Rock** (Sziklatemplom) is set in the side of Gellért Hill, opposite the entrance to the baths. The chapel dates from 1931, but in 1951 it was forcibly closed and later sealed up. After nearly 40 years, it reopened in mid-1989 and today belongs to the Pauline order, the only religious order founded in Hungary. The altar inside was made at the Zsolnay factory in Pécs (Győző Sikota, 1990).

The top of **GELLÉRT HILL** can be reached on foot via any of the (steep) paths which lead up from Kelenhegyi út. Alternatively, bus 27 goes to the summit from Villányi út, by Móricz Zsigmond körtér, 800m south of Gellért tér along Bartók Béla út (two stops on tram 47 or 49).

For centuries vines were cultivated on the slopes of the hill, until they were destroyed by an epidemic of phylloxera in the 19C. A variety of hot-water springs are found at the foot of the hill, which are used in all three baths nearby (Gellért, Rudas, and Rác). In the 19C Gellért Hill was a popular recreational area and the annual Easter Monday fair used to be held on the hill's gently sloping western side.

The **Liberation Monument**, a 14m-high female figure holding the palm of victory, stands at the top of Gellért Hill (Zsigmond Kisfaludi Strobl, 1947), it was erected to mark the liberation of the capital from the Germans in 1945 by Soviet troops. Pest was liberated on 18 January 1945 but, due to the last desperate resistance of the Germans on Castle Hill, Buda had to wait until 13 February. German units were finally driven from Hungarian territory around 4 April, which date, until 1990, used to be a public holiday.

To the sides of the Liberation Monument are large figures symbolising progress and destruction. On the back of the pedestal the names of Soviet soldiers who died during the siege of Budapest were inscribed.

Following the political changes of 1989–90 there was much argument as to whether the statue should be removed and about whether the events of 1944–45 were a 'liberation' or 'occupation' by the Soviets. In the end the city council decided to leave the monument standing, but removed the figure of a Soviet soldier which had stood below the main statue.

Recycled monument?

One of the most persistent and telling anecdotes of Budapest relates how the female figure of the Liberation Monument was, ironically, originally intended as a monument to Regent Miklós Horthy's son, István, who was killed in a plane crash in 1942 on the Russian front. After the siege of Budapest the

Soviets, so the story goes, discovered the statue in the sculptor's workshop and requisitioned it for its present function. However, the original Horthy memorial, although bearing similarities, was different from the Liberation Monument. What is true is that the sculptor Kisfaludi Strobl managed to win favour and commissions from both the pre-1945 and the post-1945 authorities, despite their conflicting political approaches to public sculpture.

The fortress known as the **Citadel** (Citadella) stands behind the Liberation Monument. It was built by the Austrians in 1851 as a symbol of their power following the defeat of the Hungarians in the War of Independence, although the architects, Ferenc Kasselik and Mátyás Zitterbarth, were both Hungarian. In 1897 the thick walls were breached in a few places, signifying that the fortress no longer served military purposes. Today it is a tourist attraction with hotel, restaurant, café and splendid look-out platforms giving a marvellous view of the city. In fact the view, with its higher and all-round perspective, is actually better than that from the more popular Fishermen's Bastion in the Castle District.

Some of the earliest inhabitants of the region, the Celts and Eravisci, used to have settlements on the hill. Their story and a potted history of Budapest's 2000 years is displayed in a series of glass cases through the entrance and on the left inside the Citadel. To the right, up the incline, is a memorial stone to the astronomer Imre Dániel Bogdanich (1762–1802). An astronomical observatory stood here from 1813 until its destruction during the 1848–49 war.

The **Gellért Monument** (Gyula Jankovits, 1904) stands two-thirds of the way down the eastern side of Gellért Hill, above the Buda end of Elizabeth Bridge. According to legend, Bishop (St) Gellért (died 1046), who had come from Italy to help King Stephen's crusade to convert the Hungarians to Christianity, was thrown down this hill to his death during a pagan rebellion eight years after the death of Stephen. The 11m bronze figure of Gellért holds a cross above a heathen Magyar accepting conversion.

The monument was one of ten public statues commissioned and paid for by Emperor Franz Josef at the turn of the century. 470,000 crowns were spent on the work which involved cutting into the hill and constructing the artificial waterfall below.

The **Rudas Baths**, one of the city's few remaining monuments of the Turkish times, is at the bottom of the hill by the end of Elizabeth Bridge (see also p 45). There were baths here even in the late 14C, then in the mid 16C Ali, the Pasha of Buda, and later Pasha Sokoli Mustapha, had new baths constructed. The octagonal pool, vaults and dome have all remained from that time. Lounging in the various pools in the dark interior (men only) takes you back in time to another world. Apart from the thermal 'Turkish' pools, there is also an ordinary (mixed) swimming pool here, which has a neo-Classical setting dating from the 1830s.

Nearby, built into the end of the bridge, is the well room where medicinal waters from the Juventus, Hungária and Attila springs can be sampled.

Taking the waters

Although therapeutic treatments only made great headway in the 19C, Budapest's thermal waters have always played a part in its history. There is archaeological evidence that Neolithic people were drawn to the warm springs along the Danube. The Romans brought their bathing habits and built conduits, aqueducts and baths. The Magyars continued the tradition, but it was the Turks who created a golden age of bathing during the period of Ottoman rule (1541–1686) and that legacy lived on.

A British traveller, Robert Townson, visited one of the former Turkish baths in 1793 and recorded the following: 'In a common bath I saw young men and maidens, old men and children, some in a state of nature, others with a fig-leaf covering, flouncing about like fish in spawning-time. But the observer must be just. I saw none of the ladies without their shifts. Some of the gentlemen were with drawers, some without; according, no doubt, to the degree of their delicacy, and as they thought themselves favoured by nature or not. But no very voluptuous ideas arise in these suffocating humid steams.'

An observer today might disagree. Some of the baths are noted gay meeting places.

The route now continues through the underpass at the end of Elizabeth Bridge (for the bridge see p 78). In the small park on the north side (part of Döbrentei tér) there is a seated **statue of Empress Elizabeth** (1837–98), wife of Franz Josef I and Queen of Hungary. Elizabeth spent much time in Hungary and even learnt the language.

Monument to a popular queen

Elizabeth was friendly with artists, aristocrats and politicians and helped pave the way for the Compromise of 1867. She was a very popular figure and so much money was collected to set up a statue after her death that there were recurring competitions for the design. One submitted by György Zala finally won in the fifth competition in 1919, but it was not until 1932 that the statue was eventually erected. It originally stood in today's March 15th Square by the bridge on the other side of the river, but in 1953 it was removed. Restored, it was placed here in 1986.

The **memorial tablet** on the ground nearby records that on 6 October 1944 Hungarian anti-fascists blew up a statue of Gyula Gömbös which stood here. Gömbös (1886–1936) was a conservative politician with fascist sympathies who was Prime Minister of Hungary from 1932 until his death. He was the first foreign statesman to visit Hitler after the latter had come to power in Germany. (6 October is a historic date in Hungary. It was on that day in 1849 that Austria took revenge on Hungary following the War of Independence by executing 13 generals at Arad in Transylvania.)

The **Rác Baths**, which takes its name from the Serbian or Rác people who used to inhabit this area, stands at the foot of Gellért Hill to the west of Döbrenti tér, across both Attila út and Krisztina krt at Hadnagy u. 8–10. The 19C exterior, designed by Miklós Ybl, belies the fact that the baths date from Turkish times. Inside, the original octagonal pool and dome still remain. The 40°C water, which comes from springs under the building, is considered beneficial in easing locomotor disorders. (Mon, Wed and Fri women only; Tues, Thurs and Sat men only.)

In front of the baths, in the corner of the park area, is a small **memorial stone** in the form of a cube. This commemorates the 51st Esperanto Congress which took place in Budapest in 1966. Hungarians were among the first to join the Esperanto movement. A century ago the world's then only Esperanto journal was published in Hungary. In the early 1950s Esperanto was suppressed as it conflicted with Stalin's theory of linguistics which deemed that the time was not ripe for an international language. Like many associations the Esperanto Society was refounded after 1956 and thereafter the language even became an optional subject in some schools.

The green area to the north of the Rác Baths is known as **THE TABÁN**. The name probably comes from the tanning workshops which existed in this area during the Turkish period. Towards the end of the 17C many Serbs fled here from the Turks and, c 1700, of the nearly 3000 inhabitants 95 per cent were Serbian. The Tabán became a densely populated, poor area, unhealthy because of a sewer that ran through it, though with a certain romantic charm for some observers. In 1908 the City Council decided to demolish the area, but the work was not finally completed until the 1930s.

A few buildings remain from the old Tabán including the **Tabán Parish Church** (Church of St Catherine of Alexandria) on Attila út. The church was planned by Keresztély Obergruber and built between 1728 and 1736 on the site of a previous medieval church which the Turks had used as a mosque. On the façade are statues of SS Gellért and Carlo Borromeo. Inside, on the right in the little window, is a copy of a 12C carving known as the Tabán Christ (the original is held by the Budapest History Museum). Further along the same wall in a window recess there is a depiction of St Florian and the 1810 fire, which swept through the Tabán destroying 600 houses and in which more than 50 people perished.

The **woman with plate statue** behind the church, in front of Apród u. 10, is a memorial to the poet Benedek Virág (1754–1830) who lived in a former house here. Virág was also a member of the Pauline order and often gave masses in the parish church.

The open junction of Apród u. and Attila út here is called SZARVAS TÉR. No. 1 on the corner is the **Stag House**, a triangular building in Louis XVI style which takes its name from the inn sign with the relief of a stag which has survived on the façade. Today the building still houses a restaurant.

Opposite the Stag House on the other side of Attila út is a **bust of Vuk Karadzic** (1787–1864), one of the pioneers of Serbian literary language (Mitric Nebojsza, 1987). Beyond this, on the far side of Kristina krt, are two graffiti-sprayed **sections of the Berlin Wall**, brought here after the wall was dramatically pulled down in late 1989.

Just below the Stag House, from Apród u., there is access via steps to the southern end of the Royal Palace. A short way up here and to the right are several Turkish grave stones, marking the bruial site of Turks who died in the 1686 siege of Buda, which ended Ottoman rule over the city.

The **Semmelweis Museum of Medical History** (Semmelweis Orvostörténeti Múzeum, tel: 175–3533; open 10.30–18.00 except Mon; no w/a) is at Apród u. 1–3, the first building on the left. The building dates from the 17C but received its present Louis XVI façade following the Tabán fire of 1810. The physician Ignác Semmelweis (see p 136), who discovered the cause of puerperal fever, was born here in 1818 and is buried here. The museum exhibits include bizarre elements like skulls, models of intestines, strange pictures of old treatments, remnants of mummies and a shrunken head. The furnishings of one of the oldest pharmacies in Pest, the Szentlélek Patika (Holy Ghost Pharmacy), founded in 1786, can be seen inside.

Apród u. leads down to YBL MIKLÓS TÉR. **No. 6** in the square, next to the museum, has a wall plaque recording that Adam Clark lived here prior to his death in June 1866. Clark, who was born in Edinburgh in 1811, came to Hungary to supervise the building of the Chain Bridge (see p 82), after which he settled in

Budapest, marrying a Hungarian. He is buried in the Kerepesi Cemetery. The present building dates from 1875–80 and was designed by Miklós Ybl.

The **Várkert** (Castle Garden) **Kiosk** stands in the middle of Ybl Miklós tér. It was originally built in 1874–79 to house the pumping station of the Castle waterworks. After splendid restoration work, it opened in 1992 as a casino and restaurant. A **statue of Miklós Ybl** (1814–91), the celebrated architect of the Opera House and many other buildings including this one, stands a short distance from the entrance (Ede Mayer, 1896).

The neo-Renaissance arcade and stairway on the other side of the road at the foot of the hill is the **Várkert Bazár**, also designed by Ybl and constructed in 1875–82. The originally open archways were intended for a display of statues. They later became a row of shops and then sculptors' studios.

The pleasant embankment walkway nearby leads to the Chain Bridge, 500m to the north. Tram 19 runs parallel, north to Batthyány tér and south back to Gellért tér.

4 · Water Town (Víziváros)—Fő utca and Batthyány tér

The narrow part of Buda between Castle Hill and the Danube has been called **Víziváros** (Water Town) since the Middle Ages. At that time it was surrounded by walls and its inhabitants were poorer than their neighbours up the hill. In the main, people here worked in various crafts and trades and, very importantly, fishing. The Turks transformed the local churches into mosques and built baths here. One of these, the Király Baths, is still functioning. Intensive building a century ago brought an end to the small-town atmosphere of Water Town, nevertheless it is an interesting area in the heart of the city.

This route (about 1.6km) begins at CLARK ÁDÁM TÉR, at the Buda end of the Chain Bridge (see p 82), continues along Fő u., the main street of Water Town, crosses the busy Batthyány tér and ends at Bem József tér. Clark Ádám tér can be reached by bus 16 from the south-east corner of Erzsébet tér in central Pest.

On the west side of Clark Ádám tér (Budapest's only square named after a British person) is the neo-Classical entrance to the 350m **Castle Hill Tunnel** (Alagút). As with the Chain Bridge, Count István Széchenyi was instrumental in promoting the concept of a tunnel through the hill, a major project for Hungary at the time, and Adam Clark was also involved in its execution. Work began in 1853 and the tunnel was officially opened in 1857. A toll was levied on the use of the tunnel until 1918.

To the left of the tunnel entrance is the **Buda Castle Funicular** (Budavári Sikló) which connects Clark Ádám tér with the former Royal Palace above. The carriages run every few minutes and the journey takes under one minute (closed on alternate Mon for maintenance; w/a available). The funicular (the second in the world) was constructed here on the initiative of Ödön, the younger son of Count István Széchenyi, and opened on 2 March 1870. It functioned continuously until late in World War II when a direct hit put it out of action. It was not until 1986 that it was reconstructed and reopened. The design of the carriages is as original, but in place of the earlier steam engine they are now operated electrically.

The large, bronze statue of an eagle-like bird, which can be seen at the top of the funicular, is a representation of the Hungarian mythical **Turul bird** (Gyula Donáth, 1905).

In the small park in front of the funicular stands the **Zero Kilometre Stone** (Miklós Borsos, 1975). It is from this spot that all Hungary's road distances from Budapest are measured.

FŐ UTCA leads north from Clark Ádám tér. **No. 1** on the right (Miklós Ybl, 1867–69) today belongs to the Central Court of the Buda Districts. **No. 3** next door was built in decorated neo-Classical style by Hugó Máltás in 1861–66. Time and pollution have taken their toll on this building which otherwise would be rather striking.

Jégverem u. is the first street to cross Fő u. The three-sided Romantic building at **No. 2** on the right was also designed by Hugó Máltás (1860–61). It was built for the widow of Dutch shipbuilder J.A. Majson who came to Hungary at the invitation of István Széchenyi. The noted 19C sculptor István Ferenczy had a studio at No. 1 opposite until 1834.

Fő u. **No. 11–13**, which today houses a district community and cultural centre, is mostly in very bad condition but its better days can be imagined by walking through the courtyards to the Danube side. Designed by István Lánzbauer, it was built in 1880 for Count Gyula Andrássy. The family kept a rich collection of European paintings here until it was nationalised in 1919.

The remains in front of the modern building at Fő u. 14–18 on the left are of a medieval house which was reconstructed in the 17C. **No. 20**, at the corner of Pala u., also originally dates from the Middle Ages, but its present form with cylindrical oriel window and reliefs is from 1811.

The Post-Modern building of the **French Institute** (Francia Intézet) is at Fő u. 17. It was designed by Frenchman George Maurios and opened in 1992 on the site of the old French Embassy, which was destroyed in the siege of 1944–45. The institute organises exhibitions, lectures, music performances and language classes. There is also a theatre, a pleasant café and a bookshop (open Mon–Fri 08.00–21.00; Sat 08.30–13.00). The French-language library, which is open to the public, has a separate entrance (open Mon–Fri 13.00–19.00; Sat 10.00–13.00).

The **former Capuchin Church and Monastery** is further along Fő u. at No. 30–32. Its present form dates from 1854–56 (Ferenc Reitter and Pál Szumrák). The originally medieval church here was used as a mosque by the Turks. On its southern wall, visible from both outside and inside, there are Turkish door and window frames. The statue of St Elizabeth on the Romantic façade dates from 1856.

CORVIN TÉR follows immediately after the church. In the square is a bronze **statue of a Hungarian warrior** from the time of the 9C Magyar conquest, drinking from an ox-horn (Barnabás Holló, 1904). On the limestone base is a relief of Lajos Millacher, a wealthy factory owner who left a small fortune in his will to the city—on the modest condition that an ornamental fountain be erected bearing his image.

The Baroque house at **No. 3** Corvin tér was built in the 18C. A statue of St John of Nepomuk stands in the niche on the façade. The adjoining neo-Classical **No. 4** has reliefs above the windows depicting King Matthias as a farmer, scholar and commander. The relief above the door, with a satyr on either side, shows the interior of an alchemist's workshop.

The **Buda Vigadó** concert hall (Mór Kallina and Aladár Árkay, 1900) stands on the north side of the square at No. 8. This is the home of the Hungarian State Folk Ensemble, whose regular performances here are always colourful and lively.

The neo-Gothic **Calvinist Church** in Szilágyi Dezső tér a few metres along Fő u. was built in 1893–96 and designed by Sámuel Pecz, who, unusually for a church of this denomination, employed the style of medieval Catholic church architecture. The city itself provided the site by the Danube embankment. As the river was so close, deep foundations were laid and the earth obtained was used to build the terrace mound around the church. The building was seriously damaged in World War II and was not fully restored until the 1980s. The roof contains coloured ceramic tiles from the Zsolnay factory.

There is a small statue of Pecz atop a drinking fountain at the south-west corner of the square (Béla Berán, 1919). The architect is portrayed in the attire of a medieval master builder, a costume the sculptor claimed to have seen him in once at a fancy dress ball.

> The stretch of the Danube embankment by Szilágyi Dezső tér is one of the spots where many Hungarian Jews and anti-fascists were brought and shot during World War II. Erzsébet Róna, the daughter of József Róna, who sculpted the equestrian statue of Eugene of Savoy in front of the Royal Palace, has recorded how she was arrested in January 1945 by the Hungarian Arrow Cross and brought here. 'The Arrow Cross were right behind us with their guns....We stood in line obediently, with our faces to the Danube. Nobody said a word because it happened so suddenly, then a command, and they shot. Those who were hit fell down at once....I was not hit....[but] instinctively I dropped to my side on one arm and remained motionless. They believed that I was dead....Anyone they saw moving was given a second shot.' She was dumped in the Danube, but luckily the water was shallow and she later managed to crawl to safety.

Vám u. crosses Fő u. 50m after Szilágyi Dezső tér. The building of **MVM** (Hungarian Electricity Works) to the left shows an ingenious use of the narrow space (Iván Szabó, 1974). Beyond this building, at the junction of Vám u. and Iskola u., is a curious monument called **The Iron Block** (Vastuskó). Legend has it that wandering apprentices visiting Buda would drive a nail into the wooden block here, but no one really knows what its function was. This one is actually a copy, the original is in the Kiscell Museum.

No. 37/c Fő u. has reliefs above the first-floor level of Danaides-type figures. To the bottom right is the symbol of the sculptress, Alice Lux. The modern building opposite today belongs to the Environment Ministry (Dezső Dul, 1972).

Fő u. now enters BATTHYÁNY TÉR, the historic centre of the Water Town district. Like many streets and squares in Budapest it has had a variety of names. It was once called Bomba (bomb) tér because a cannon and ammunition depot was situated here. In the 18C it was the site of a market and hence called Upper Market Square. The present name refers to Count Lajos Batthyány, the Prime Minister of the 1848 Hungarian government.

The terminus of the HÉV suburban rail line which goes north to Szentendre is situated here. It shares an entrance with the Batthyány tér metro station, which is on the No. 2 (red) line.

The twin-towered **Church of St Anne** (Szent Anna templom) in the square is one of Budapest's major Baroque monuments. It was built for the Jesuits from

1740 under the direction of Kristóf Hamon, Mátyás Nepauer and Mihály Hamm, though the original architect is unknown. Work was hindered by financial difficulties, an earthquake in 1763 and, not least, by the dissolution of the Jesuit order in 1773. Thus consecration only occurred in 1805. The façade of the church was seriously damaged during World War II, but it has been meticulously restored.

The Buda coat of arms can be seen in the tympanum and above it the triangular God's eye motif between two kneeling angels. A statue of St Anne with the child Mary stands in a niche in the middle of the façade and above the entrance are allegorical figures of Faith, Hope and Charity.

The high altar has a group of statues representing the young Mary being presented by her mother, St Anne, in the Temple in Jerusalem. It is the work of Károly Bebó and was completed in 1773. Bebó also built the pulpit, although the reliefs on it were added later. The painting of the Holy Trinity in the cupola of the chancel is by Gergely Vogl (1771), while the ceiling frescoes depicting the life of St Anne and the triumph of the Eucharist were only added in 1928 by Pál C. Molnár and Béla Kontuly.

The building adjoining the church, **No. 7** Batthyány tér, was adapted from a former tavern in 1724 by Henrik Ferenc Fiedler. Today it houses the presbytery and the *Angelika Café* (entrance on the Danube side). The relief on the façade facing the square is in memory of the Jesuit Ferenc Faludi (1704–79), a poet, prose-writer and translator.

The **market hall** on the west side of the square has been standing here since 1902, at which time it was the first such large covered market in Buda. Severely damaged in the war it remained closed for many years and functioned only intermittently. Totally reconstructed inside, it finally reopened in 1975 as Budapest's then largest supermarket.

To the right of the market hall is a Louis XVI-style house built in the 1790s. The neighbouring two-storey late Baroque building with Rococo ornamentation at No. 4 is the **former White Cross Inn**, which acquired its present shape around 1770. The asymmetrical character indicates that it was formed from two buildings. In the late 18C the inn was a popular and elegant place of entertainment where theatrical performances were given. Tradition has it that Casanova once stayed here, hence the name of the present-day night club on the ground floor. The neighbouring, three-storey, Louis XVI-style dwelling house at No. 3 was constructed in the 1790s by the master builder Kristóf Hikisch for his own use. The reliefs above the ground floor symbolise the four seasons.

The large red building on the north side of Batthyány tér is a former Franciscan monastery and later hospital of the Nuns of St Elizabeth. It was built in stages throughout the 18C. In front of the building, facing the square, is a seated **statue of Ferenc Kölcsey** (Ede Kallós, 1939). Kölcsey (1790–1838) was the author of the Hungarian national anthem (*Himnusz*), written in 1823. The words on the statue, however, are from another, 1838 work of the poet, entitled *Huszt*, the name of a town then in Hungary but today across the border in Ukraine. They read: 'Look to the distant future and confront the present wisely; Produce, create, enrich— from this our homeland will flourish and be brighter.'

The route continues north along Fő u., which leaves Batthyány tér at its northwest corner. On the right is the **Church of the St Elizabeth Nuns**, built between 1731 and 1757. It originally belonged to the Franciscans, hence the statues of SS Francis of Assisi and Anthony of Padua on the façade between the image of the Immaculata. The interior is very rich in Baroque decoration and is particularly striking since restoration was completed in the early 1990s. All the more disappointing then that, except during mass times, access is usually limited to the porch.

The pulpit and the carvings on the benches were the work of Franciscan friars. The main altarpiece depicts St Francis receiving the stigmata. The chancel walls have illusionistic frescoes including pictures of friars. A fresco to the right of the chancel depicts a fire of 1810 with St Florian protecting the Christians.

The three-storey building next to the church on the corner of Csalogány u. is the **former Marczibányi alms-house**. It was built by philanthropist István Marczibányi (1752–1810) for charitable purposes. The inscription above the door reads 'A shelter for the defenceless ill, 1805'. In recent times the building has been returned to the Sisters of St Elizabeth order.

NAGY IMRE TÉR is a few metres further along Fő u. The square is named after Hungary's Prime Minister during the 1956 Uprising who was subsequently executed. It has had this name since 1991 and recalls that it was in the large building of the **Military Court of Justice** on the north side of the square (Fő u. 70–78) where Imre Nagy was tried in secret and condemned to death in June 1958. The massive building (Jenő Hübner, 1915) was a judicial centre and police headquarters for many years and was used by both the Gestapo prior to 1945 and the secret police in Hungary's Stalinist period.

The red-brick, Post-Modern building overlooking the west side of Nagy Imre tér belongs to the **Ministry of Foreign Affairs** (György Guczoghy, 1987–90). The large building on the south side of the square was designed by István Janáky and Jenő Szendrói and constructed at great speed during the harsh winter of 1941–42 for the then Ministry of Light Industry.

The attractive block of flats in Modern style between Nagy Imre tér and the Danube, across the road from the petrol station, is unusual in that it was built in the years of economic hardship following the Second World War (Pál Németh *et al.*, 1948).

The **Király Baths** at Fő u. 82–86 is one of Budapest's few remaining buildings from the Turkish period. Construction started under Pasha Arshlan in 1566 and was finished by Pasha Sokoli Mustapha c 1570. For defence reasons, the baths were built inside the then walls of Water Town and water had to be piped in from springs to the north where the Lukács Baths now stands. The surviving Turkish parts are in the wing which faces Ganz u. The neo-Classical wing with Ionic pilasters and tympanum facing Fő u. was built in 1826. The present name of the baths (King Baths) recalls the 19C owners, the König family, who later adopted the

Király Baths on Fő utca—one of the city's few genuine Turkish remains

Hungarian equivalent of their name. The original 16C Turkish pool is still in use. (Women only Tues, Thurs and Sat; other days men only. Closed Sun.)

Across Ganz u. is the Baroque **Chapel of St Florian** (Mátyás Nepauer, 1760) which is today a Greek Catholic parish church. On the façade are statues of SS Blaise, Florian and Nicholas.

Fő u. ends in BEM JÓZSEF TÉR, and a **statue of Bem** himself stands in the middle of the square (János Istók, 1934) showing the wounded general with his arm in a sling.

A friend of Hungary

Josef Bem (1794–1850) was a Polish general who fought in the Polish uprising of 1830–31, then against the Habsburgs in the 1848 Vienna revolt and later with the Hungarians during the 1848–49 War of Independence. Notwithstanding, and maybe even helped by his foreign origins, Bem's role in the war ensured for him a prominent place in the pantheon of Hungary's 19C heroes. Under his command the revolutionary army managed to liberate almost the entire territory of Transylvania in a period of three months. During that campaign Sándor Petőfi was his aide-de-camp and his poem about Bem is engraved on the back of the pedestal. After the defeat of the 1848–49 war Bem went into exile, becoming a Muslim and a Turkish citizen. He fought in Syria, then a Turkish province, helping, ironically, to put down a rebellion against Turkish rule. He is buried in Syria at Aleppo.

One of the major events of the 1956 Uprising took place in Bem József tér. On 23 October, the first day of the revolt, a huge protest rally gathered in front of Bem's statue. The events of 1956 were partly sparked off by sympathy with political developments unfolding at that time in Poland.

The **Foundry Museum** (Öntödei Múzeum) is 200m away at No. 20 Bem József u., which runs westwards from the square (open Mon–Fri 09.00–16.30; weekends 10.00–16.30; w/a good after three steps). In 1844 the Swiss cast-iron worker Abraham Ganz established a foundry here which became the core of the internationally known Ganz Machine Works. The foundry functioned until 1964, after which it was turned into a museum. The original wooden structure can be seen inside as well as jib cranes and ladles in their original setting. The museum exhibits the history of foundry and metal work in Hungary and has a collection of stoves made in different regions.

5 · The Pest Embankment—from Elizabeth Bridge to the Chain Bridge

This route (about 1km) covers one of the most popular traditional spots for strolling in the city—the pedestrianised way by the Danube known as The Corso. The views from here of the bridges, the river, Gellért Hill and Castle Hill are superb.

The striking, white, 380m **Elizabeth Bridge** (Erzsébet híd) was designed by Pál Sávoly and opened in 1964. It was built on the site of a former chain bridge of the same name which opened in 1903 and which, until 1926, was the largest single-span bridge in Europe. That bridge, the construction of which was accompanied by considerable urban redevelopment on the Pest side, was destroyed by the Germans in January 1945 as they retreated from Pest to Buda. Of all the similarly destroyed

Budapest bridges, Elizabeth Bridge was the only one not to be reconstructed according to its original design.

The **Inner City Parish Church** (Belvárosi plébániatemplom) stands by the Pest end of the bridge. The church, which is usually open every day, traces its roots back much farther than others in the city.

History

At the end of the 12C, a triple-aisled Romanesque church was built here and in 1211 Princess (later Saint) Elizabeth of the House of Árpád was betrothed here to Louis, Marquis of Thüringia. History has not recorded what she thought of the matter, since she was only four at the time! (He was 11.)

In the 14C the church was rebuilt in Gothic style and attained its present size. The Turks used the church as a mosque, but later they returned it and for a while it was the only Christian church in Pest. Following the expulsion of the Turks from the city in 1686 the church was damaged and in 1723 it burnt down. In the following decade it was partly rebuilt in Baroque style resulting in the present curious combination of Gothic rear and Baroque front.

Inside, the neo-Classical organ loft dates from the 1830s. War damage necessitated reconstruction after 1945 and the high altar dates from that time.

Above the main entrance there is a group of statues representing the Holy Trinity, while at the rear, on the exterior chancel wall, there is a large relief of St Florian by Antal Horger. Florian is the patron of fire-fighters and the relief was placed here after the 1723 fire.

Inside, you can see the Baroque barrel-vaulted nave and the Gothic chancel with its ogival vaults. The Doric columns just beyond the entrance are the work of neo-Classical architect János Hild and date from 1835. On the right there are three small chapels which have Baroque interiors, while in the fourth there is a red marble and white limestone Renaissance tabernacle niche commissioned by the town of Pest in 1507. It is decorated with the arms of Pest. The next chapel is Gothic.

Just along the row of sedilia which stretches around the interior of the chancel wall there is a Turkish prayer-niche (mihrab) which dates from when the church was used as a mosque.

The high altar is the work of sculptor Károly Antal and painter Pál C. Molnár (1948). On its left is a reconstructed Gothic tabernacle. The pulpit (1808) is a good example of early Gothic revival and is the work of Fülöp Ungradt, a Pest master craftsman. The two statues by the arch at the front of the chancel are of St Joseph and the Virgin Mary. Both are by József Damkó (1900).

On the left the first chapel beyond the entrance to the chancel has fragments of frescoes which were originally in other parts of the church and a baptismal font with small bronze sculptures (Béni Ferenczy, 1955). In the next chapel towards the entrance is another Renaissance tabernacle commissioned by the parish priest, András Nagyrévi, in 1500. This and the tabernacle on the other side are rare surviving examples of Renaissance work in Hungary. In the chapel nearest the entrance is the neo-Classical tomb of newspaper editor István Kultsár (1760–1828). It was constructed in 1835 by István Ferenczy, one of the leading Hungarian sculptors of the period.

MÁRCIUS 15 TÉR (March 15th Square) is the name of the area in which the church stands (the square actually covers both sides of the bridge abutment). The name refers to the date in 1848 when the national revolution against Austrian rule began.

Just to the north of the church is the small, sunken, open-air museum called **Contra-Aquincum**. This was the name of the Roman fortress built in 294 under Emperor Diocletian to help defend the Imperial border which ran along the Danube. The display shows the system of Roman fortifications in the area. Nearby is a bronze sculpture/fountain symbolising the Roman–Barbarian struggle (István Tar, 1971).

The large building on the east side of the square belongs to the Arts Faculty of the Eötvös Loránd University and at the far north-east corner of the square (Pesti Barnabás u. 2) is the yellow, two-storey **Százéves Étterem** (*100-Year-Old Restaurant*). This is one of the oldest surviving non-ecclesiastical Baroque buildings in Pest. It was designed by András Mayerhoffer in 1755 for Baron János Péterffy whose family coat of arms can be seen on the tympanum. Note the tablet to the right of the gate showing the water level during the great flood of 1838. There has been a restaurant here since 1831.

PETŐFI TÉR is at the north-west corner of March 15th Square. The **statue of Sándor Petőfi** with raised arm is by Adolf Huszár to the design of Miklós Izsó (1882). Petőfi (1823-49) is perhaps the closest there is to being Hungary's 'national poet', although, in fact, he was of Slovak descent.

Sandor Petőfi—the people's poet

Petőfi's popularity stemmed both from his (often criticised) use of everyday language and from his political involvement. Love and liberty were his great themes and in pursuit of the latter he became one of the leaders of the youthful rebellion in Pest which sparked off the Hungarian Uprising against Austrian rule in 1848. His moving 'National Song' (*Nemzeti Dal*) captured the feel of the times with rousing lines such as 'Rise up Hungarians...your home-land calls...it's now or never...Hungarians will be slaves no more!'

Petőfi took up arms during the subsequent War of Independence and died in battle. His memory lived on, however, and indeed still lives on. His verses are used for teaching from an early age in Hungarian schools and in hundreds of towns and villages throughout the land his memory is recalled not only by countless street names and statues, but also by numerous memorial plaques recording that he wrote this here, or did that there.

Erecting the statue was a political statement in itself. In the decades following the 1848–49 war the Austrian authorities were obviously not keen. The renowned violinist Ede Remény was a prime mover and raised enormous amounts of money for the project on his European tours.

Petőfi is depicted with a scroll in one hand and with the other raised as if proclaiming the 'National Song'. The patriotic mood and its central location help explain why the statue has often been chosen as the site for political demonstrations.

A large, albeit illegal, anti-fascist rally assembled here in 1942. The date chosen was 15 March, the anniversary of the 1848 rebellion. In 1956 the statue was one of the initial rallying points on the first day of the Uprising and during the Kádár era unofficial demonstrations were often organised by oppositionists in front of the statue on 15 March.

Behind the statue to the right stands the **Greek Orthodox Church**, Hungary's largest Orthodox place of worship. Construction started in 1791 to the plans of József Jung, though the façade was transformed in 1872–73 by Miklós Ybl when two spires were added, one of which was destroyed in World War II. The richly decorated iconostasis (1797–99) is the work of Serbian woodcarver Miklós Jankovich. The pictures were added by Viennese artist Anton Kochmeister c 1801.

To the left of the church, at Petőfi tér 2, there is a Non-Stop IBUSZ office, open 24 hours a day for booking accommodation and other tourist services.

The route now proceeds north from Petőfi tér, along the pedestrianised upper embankment, known as **The Corso** (Duna-korzó). The embankment was built up in its present form in the second half of the 19C. The tramway along here was constructed in 1900 on a form of viaduct to allow space for storehouses underneath by the river.

From the late 19C to the Second World War, the Corso was a favourite place for Budapest promenaders. Fashionable hotels along here and nearby, such as the Carlton, Bristol, English Queen, Europe and Grand Duke Stephen, received guests from all over the world. It was a place to stroll and be seen for both visitors and locals alike. Some of that atmosphere has been revived in recent years.

One of the attractions of the Corso has always been the splendid view it gives of the right bank of the Danube. International recognition of this beauty came in 1988 when Castle Hill and the entire Danube panorama from Liberty Bridge to Margaret Bridge were added to Unesco's World Heritage List, alongside such places as the Acropolis in Athens and London's Westminster.

The large **Budapest Marriot Hotel** stands on the Corso where two of the old hotels, the Bristol and the Carlton, used to be before the Second World War. Designed by József Finta and built in 1969 it was, when it opened originally as The Intercontinental, the first of the large modern hotels constructed in recent times.

VIGADÓ TÉR is to the north beyond the hotel. The **Vigadó Concert Hall** (Pesti Vigadó) was designed by Frigyes Feszl and built in 1859–64 to replace a former concert hall on the same site which burnt down during the War of Independence of 1848–49. The hall has witnessed many premiers and performances by internationally renowned artists, and is still a major concert venue today.

The building was badly damaged by fire towards the end of World War II and, although Feszl's Romantic exterior was reconstructed as original the inside was completely redesigned, though, as a reflection of how long it took to complete some post-war reconstruction, the building did not actually reopen until 1980.

The richly decorated exterior includes reliefs of dancers on the columns (Károly Alexy, 1863–64) and, along the frieze-like ledge, a series of busts of various Hungarian rulers and prominent personalities. In the centre is the old Hungarian coat of arms.

In 1913 the Vigadó hosted the International Women's Suffrage Conference and the following Easter the famous English 'votes for women' campaigner and socialist activist Sylvia Pankhurst lectured here. She also visited public welfare projects for orphans, which she found positive, and investigated the conditions of women prisoners, which struck her as 'a sad experience'.

The small statue of a child with jester-like hat, seated on the railings by the tramline in Vigadó tér is entitled **Little Princess** (László Marton, 1989).

The Pest embankment was almost completely destroyed during the siege of Budapest in 1944–45. The battle raged between the Soviet Army on this side and the retreating Germans holed up on Castle Hill and Gellért Hill across the river. The building stretching along the Corso to the north of Vigadó tér is the only one remaining from the pre-war era, and gives some idea of what the embankment looked like in the old days.

Beyond this, on the ground, there is a large **bronze anchor**. It was placed here in 1990 as a memorial to the Hungarian seamen who have lost their lives at sea. (Although Hungary is landlocked, it has a small merchant navy operating on the Danube and on the high seas.)

Nearby stands Pál Pátzay's 1937 female statue entitled **Danube Wind**. Behind this rises the dark-glass-fronted **Forum Hotel** (József Finta, 1981). The popular coffee shop on the first floor is in the style of an old Viennese coffee-house.

In front of the hotel's main entrance is a bronze **statue of Baron József Eötvös** (1813–71), a statesman, scholar and writer, Minister of Culture in 1848 and after 1867, and from 1866 President of the Academy of Sciences (Adolf Huszár, 1879). As early as 1868 Eötvös's Public Education Act established state-controlled compulsory elementary schooling. However, his Nationalities Act of the same year was more controversial. It declared that all Hungary's citizens belonged to the 'united Magyar nation' and did not recognise the right to autonomy of non-Magyar peoples.

In the summer months the **Kossuth Museum Ship** is moored at the embankment near the Forum Hotel. Founded in 1986 as part of the Transport Museum, the museum (itself a steamship built in 1913) is devoted to the history of steam shipping on the Danube.

The **CHAIN BRIDGE** (Széchenyi lánchíd) is at the northern end of the Corso. Built in 1839–49 this was the city's first permanent river crossing. Today the outline of the Chain Bridge is one of the most commonly used symbols of Budapest.

History

The idea of a permanent bridge was developed by Hungary's great 19C reformer, Count István Széchenyi. In 1820 bad weather had forced him to wait eight days before he could cross the river by ferry to attend his father's funeral.

A great Anglophile, he commissioned William Tierney Clark, an Englishman, to design the bridge, and the Scottish engineer Adam Clark (no relation) was brought to Hungary to supervise the construction. The building of the bridge aroused much public interest and was seen as a symbol of economic and social progress.

In May 1849 during the War of Independence and before the bridge was finally completed, the Austrians planned to blow it up. Adam Clark thwarted their plans by having the chain-lockers flooded with water. When it finally opened on 21 November 1849 the bridge, at nearly 380m, was one of the largest suspension bridges of the time. The similarity with London's Hammersmith Bridge is not coincidental—Tierney Clark designed that one, too, and it was the basis of his plans for the Chain Bridge.

When the bridge opened, a controversial toll was levied on all who used it, thus breaching the privileges of those nobility who had previously been exempt from such taxes. In practice tolls ceased in 1918, though they were not legally abolished for a further two years.

The bridge was reconstructed during the 1914–18 War, since when it has officially been called the Széchenyi Chain Bridge. Destroyed by the Germans in World War II, it was reconstructed and reopened on 21 November 1949, the centenary of its original inauguaration.

Legend has it that the lion statues at either end of the bridge (János

Marschalkó, 1850) have no tongues, for the shame of which the sculptor drowned himself in the river. Others say if you look closely you can find them.

ROOSEVELT TÉR is at the Pest end of the Chain Bridge. The name, one the few American or English place-names in Budapest, dates from 1947. In 1867, for the coronation of Emperor Franz Josef as King of Hungary, a 'coronation hill' was constructed here from earth brought from all parts of the country. The newly crowned king flourished the sword of St Stephen in all directions, pledging he would protect the country. The historic soil was later dug into the earth.

On 28 October 1918 the 'Battle of the Chain Bridge' (lánchídi csata), one of the main events of that year's Republican Revolution, took place here. Demonstrators were attacked by mounted police and fired on; three were killed and many injured. The incident sparked off a mass protest strike the following day.

The **Atrium-Hyatt Hotel** (Lajos Zalavári, 1981) faces the southern end of the square. Inside, hanging from the roof of the high atrium, is a life-size copy of one of the first aeroplanes to fly in Hungary.

Moving anti-clockwise around the square, the large building at No. 3–4, at the corner of József Attila u., is today the **Interior Ministry**, though it was originally built as the Pest Hungarian Commercial Bank (Zsigmond Quittner and Ignác Alpár, 1907).

The impressive Art Nouveau building next-door at No. 5–6 is known as the **Gresham Palace**. It was built in 1907 to the plans of Zsigmond Quittner and the Vágó brothers, József and László, for the London Gresham Life Assurance Company. At the top of the façade there is a curious relief of a male head with Elizabethan ruff. The work of Ede Telcs, it represents the English financier Sir Thomas Gresham (died 1579), the founder of the Royal Exchange in London, and the originator of Gresham's law (bad money drives out good). The façade generally is badly in need of repair, but close examination reveals its original richness.

Inside the gateway on the right, a plaque in English testifies to the building's origins and lists the company directors. A plaque opposite details the builders and directors of the company's Hungarian branch, which was founded in 1867.

The building was designed with the latest technology available. The luxury apartments above the offices were equipped with a modern dust extraction system and a form of central heating. Some of the original glory can be sensed through the entrance passageway which leads to a huge T-shaped glass-roofed arcade, although today this is in a sad state of disrepair (there are plans to renovate the whole building). The beautiful, wrought-iron 'peacock' gate at the Zrínyi u. end, to the left, is original. On the second floor of the 'Kossuth' stairway by this gate there is a fine stained glass window by Miksa Róth depicting Lajos Kossuth

The furnishings of an 1885 pharmacy can be seen in the window of the National Pharmacy Institute at Zrínyi u. 3, which runs along the north side of the Gresham Palace.

The neo-Renaissance **Hungarian Academy of Sciences** (Magyar Tudományos Akadémia, or simply MTA) stands on the north side of Roosevelt tér. On the main façade are statues representing the original six departments of the Academy: law, sciences, mathematics, philosophy, linguistics and history. At the corners, from the Danube side, are Newton, Lomonosov, Galilei, Révay (a Hungarian linguist), Descartes and Leibnitz.

History

The Academy and its building both have interesting histories. It was on 3 November 1825 when Count István Széchenyi astounded his fellow deputies in the Hungarian Diet (Parliament) in Pozsony (today Bratislava) with the announcement that he was prepared to offer a year's income towards the establishment of a learned society for the development of Hungarian arts, science, language and literature. Thus was born the Hungarian Academy of Sciences. It was the time of Hungary's great Reform Period and the Learned Society was seen as a national project to revitalise the intellectual life of the country.

In the early decades of its existence the Academy had no permanent home of its own. Then in 1859 a committee was established to organise the building of one. A closed tender was offered to three architects, Imre Henszlmann, an Academy associate, Heinrich Ferstel, designer of Vienna's Votive Church, and Miklós Ybl who was later to design the Budapest Opera House. Two other architects, Antal Skalnitzky and Frigyes Feszl, designer of the Vigadó Concert Hall by the Danube, were bold enough to submit plans without invitation. However, the committee, dissatisfied with all the proposals, invited further contributions from Leo von Klenze of Munich and Friedrich August Stüler, the architect of Berlin's National Gallery and Stockholm's National Museum.

In the end Stüler's design was accepted but the decision aroused great public controversy. Some were dismayed that a foreigner had been chosen; others argued as to whether neo-Renaissance or neo-Gothic was a more appropriate style for a Hungarian national institution, although, ironically, neither style bore any relation to indigenous Hungarian traditions.

Despite the controversy, Stüler's design was put into effect and the Academy building was formally inaugurated on 11 December 1865.

On the right side of the building, facing Akadémia u., there is a large detailed bronze **high relief** (Barnabás Holló, 1893) of the scene at Pozsony in 1825. In the foreground, dressed in Hussar officer's uniform, stands Széchenyi as he offers his income for a year to help establish the Academy.

Akadémia u. **No. 1** was built in neo-Classical style with Corinthian pilasters in 1835 (Mátyás Zitterbarth Jr). The upper floors were added in 1927–28. A wall plaque recalls that Josef Bem, the Polish general who fought with the Hungarians in the War of Independence, stayed here in 1848 when it was a hotel.

No. 3, also neo-Classical, was designed by József Hild in 1836. Hild (1789–1867) was one of the chief architects involved in the development of this part of Pest in the first half of the 19C. The house was the birthplace of György Hevesy (1885–1966), a colleague of both Ernest Rutherford and Niels Bohr, the discoverer of the element hafnium and the recipient of a Nobel Prize in 1943.

There are two statues amidst the trees in the middle of Roosevelt tér. In the southern part is a large seated **statue of Ferenc Deák** who was largely responsible for the so-called Compromise of 1867, whereby the Austrian Empire was transformed into the Dual Monarchy and Hungary gained autonomy from Austria in domestic affairs.

The side-statues show Justice (front), Patriotism (back), Popular Education and National Progress (left) and on the right Compromise (children with the Austrian and Hungarian coats of arms clasping hands). The ensemble is the work of Adolf Huszár, Ede Mayer and Adolf Kessler (1887).

The nation's sage

Ferenc Deák (1803–76) was a well-to-do landowner who had studied law and worked in the county civil service. After 1833 he was a deputy and leader of the liberal opposition. In the 1848 government he was Minister of Justice, but being of moderate persuasion he retired from public life during the War of Independence. During the 1860s he was the advocate of compromise with Austria, which finally came about in 1867. Afterwards he accepted no office, but as a politician enjoying great prestige (he was known as 'the nation's sage'—*a haza bölcse*) he was for a long time an influential figure and promoted a number of liberal laws.

In the northern part of the square stands a **statue of Count István Széchenyi**, Hungary's leading social and economic reformer of the first half of the 19C. The four secondary figures represent Széchenyi's varied fields of activity: Minerva (trade), Neptune (navigation), Vulcan (industry) and Ceres (agriculture). The Academy of Sciences decided to raise a statue to Széchenyi two days after his death in 1860 but it was not until 20 years later that the bronze and granite statue by József Engel was finally unveiled.

The greatest Hungarian

István Széchenyi (1791–1860) was involved with almost all the major projects of the Reform Period of 1825–48, determined as he was to drag Hungary, even if kicking and screaming, into the 19C.

A great Anglophile, he visited England several times and introduced many technical novelties from Britain to Hungary, including domestic gas-lighting, bathrooms and flush lavatories. He established the country's first stud and encouraged English trainers and jockeys to move to Hungary. Similarly, he brought engineers and shipping experts to help extend the navigation channels on the Danube. His major projects involved the building of the Chain Bridge, the founding of the Academy of Sciences and the promotion of a modern financial and banking system. Lajos Kossuth, although a political rival, once described Széchenyi as 'the greatest Hungarian', a characterisation which many still believe holds true.

Széchenyi distrusted Kossuth's demands for the overthrow of the Habsburgs, nevertheless he joined the revolutionary government of 1848. Subsequently persecuted by the Austrians, he ended up an inmate of an asylum at Döbling near Vienna, though even from here he managed to get articles published anonymously in the London *Times*. Following one police raid a relapse occurred and on 8 April 1860 he put a bullet through his head.

His funeral deeply moved the whole country. Tens of thousands of people went to pay their respects as he was laid to rest on his estate at Nagycenk, near Sopron in western Hungary.

The two busts across the road behind Széchenyi are of the linguist Gábor Szarvas (on the left) and the historian Ferenc Salamon (both by Gyula Jankovits, 1899 and 1902 respectively).

6 · The Inner City (Belváros)

This route describes a walk around the heart of the historic inner city of Pest (Belváros), the central area bounded by the Little Boulevard (Kiskörút) and the Danube. Today this area is the shopping centre of Budapest and also houses many of the city's travel bureaux, tourist offices and foreign airline companies.

The route is divided into two walks—one (1.5km) north, the other (1km) south of Ferenciek tere. They can be taken either together or separately.

A. North of Ferenciek tere

This is the busier part of the Inner City, and includes Váci utca, Budapest's most fashionable shopping street and popular promenade, and the equally popular Vörösmarty tér.

The walk begins on VÁCI UTCA, at the junction of Kígyó u., 150m from Ferenciek tere (metro station here). The bronze statue of a boy on the fountain by the junction is the work of Béni Ferenczy (1977).

The large building on the west side of the street is the **Eötvös Loránd University Arts Faculty**. Designed by Dezső Hütl and built during World War I, it has been occupied by the university since 1950. Prior to that it was a Piarist secondary school which, when it was founded in 1717, was one of Pest's earliest secondary educational establishments. It became an important centre for teaching both the Hungarian language and the sciences. The physicist Loránd Eötvös, after whom the university is named, studied here in 1857–65 (see also p 96).

The old school building was demolished early in the 20C as part of the redevelopment linked with the construction of the first Elizabeth Bridge. The present building dates from 1913–17. In 1948 the Piarist school was nationalised, though the order was given another school in Budapest. Above the arch facing Váci u. there is a statue of St Joseph Calasanctius, the founder of the Piarist Order.

The chemist's at **No. 34** on the corner of Kígyó u. traces its origins to 1686 and the Szentháromság (Holy Trinity) Pharmacy, the oldest pharmacy in Pest. In the middle of the block across Kígyó u. is the Libri Bookshop, which sells imported titles and books published in Hungary in foreign languages.

The rich Eclectic building at **No. 28** Váci u., on the corner of Párizsi u., was designed by Imre Steindl and built in 1877. An 1889 guidebook carried an advertisement for Mátyás Hezella's general shop here, saying that all manner of English gentlemen's tennis, riding, cricket and croquet sports equipment was available and that the gunpowder for shooting came directly from the English Curtis & Harvey Co. The second-hand bookshop, which today occupies part of the folk art shop here, contains many works in foreign languages.

Eternal elegance

It took some time after World War II before Váci u. returned to its former status as the most fashionable street in Pest, which it had enjoyed for many decades. In the record of his travels in 1834, the Austrian painter F.S. Chrismar commented on the animated life he found in central Pest: 'It is especially pleasant to walk along Váci street in fine weather, in the noonday hours, when everyone belonging to the elegant world of Pest is about. Here, dressed in all their finery, the beauties of the country stroll past the elegant shop-windows to look at the articles of luxury and fashion. The tastefully arranged windows provide a brilliant frame to the two sides of the street.' If the artist returned today, he might think that very little had changed!

No. 24 Váci u. dates from 1928 and was designed by the then 60-year-old Emil Vidor, one of the most ardent devotees of the Hungarian Secessionist school. By the late 1920s, however, this style was no longer fashionable and he designed this building in the then more popular Modern style.

The Studium Akadémia Bookshop at **No. 22** stands on the site of a former watchmaker's shop. In 1857 the first public clock in Pest was erected here. It was lit by gas at night until midnight. The bookshop's wooden frontage dates from when the premises were occupied by a funeral director's. Everything has been restored except the vultures which used to perch above the lamps—a rather morbid touch for an undertaker's!

The neighbouring Post-Modern **Taverna Hotel** was designed by József Finta and opened in 1987. The same architect planned the International Trade Centre (1985) opposite at **No. 19–21**. The wall plaque records that two noted 19C poets, Kisfaludy and Vörösmarty, both died in the building which used to stand here.

No. 18 next to the hotel, decorated with blue ceramic tiles, was designed by Bertalan Gál and built in 1907; the Fontana Department Store at **No. 16** (György Vedres) dates to 1984. The bronze statue of the **Hermes Fountain** next to the store is mid 19C, and was orginally an emblem of the Merkur Bank which used to be nearby.

The decorated façade of **No. 15** opposite the Fontana building (Géza Majorossy and Elek Hofhauser, 1901) includes wooden panelling adorned with floral carving and a proud winged lion. A knight appears above, as if stepping out of a niche. There are large tulip motifs under the cornice in coloured glazed majolica.

No. 13 next door is the oldest building in Váci u. It was designed c 1805 in neo-Classical style by Ferenc Schorndorfer, although its appearance has changed much over the years. Round the corner on the Régi posta u. side are four original inset reliefs above the windows. Further along this side street, **No. 13** is a rare example of Bauhaus-type architecture in central Pest (Lajos Kozma, 1937). The coloured ceramic of the old post coach above the door is by Margit Kovács.

The striking building at Aranykéz u. 2, on the corner of Régi posta u., dates from 1930 and is the work of Miklós and Ernő Román. The McDonalds in Régi posta u. opened in 1988 and was the first Western fast-food outlet to appear in Budapest. For a while it had the largest turnover of any McDonalds in the world.

The **Folkart Centrum**, at Váci u. 14, is one of the largest shops in Budapest for folk and craft goods (open daily 09.30–19.00). The building (Albert Kőrössy, 1913) once housed the shop of Marcell Breitfeld, an attention-grabbing fur-trader. In 1931 he installed a mini putting green in the window where he employed fur-draped models to play golf.

The richly decorated No. 11a on the left is the **Thonet House**, which was built in 1888–90 to the designs of Ödön Lechner and Gyula Pártos, the architects who later designed the Applied Arts Museum. The building, panelled in coloured majolica and including intricate carving, was constructed for the furniture-making company of Jakab Thonet. Miraculously it escaped damage in World War II and it stands today as original.

The **Philantia florist's** next door opened in 1905 and is the oldest flower shop in Budapest; the interior is original Art Nouveau. The large building at **No. 9**, of which the flower shop occupies a part, today houses the Pest Theatre (Pesti Színház). The site was formerly occupied by the Inn of the Seven Electors, a gathering place noted for its magnificent balls. A 12-year-old Ferenc Liszt gave a concert here in 1823. The present building is the work of József Hild and was constructed in 1840. In the last four decades of the 19C it functioned as the National Hotel. A cinema was added in 1913 which was rebuilt for the theatre in the 1960s.

The Gondolat Bookshop at **No. 10** opposite is on a site which has been occupied by a bookshop for many decades; in the 1930s the Librarie Française bookshop was situated here. The plaque in the window says that the writers Attila József, Lajos Kassák and Miklós Radnóti often used to frequent the premises.

No. 8 next door (Ferenc Fazekas and Gyula Katona Mihály, 1906–09) has typical turn-of-the-century Art Nouveau sculptoral decoration on its upper floors.

KRISTÓF TÉR, on the east side of Váci u, derives its name from a former pharmacy belonging to one Kristóf Nagy. In the middle of the small square stands László Dunaisky's 1862 **Fisher-girl statue**. It originally adorned a well at a fish market nearby on the embankment. Known locally as '*Rézi Fischer*', it aroused some criticism from those who would have preferred to see a masculine figure representing the fish trade. Others, more pointedly, observed that her flowing robes were hardly the sort of clothes actually worn by a working woman. Restored by Sándor Lovas, the statue was placed here in 1985.

No. 6 in the square (Albert Kőrössy and Géza Kiss, 1910) is rather puritan apart from unusual decoration right at the top. Several reliefs are related to hunting, as are the strange bear heads on the ledge.

Türr István u. leads off Váci u. opposite Kristóf tér.

From war to water

István Türr (1825–1908) fought in the 1848–49 War of Independence after which he went into exile. He served the British during the Crimean War and British intervention saved his life in 1856 after he had been captured by the Austrians in Romania. Having fought alongside Garibaldi in Italy in 1860 he returned to Hungary following the Compromise of 1867. He was involved in developing the canal system in Hungary and he even also participated in the preparatory plans for the construction of the Panama Canal.

The Vác Gate, one of the major gates in the old medieval Pest walls, stood at the end of Váci u. It was pulled down in 1870 but an outline of it can be seen on the ground here.

The massive building on the left, known as the **Bank Palace**, is one of the most sumptuous bank buildings erected in Budapest. It was designed in 1913–15 for the First Pest Savings Bank Association by Ignác Alpár who won an international tender from among ten architects. Alpár, who also designed the former Stock Exchange and the National Bank in Szabadság tér, wrote that it was his biggest project and that after the First World War such expensive building would probably no longer be undertaken. A whole series of master craftsmen were employed. The bronze gate of the main entrance (round the corner in Deák Ferenc u.) is the work of Gyula Jungfer. The reliefs above the first-floor level are by Géza Maróty. The rich interior is by Ödön Faragó and the windows are by stained glass maker Miksa Róth.

Although partly burnt at the end of World War II the building has been carefully restored. Today it is occupied by Budapest Bank and the State Development Bank. It also houses, on the ground floor, the **Budapest Stock Exchange**, which reappeared in 1990 after over four decades of non-existence. Visitors are able to observe the workings of the exchange (open Mon–Fri 10.30–13.00).

The corner building on the other side of Váci u. was built in 1877 to the design of Mór Kallina. Critics thought the building too simple and not ornate enough having just one balcony on the north side overlooking the large square. Ironically that balcony played a larger role in history than the critics might have guessed, for during World War I the supporters of the radical liberal politician Mihály Károlyi, who became Prime Minister in 1918, had an office in the building and Károlyi himself often used to address the crowds in the square from the balcony above.

Váci u. ends in VÖRÖSMARTY TÉR, a large, pleasant, traffic-free square popular with street musicians and artists in the summer. In the middle of the square is Ede Telc's 1908 Carrara marble **statue of Mihály Vörösmarty** (1800–55), one of the leading literary figures of the Reform Period. Carved on the front of the monument are Vörösmarty's famous words 'Rendületlenül légy híve hazádnak, óh Magyar' (Be always faithful to your country, oh Magyar), the opening lines of his *Szózat* (Appeal) which is regarded almost as a second national anthem. The small, dark, round spot below the inscription is alleged to be a patriotic beggar's 'lucky coin' donated to help erect the statue.

On the ground floor of the modern building facing the statue (Elemér Tallós and Tibor Hübner, 1971) there is a concert ticket agency (through the glass swing doors). The German Theatre of Pest used to stand on this site; Beethoven composed an overture for its opening in 1812. The **Luxus Department Store** stands behind the statue on the east side of the square (Flóris Korb and Kálmán Giergl, 1911).

One of Budapest's most famous confectioners and cafés, the **Gerbeaud**, occupies the ground floor of the large building on the north side of Vörösmarty tér. It was founded in 1858 by Henrik Kugler, a pioneer of the Hungarian confectionery industry, and moved here in 1870. It was bought by the Swiss Emil Gerbeaud in 1884 and from the turn of the century Gerbeaud's became well known both as a meeting place and for the quality of its cakes. The interior furnishings date from the turn of the century. A couple of portraits of Gerbaud himself hang on the walls. Nationalised after 1945, the café was called the 'Vörösmarty' until it reverted to its old name in 1984. The building itself dates from 1861 and was designed by József Hild, orginally for the Pest Hungarian Commercial Bank.

Vörösmarty tér has had many names and appearances over the years, as is shown by the old pictures on the large round pillar by the edge of the trees towards the north-east corner. The ornamental lion fountain nearby (Ágnes Péter, 1984) is always popular with children.

JÓZSEF NÁDOR TÉR, a pleasant and surprisingly quiet square, is 50m along the short road due north of the fountain. The first corner building here, at **No. 7**, dates from 1833 and was designed by Lőrinc Zofahl. It was beautifully restored for Credit Lyonnais in 1992–93. The attractive stairway can be viewed from just inside the entrance.

The Romantic building opposite, at **No. 5–6**, which overlooks the south end of the square (Hugó Máltás, 1859) originally only had four storeys; the fifth was added in 1922. Medieval and Baroque motifs decorate the window-frames and the balustrades of the balconies. The lavishly decorated façade was fully restored in 1994.

In the middle of the square stands a **statue of Archduke Joseph**, grandson of Maria Theresa and son of Leopold II, who was appointed Palatine (the king's deputy) of Hungary at the age of 20 in 1796. He had plans for the development of Pest drawn up by architect János Hild and in 1808 he was instrumental in setting

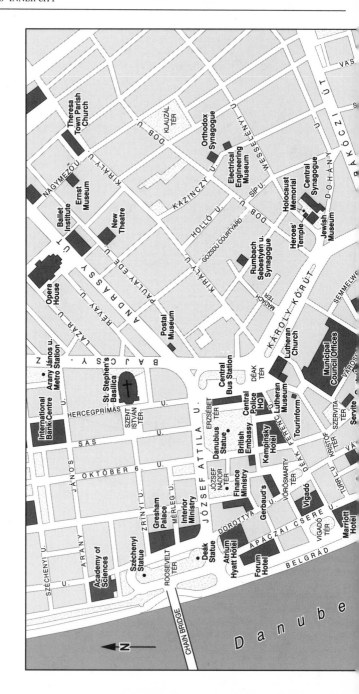

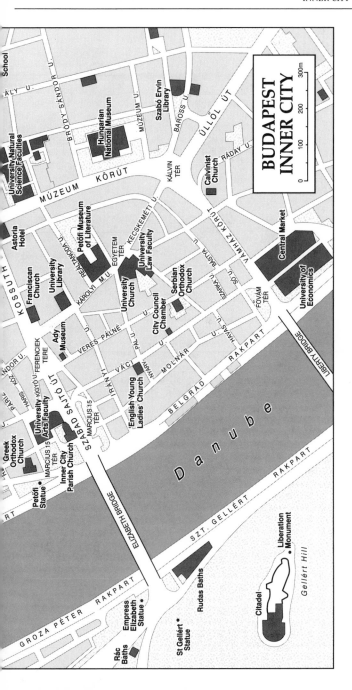

up the Beautification Commission, a public body of unpaid, enthusiastic citizens of various professions devoted to urban renewal and development. He died in Buda in 1847.

> The statue, which shows Joseph in the ceremonial costume of the Order of St Stephen, is the work of Munich sculptor, Johann Halbig. It was the first public statue of a secular person to be commissioned in Pest. It was completed in 1858, but arguments between the city and national authorities as to who should pay for it meant it was not erected until 1869. Paradoxically, it was placed facing south, though much of Joseph's work had involved developing Pest to the north. The city council considered turning it in the 1920s but it remains today as originally erected.

The large building at No. 2–4, dominating the west side of the square, is the **Ministry of Finance**. It was designed in 1913 by Ignác Alpár for the Hungarian General Credit Bank and is another example of the massive building projects commissioned for financial institutions in Budapest before the Great War. The foundations alone took a year as the two-storey vaults went below the level of the Danube. The sculptural decoration includes a statue of Mercury, the god of commerce, holding a model of the entire building (middle statue on the top ledge overlooking the square).

No. 1 next door is a characteristic example of neo-Classical Pest architecture and was designed by József Hild in 1824. The building overlooking the north end of the square (József Attila u. 8) is an early example of Art Nouveau in the city (Artúr Meinig, c 1898). It was built for the Hungarian General Savings Bank and thus has the charateristic savers' beehive motif on the façade. The attractive iron-work is by Gyula Jungfer.

At József Nádor tér 11 there is a Herend porcelain shop specialising in products of the noted factory at Herend in south-west Hungary.

The walk now continues through the archway in the middle of the east side of the square to reach ERZSÉBET TÉR, which at 20,000sq m is one of the biggest squares in the city centre. At one time a cemetery, by the 19C it had become a market place. Today its eastern side is occupied by the unimposing **Central Bus Station** (István Nyíri, 1948). Before 1990 the square bore the name of Karl Marx's colleague Engels, and for seven years up to 1953 it was even called Stalin Square.

The large **Danubius Fountain** in the square's park area was designed in the early 1880s by Miklós Ybl, the secondary figures being the work of Leo Feszler and Béla Brestyánszky. The lower basin was carved out of a single piece of rock weighing 100 tonnes. Its transportation on a specially contructed cart from Budakalász some 15km away was a public event. The fountain originally stood in Kálvin tér but was badly damaged in the Second World War; resculpted, it was placed here in 1959. The male figure at the top represents the Danube and the sitting female figures the Tisza, Dráva and Száva, the three largest rivers after the Danube in pre-1920 Hungary.

One of Budapest's most attractive Post-Modern buildings, the luxury **Kempinski Hotel**, overlooks the south side of Erzsébet tér (József Finta and Antal Puhl, 1992). The corner building just to the west, at Harmincad u. 6, is the **British Embassy**. The street name means 'one thirtieth' and comes from an ancient form of toll. The embassy building dates from c 1908 and was designed by Károly Rainer for the Domestic Bank. As the name might suggest, all the materials used and the labour employed were Hungarian.

Basil Davidson in his autobiographical wartime memoir, *Special Operations Europe—Scenes from the anti-Nazi war*, recalls an ironic incident about the British Legation which was then based here. He had been sent to Budapest to assist the underground resistance while officially running a news service for Britain. Early in 1941 he was called to the Legation and told that the plastic for explosives intended for the Resistance, which had been stored at the Legation, had been dumped in the Danube and that if he did not cease his clandestine activities he would be denounced to the Hungarian police. The Minister (not named) sincerely believed that Britain would soon lose the war, a not uncommon attitude in Central Europe at that particular time.

British officials in Budapest certainly seem to have been a mixed bunch over the years. Harold Nicolson's father, Lord Carnock, was British Consul at one point in the time of the Dual Monarchy, when the Hungarian authorities were not noted for their liberalism. 'I should be a Socialist of the deepest magenta if I were a worker here,' he once confided.

The route continues south along Bécsi u. **No. 4**, on the corner of Deák Ferenc u., is the Chemolimpex Building (Zoltán Gulyás, 1964). Its Modernist style became, in the words of one commentator, 'a repository of architectural cliché', copied on countless occasions in Hungary over the following 20 years (though note the rather Post-Modernist glass pyramid in the middle).

Bécsi u. leads to SZERVITA TÉR. In the centre of this small square stands an **Immaculata column**. It originally dates from 1729, though the present structure is a copy made in 1943. At the base are figures of Joseph, Anne and Joachim.

No. 2 Szervita tér, which prefigures Modernism (Dávid and Zsigmond Jónas, c 1908), was originally built for a small department store. **No. 3** next door is the former 'Turkish Bank House', built in 1906 and designed by Henrik Böhm and Ármin Hegedüs. It incorporated huge (for the time) glass surfaces mounted on a reinforced concrete structure. At the top on the gable is one of Budapest's most striking and colourful Secessionist mosaics. The work of Miksa Róth, it depicts a glorified **Patrona Hungariae** (Our Lady, Patron of Hungary), surrounded by angels and shepherds. Among the figures here are also representations of Prince Ferenc Rákóczi, István Széchenyi and Lajos Kossuth.

No. 5 Szervita tér, the **Rózsavölgyi Building**, was designed by Béla Lajta in 1910–11. With its architectonic horizontal distinction between retail, office and residential levels, it is considered a precursor of Modernism in Hungarian architecture. Lajta had spent time in both England and Germany and was well acquainted with European trends. Although he is often regarded as the local father of Modernism, the ceramic decorations on the upper floors betray his earlier connections with Ödön Lechner's school. On the ground floor is a chemist's and the old-established Rózsavölgyi music shop, from which the building derives its name. Apart from recorded music, it stocks a large range of music books and scores.

The **Servite Church** in the square was built between 1725 and 1732 to the designs of János Hölbling and György Pauer. The large relief by the entrance is a memorial to the members of the VIIth Wilhelm Hussar Regiment who fell in World War I (János Istók, 1930). Above the level of the door to the right and the left are statues of SS Anne and Peregrin. At the top stand SS Augustine and Philip. Although the façade was rebuilt in the early 1870s, the interior has retained its rich Baroque character. The huge main altar is by J. Hotzandorfer and was brought by boat from Vienna in 1741.

The modern building (1975) to the right of the church belongs to the telephone authority; various services are available on the first floor (public telex and fax, international directories etc.). Adjoining it, at Petőfi Sándor u. 13–19, is the neo-Renaissance building of the **Central Post Office** (Antal Skalniczky, 1875).

VÁROSHÁZ UTCA leaves Szervita tér from the north side of the church. The building which stretches for nearly 200m along here houses the **Municipal Council Offices**. Designed in the early 18C by Anton Erhard Martinelli as a hospital for veterans of the anti-Turkish war, it is the largest Baroque building in Budapest, though much of the original ornamentation was destroyed in World War II, which accounts for the rather plain appearance today. Just inside the third, southernmost gateway is a 1785 statue of Pallas Athene by Italian-born sculptor Carlo Adami. It originally stood by the old Buda Town Hall near the Matthias Church, hence the Buda coat of arms on the goddess' shield.

In the small square (Kamermayer Károly tér) at the far end of the Council building is an aluminium **statue of Károly Kamermayer** (1829–97), the first mayor of the united city when Buda, Óbuda and Pest were administratively joined in 1873 (Béla Szabados, 1942).

Pilvax köz opposite is the site of the former Pilvax Coffee House, a popular 19C meeting place for political radicals. 'If you write,' Sándor Petőfi once advised János Arany in a letter of 1847, 'then address the letter to the Pilvax. It is more likely to reach me, as I am more often here than at home.'

It was from here that Petőfi and the revolutionary youth set out on 15 March 1848. The original coffee-house was pulled down in 1911 though one of the tables and various memorabilia are kept in the Petőfi Literary Museum on Károlyi Mihály u. Inside today's *Pilvax Restaurant*, half-way down the street, there are archive pictures and other items recalling the 19C atmosphere.

The **Pest County Hall** stands at Városház u. 7, beyond Kamermayer Károly tér. It was built in several stages in the first half of the 19C and is one of the best examples of neo-Classical civic architecture in Pest. The section facing the street, with its six Corinthian columns and tympanum is the work of Mátyás Zitterbarth Jr (1838–42). The building has three courtyards, the first of which has an attractive colonnade. It can be viewed during working hours.

The walk now passes through the gateway of the **Trattner Building** at Városház u. 6 and through its two inner courtyards. This large neo-Classical building was constructed in the 1830s to the plans of József Hild. For more than 30 years until 1865 it was the home of the Academy of Sciences. The Trattner Printing House, also based here, was associated with the magazine *Tudományos Gyűjtemény* (Scientific Collection), an important critical, literary and historical journal of the 19C and a forum for young Pest writers. Damaged by cannon fire in 1849, the building was later restored by Hild.

The far gateway leads to Petőfi Sándor u. To the left is Ferenciek tere.

B. South of Ferenciek tere

This part of the inner city is somewhat quieter and the items of interest are more widespread. Included, however, are the important Petőfi Literature Museum and University Church (nearest metro station: blue line—Ferenciek tere).

For the Franciscan Church and Ferenciek tere see p 132. The Catholic Repository is next to the church. Beyond it is the *Kárpátia restaurant* which has a striking, pseudo-Gothic interior, stained glass windows and all, dating from the mid 1920s.

Further along, at Ferenciek tere 6, stands the **University Library**, which was originally founded in 1635. The present building was designed by Antal Skalnitzky and Henrik Koch and constructed in 1873–76. It was beautifully restored in 1991, though traffic pollution has clearly taken its toll even since then. A glance of the less-damaged interior can be had through the entrance.

KÁROLYI MIHÁLY UTCA leads south from Ferenciek tere. The **Petőfi Museum of Literature** (Petőfi Iródalmi Múzeum) occupies the former Károlyi Mansion 100m along here at No. 16 (tel: 117–3611; open 10.00–18.00 except Mon; no café; w/a very difficult; occasional concerts in courtyard). The building was originally Baroque, the work of András Mayerhoffer in 1759–68, though Anton Riegl of Vienna rebuilt it in neo-Classical style in 1832. The museum has permanent exhibitions about three of Hungary's great poets—Sándor Petőfi, Endre Ady and Attila József. There is also an exhibition about the Károlyi Mansion itself. Count Mihály Károlyi, the liberal progressive politician and President of the 1918–19 Hungarian Republic, was born here in 1875 (see also p 119). The Károlyi

Eye-catching domes in Ferenciek tere. On the left, the University Library

memorial plaque on the north wall of the building is by Viktor Kalló (1964).

The Austrian general Julius Haynau, who was sent to counter the Hungarians in the 1848–49 War of Independence, had his headquarters in this building. The relief on the south side, by Henszlmann u., shows the arrest which took place here of Count Lajos Batthyány, the Prime Minister of the first independent Hungarian government in 1848. Batthyány was later executed, on 6 October 1849.

Károlyi Mihály u. ends at EGYETEM TÉR. The façade of one of the most impressive pieces of Baroque architecure in the city, the **University Church** (Egyetemi templom) is at an angle at the corner of the square. Consecrated in 1748 it was built for the Pauline order, the only religious order founded in Hungary (by Canon Eusebius in 1263). The design is attributed to András Mayerhoffer. Above the tympanum at the top of the façade are statues of St Paul and St Anthony. Between them is the Pauline arms, a palm tree with a raven between two lions. The door is particularly beautiful with its carved wooden interior porch. The now somewhat dilapidated frescoes on the ceiling show scenes from the life of Mary (Johann Bergl, 1776).

The statues on the high altar are the work of József Hebenstreit who also carved the stalls in the chancel. Above the altar is a copy of the Black Madonna of Czestochowa painted on copper (c 1720). The richly decorated pulpit on the right and the carvings on the pews are the work of the Pauline monks who also made the balustrade in the organ loft, the Louis XVI confessionals on each side and all the other interior carvings of the church.

The church appears to be built into the large building at Egyetem tér 1–3. This is the **Law Faculty** of the Loránd Eötvös University, built in 1888–89. The University was originally founded in 1635 in Nagyszombat (today Trnava in Slovakia) by Péter Pázmány, the Archbishop of Esztergom. In 1777 it moved to Buda, and in 1784 to Pest where it occupied the former Pauline Monastery near the present building. Loránd Eötvös (1848–1919) was a physicist noted for his invention of the torsion pendulum used in geological research and his theories concerning the measurement of gravity and magnetism.

On the corner, between the faculty building and the church there is a dramatic, typically inter-war, patriotic **bronze relief** dedicated to the students who died fighting in World War I (György Zala, 1930).

Szerb u. runs from the square along the south side of the university. On the corner of Veres Pálné u., 150m along here, there is a walled garden in the middle of which stands the **Serbian Orthodox Church** (normally closed apart from service times). Large numbers of Serbs fleeing from the Turks arrived in Pest in the late 17C, but the church was not completed until the middle of the 18C. It is probably the work of András Mayerhoffer. The iconostasis has carvings dating from 1845; the paintings (1856–57), which show Italian Renaissance influence, are by Károly Sterio, a painter of Greek origins.

The Baroque Serbian Orthodox Church lies hidden in a quiet corner of Pests's inner city

Szerb u. ends in the southern section of VÁCI UTCA, which is not nearly so elegant as its northern counterpart, though there are plans to pedestrianise and upgrade it. The **City Council Chamber** is to the right at 62–64. It was built in 1870–75 to plans by Imre Steindl, architect of the Parliament, for the unification of Pest, Buda and Óbuda in 1873. Disagreements meant that Steindl had to change from decorated brick neo-Renaissance (exterior) to cast-iron neo-Gothic (interior), hence the delay.

Further to the north, on the corner of Váci u. and Nyáry Pál u., stands the Baroque **Church of St Michael** (Szent Mihály templom), formerly called, curiously, the 'Church of the English Young Ladies' (Angolkisasszonyok temploma). The reference is to the Mary Ward Nuns, or Institute of the Blessed Virgin Mary.

In 1611 the Englishwoman Mary Ward, a member of a Yorkshire Catholic recusant family and a niece of two of Guy Fawkes's fellow conspirators, founded an order of nuns in the Netherlands for the education of young girls. In 1774 Maria Theresa gave part of the Royal Palace in Buda to the nuns, then in 1787 they resettled in the former monastery of the (disbanded) Dominicans next to the church. Until 1948 there was a school and teachers' training college here named after the founder of the order (Ward-Kollégium). The church itself dates from 1747–49. The statue above the gate is of Patrona Hungariae (Our Lady, Patroness of Hungary). The carved benches inside are the work of friars and also date from the mid 18C.

100m to the north, on the corner of the building at Váci u. 43, is a **bronze plaque** recording that Charles XII of Sweden spent a night here in November 1714 during his return from exile in Turkey (Ottó Jarl, 1924).

The large building at **No. 38** is the former Officers' Club which was founded in 1861 and moved here in 1899 after the completion of the building. The patriotic slogan 'A Haza Minden Előtt' (The Homeland Before Everything) can still be seen high up on the façade.

In June 1956 the radical intellectual Petőfi Circle held a noted meeting here prefiguring the uprising later in October. Thousands of people tried to attend and the speeches, which continued until late into the night, had to be relayed into the surrounding streets by loudspeaker.

VERES PÁLNÉ UTCA is 100m to the east along Irányi u. A few metres to the right is Szivárvány köz (Rainbow Alley) one of the narrowest streets in Budapest. To the left, on the first floor of No. 4–6, is the small **Ady Memorial Museum** (Ady Emlékmúzeum; open Wed–Sun 10.00–18.00). The poet and social critic Endre Ady (1877–1919) lived the last two years of his life here. Ady was one of the outstanding Hungarian poets of the early 20C, as well as being a noted radical publicist who was outraged by the misery of poverty, economic backwardness and corruption in public life. His appearance on the scene coincided with and encouraged the emergence of a radical democratic intelligentsia, one result of which was the establishment of *Nyugat* (Occident), the progressive literary journal. The bronze memorial tablet outside is the work of sculptor Imre Varga and was placed here in 1977 when the museum opened.

Ferenciek tere is a short distance to the north.

7 · The Little Boulevard (Kiskörút)

This route (about 1.5km) starts at Deák tér in the city centre (metro station here) and runs the length of the Little Boulevard—Károly krt, Múzeum krt, Vámház krt—ending at Liberty Bridge (Szabadság híd), and includes the Hungarian National Museum. It follows the line of the ancient medieval town walls of Pest, parts of which can still be seen. Trams 47 and 49 run the entire length.

DEÁK TÉR has had a variety of strange names (e.g. Cabbage Market) but since 1874 has been named after the Hungarian politician Ferenc Deák (1803–76). In 1883 the square had the dubious distinction of having the first public toilet in Budapest.

The busy Deák tér metro station is Budapest's only underground interchange; all three lines meet here. In the underpass there is a small **Underground Museum** (Földalatti Múzeum), dealing with the history of Budapest's underground rail network. Entrance is one metro ticket or the cost equivalent in cash (tel: 342–2130; open 10.00–18.00 except Mon).

The neo-Classical **Lutheran Church** (Evangélikus templom) in Deák tér was designed by János Krausz and then Mihály Pollack, and built slowly between 1799 and 1808. Delays were due to the financial burden on the relatively small Lutheran congregation. Vienna-born Pollack had only been in Hungary for a year when he received this commission; he later went on to design many neo-Classical public buildings which helped shape the face of the city at that time. The church is one of his earliest productions. In the great Pest flood of 1838 many people found refuge here as it stood above street level.

The façade with its Doric pillars and tympanum was added later, by József Hild in 1856. The neo-Classical high altar, however, is Pollack's work. The large altarpiece is a copy of Raphael's Transfiguration (Franz Sales Lochbihler, 1811).

The building is normally only open for worship, but occasionally concerts are given inside and these are usually advertised on the front door.

Pest's first horse-drawn tram set off from outside the church in July 1866. The line, the third of its kind in Europe, ran all the way to Újpest on the outskirts. The new service was frequent (every five minutes) and aroused so much curiosity you had to book a ticket in advance!

The **National Lutheran Museum** (Evangélikus Országos Múzeum) adjoins the church (tel: 117–4173; open 10.00–18.00 except Mon). The permanent exhibition, 'Lutheranism in Hungarian Culture', includes a facsimile of the last will and testament of Martin Luther. The original is held in Budapest, in the local Lutheran archives. It was bought at a Helmstedt auction by Miklós Jankovich, a Catholic collector who later donated it to the Lutheran community.

The highly decorated 'German Jugenstil' building opposite the museum at **No. 3** Deák tér is the former Modern and Breitner department store (Sámuel Révész and József Kollár, 1910). The ground floor used to house the GDR (East German) Cultural Centre. It was a sign of the times when that was replaced by an exclusive VW–Porsche car showroom.

On its right, at Deák tér 2, is the **Budapest Central Police Headquarters**. Designed by Móric Pogány and Emil Tőry it was originally built in 1913 for the Adria Insurance Company; insurance companies were among the prime builders in Budapest in the years before World War I. Another such company, Anker Insurance, put up the large, columned building opposite the police headquarters on the far side of Deák tér (Ignác Alpár, 1907).

At the northern edge of the square is a half-seated/half-standing **statue of Endre Bajcsy-Zsilinszky**, a politician and anti-fascist activist who was killed by the Nazis (Sándor Győrfi, 1986). Bajcsy-Zsilinszky (1886–1944) had a rather varied career. In the 1920s he was a right-wing activist and editor. In the following decade he swung to the left and joined the anti-government forces. During the war he advocated unity with the Communists and formed a committee to direct the armed struggle against the Germans.

On the base of the statue, erected on the centenary of his birth, are the words of the 19C Hungarian poet Ferenc Kölcsey, 'A Haza Minden Előtt' (The homeland before everything).

Sütő u. is the pedestrianised street leading off Deák tér by the side of the Lutheran Museum. **Tourinform**, the central tourist information office is at No. 2 on the right. Tourinform deals with all tourist enquiries. The staff are invariably very helpful and English is spoken. Open daily 08.00–20.00; Oct–Mar early closing at 15.00 on Sat and Sun; tel: 117–9800.

In the small square just beyond Tourinform stands the Danaides fountain

(Ferenc Sidló, 1933). To its rear, overlooking the square, is the **Lutheran School**. Nationalised after World War II, it became a denominational school once again in 1993. Among its many famous past pupils was the Marxist philosopher György Lukács (1885–1971) who appears to have been a rebel even in youth. He once recalled that some of the leading personalities of Hungarian literary orthodoxy taught here and that his 'attempts at intellectual self-liberation took on accents glorifying international modernism in opposition to a Hungarianness I considered stupidly conservative'. His homework elicited 'violent professional uproar' (see also page 104).

The route now continues along KÁROLY KÖRÚT which leaves Deák tér by the side of the Lutheran Church.

The huge complex of red-brick buildings a short way on the left and surrounding MADÁCH TÉR was designed by Gyula Wälder in 1938. The plan was to make this the 'gateway' of a new avenue which would sweep towards the City Park in parallel with Andrássy út. The plans were shelved during the Second World War and the present buildings are all that remain. Two Post-Modern office blocks are through the archway—the Madách Trade Centre (János Pomsár, 1994) and, to its left, the Rumbach Centre (László Benczúr, 1993).

200m along the körút the impressive onion-dome towers of the **Dohány u. Synagogue** come into view (see p 105).

The Broadway Cinema occupies the corner ground floor of the massive **No. 3/a** Károly krt, which was originally constructed as apartments for the Victoria Insurance Co. (Guidó Hoepfner and Géza György, 1912). The reliefs are by Ede Margó.

Károly krt now approaches the 'Astoria' junction (for the hotel see p 134). The last building on the left, set back from the road at **No. 1** was built in 1936. It was occupied by the financial aristocracy of the day, and was popularly known as the 'Golden House', it being alleged that you needed a kilo of gold to buy a flat here.

Crossing the junction the Litte Boulevard now continues as MÚZEUM KÖRÚT. In the wave of office-building which hit Budapest in the 1990s the **East–West Trade Centre** immediately on the left here was one of the first (Lajos Zalaváry, 1991). Note how the building complements the aforementioned 'Golden House' with the similarity of its form.

The complex of large buildings erected in the 1880s at Nos 4–8 on the left of Múzeum krt today houses the **University Natural Sciences Faculty**. In the grounds, through the gate, stands a memorial to teachers who fell in World War I (Béla Horváth, 1936). 50m beyond this is a most curious building, the **Gólyavár** ('Stork Castle'—'stork' in Hungarian is the equivalent of university 'fresher'). It was built in six months in 1897 to the design of Samu Pecz, a professor at the Technical University, which was then based here. The building played a role in the build-up to the 1918–19 revolutionary upheaval. Radical intellectuals often used to meet here and hold lectures.

No. 7, on the other side of Múzeum krt (Miklós Ybl, 1852), has been described as 'representative of the finest instances of Romantic architecture in Hungary'—at the time of writing it is so dilapidated that you hardly notice it. Yet close observation reveals griffins under the balconies and a lavishly decorated cornice. In the equally dilapidated through-courtyard you can (almost) imagine you are in a Venetian palace.

In the courtyard of **No. 21** a section of the 15C medieval city wall can still be seen.

The **Múzeum Kávéház** opposite, at No. 12, is one of the oldest coffee-houses in Pest, dating from 1885. Although reconstructed and more of a restaurant today, you can still see original Zsolnay ceramic wall decoration as well as ceiling frescoes by Károly Lotz.

BRÓDY SÁNDOR UTCA runs to the left here. This narrow street witnessed one of the major events of the 1956 Uprising. The first shooting occurred here when a crowd, incensed by an inflammatory broadcast of Party First Secretary Ernő Gerő, besieged the radio building (No. 7) on the evening of 23 October, the first day of the revolt.

The neo-Renaissance **No. 8** here today houses the Italian Cultural Institute, though it was originally built in 1865–66 for the Chamber of Deputies, the lower of the two houses of Parliament.

Following Miklós Ybl's plans, construction began in September 1865. The project was regarded as a national concern. 800 people worked on the building and despite a strike for higher pay by the Hungarian carpenters, which necessitated the importing of Austrian furniture, the building was ready for use by the following March. MPs met here until the new Parliament building by the Danube was opened in 1901.

However, it was not the last the building saw of political gatherings. A public meeting was called here in November 1918 by the Feminist Association, a leaflet advertising the event declaring: 'All (recently enfranchised) women should be there who want to use their political rights in the interest of society.' The Association had been formed in 1904 with the primary aim of securing votes for women.

HUNGARIAN NATIONAL MUSEUM

The large neo-Classical building of the **Hungarian National Museum** (Magyar Nemzeti Múzeum) stands on Múzeum krt, immediately after Bródy Sándor u. (tel: 138–2122; open 10.00–18.00 except Mon; small café; w/a difficult; free concerts on various days). The collection dates from 1802 when Count Ferenc Széchényi (1754–1820), the father of István Széchenyi and himself a promoter of Hungarian national identity, donated his own huge collection of prints, manuscripts, maps, coats of arms and coins to the nation for the founding of a national museum and library.

History

Construction of the museum began in 1837 to the designs of Mihály Pollack (1773–1855), who, although born in Vienna and trained in Italy, adopted Hungary as his homeland. His neo-Classical public buildings and town houses typified the architecture of the Reform Period in the second quarter of the 19C. When the museum was opened in 1847 it was the fourth such national museum built in Europe.

Shortly after its opening, the museum became the scene of one of the most celebrated events of the 1848 revolution. It was here, or so the story goes, from the wide steps of the building, that a huge crowd was addressed by the young revolutionary leader of Pest, the poet Sándor Petőfi, who recited his rousing Nemzeti Dal (National Song). The event, the place and the poem have all found their place in Hungarian history and usually every year on 15 March the museum is decked out with the national colours and an open-air rally and/or performance takes place on the steps recalling the events of 1848.

The façade of the museum is dominated by a huge central portico with eight Corinthian columns supporting a large tympanum with statues. The central seated figure is Pannonia (the name of the Roman province occupying today's western Hungary). The figures on each side represent the sciences and arts.

Major interior renovation in the mid 1990s involved the closure of the main exhibitions. However, a new permanent exhibition, **A History of Hungary from 1000 to 1990**, was due to open in 1996, covering all the political stages of Hungarian history to recent times—King Stephen and the founding of the state, the flowering Renaissance period under King Matthias Corvinus, the 150-year Turkish occupation, the Rákóczi War of Independence against the Habsburgs, the Revolution and War of Independence of 1848–49, the 1867 'Compromise' with Austria, the two world wars, the 1956 Uprising and the subsequent decades.

In addition to the above, there are plans to open another permanent display in the late 1990s covering the history of the Carpathian Basin prior to the Magyar conquest.

The Hungarian Crown Jewels and Coronation Regalia are on permanent display in the museum. The central piece is the Hungarian crown, one of the oldest royal crowns in existence. It is made up of an upper, Roman crown and a lower, Byzantine portion. The upper part is believed to have been sent by Pope Sylvester II to King Stephen I for his coronation in AD 1000. It is made up of gold bands set with gems and pearls, and has cloisonné enamel images of eight apostles. On top is a gold cross bent to one side (no one knows the explanation). The leaning cross features prominently on Hungary's traditional coat of arms, officially readopted in 1990 (a curiosity in itself—a republic with 'monarchical' arms).

The lower crown was sent to King Géza I in 1074 as a gift from the Byzantine emperor. It is a gold diadem set with precious stones and gold enamel images of archangels and saints. Along the upper edge are images of Christ Enthroned, the Byzantine emperor Michael Duca, Constantine the Great and Géza I. The two crowns were probably joined together sometime during the 12C.

The crown was used for centuries at the coronation of Hungarian kings. Possession and being crowned with it was always a matter of great political significance. Several times it has been removed from the country; the most recent absence lasted 34 years. At the end of World War II it was taken by Hungarian Nazis to Germany from where it was taken to the USA and kept in Fort Knox. It was not returned to Hungary until January 1978, after US–Hungarian relations had been normalised for some time.

Other items on display include the Byzantium silk coronation robe, the sceptre with a rock crystal head and gold setting, a 14C gold-plated bronze orb and a 16C sword made in Venice.

The **Museum Garden** surrounding the National Museum (gates open 06.00–21.00) has been a popular place of tranquillity since it was laid out in 1856. A nationwide campaign was organised to create the garden. Ferenc Liszt and Ferenc Erkel both gave concerts to help raise funds.

The large bronze and limestone statue in front of the museum, overlooking Múzeum krt, is of the poet **János Arany** (Alajos Stróbl, 1893). The side figures represent Miklós Toldi and Piroska Rozgonyi, characters in his epic work of Hungarian chivalry, the *Toldi Trilogy*. Arany (1817–82), one of the classic figures of Hungarian literature, was an epic poet and ballad writer. He translated many works of Shakespeare and was instrumental in the publication of the bard's first complete works in Hungarian.

Almost all the statues and busts in the garden surrounding the museum are of noted Hungarian literary, political or scientific figures. Curiously, there is also a bust of Italian nationalist leader Garibaldi (to the right of the steps). But there is a Hungarian connection—a relief shows him shaking hands with István Türr, a Hungarian who fought at his side in Italy.

Another curiosity is the marble column standing to the left of the museum steps. This is from the Forum in Rome and was brought here in 1929. Indicative of political changes is the fact that pre-1945 guidebooks described it as 'a gift from Mussolini' while later ones preferred 'from the city of Rome'.

Múzeum krt ends at KÁLVIN TÉR, one of the main junctions of central Pest. The Kecskemét Gate, part of the old city walls, used to stand here until it was pulled down in 1794. The Korona Hotel (Csaba Csontos, 1990) today occupies the site where the gate used to stand.

The square received its present name in 1874 from the single-nave **Calvinist Church** (Református templom) here. Designed by József Hofrichter it was built between 1816 and 1830, although the entrance and tympanum were added by József Hild in 1848 and the spire dates from 1859. Hild also added the upper part of the pulpit (1831) and the organ loft (1854). The neo-Gothic sepulchre of the Countess Zichy can be found in the wall of the church on the left. The statue is by Frenchman Raymond Gayard and the framework by Frigyes Feszl (1854). The church is normally closed outside worship times.

BAROSS UTCA is the first street to the left from Kálvin tér. 150m along here is the neo-Baroque **Municipal Szabó Ervin Library** (Artur Meining, 1887). The library is a public lending social sciences library with over 100 branches throughout the city; it has a specialist collection of material on Budapest. An information service covering virtually all fields also operates here. It is mainly used by Hungarians, but English-speaking members of staff can probably be found. The rich interior is worth viewing. The large wrought-iron gates (1897) of the library are a good example of the fine work of Gyula Jungfer.

Ervin Szabó

Ervin Szabó (1877–1918) was a social scientist, a recognised authority on statistics and librarianship, and the library's first director. A prominent and popular political writer and activist in the pre-1918 decades, and a rather dissident member of the orthodox Social Democratic Party, he attempted to bridge the gap between the Marxist and anarchist traditions. When he died, all work in Budapest stopped for a while as a sign of mourning. There is a marble relief of him on the wall of the library (Gyula Kiss Kovács, 1954).

The bronze and limestone **Fountain of Justice** in front of the library is by István Szentgyörgyi and depicts Justitia, the goddess of justice, with sword and scales. It was placed here in 1929 as a reminder of the injustice many Hungarians felt had been inflicted by the Treaty of Trianon after World War I, under which Hungary lost about two-thirds of her territory and over half her population.

Originally there was a side relief on the fountain of the first Lord Rothermere, who befriended post-Trianon Hungary in the 1920s and campaigned in his *Daily Mail* for the return to Hungary of the lost territories. Such was the popularity of the British lord in Hungary that he received a letter of gratitude signed by over a million Hungarians and at one point was even offered the Hungarian crown!

The relief of Rothermere and an inscription in his honour around the rim of the fountain were removed in 1949, when the irredentist policies of the inter-war period were no longer in favour.

Returning to Kálvin tér, the two stone lions above the entrance to the two-storey building at **No. 9** are a reminder that the building, until 1881, used to be the Two Lions Inn (Mátyás Zitterbarth, 1816–18). Hector Berlioz is believed to have first heard the 'Rákóczi Song' here after which he composed his 'Rákóczi March'. In the courtyard through the gateway is a row of old, single-storey 19C houses and a lonely seated female figure from the Danubius fountain, which originally stood in Kálvin tér. Damaged, like much of the area, in World War II, the fountain was eventually restored and today stands in the centre of Erzsébet tér.

The Little Boulevard continues from Kálvin tér as VÁMHÁZ KÖRÚT. In the courtyard of the neo-Classical building at **No. 16** an impressive, free-standing section of the 15C Pest town wall can be seen.

100m beyond this, Veres Pálné u. runs to the right. This street is named after Hermina Beniczky (1815–95), a pioneer of education for girls in Hungary. (Ironically, in view of this, she is usually referred to through the name of her husband, Pál Veres.) The wall tablet at the corner of the street records that at No. 36 she founded the National Association for Female Education and at No. 38 the first high school for girls.

The neo-Classical building farther along the körút at **No. 2** was built as the Nádor Hotel in 1840 to the design of Ferenc Kasselik. The building is a characteristic example of mid-19C Pest architecture.

Opposite, at No. 1–3, there is the massive, station-like building of the **Central Market Hall** (Samu Pecz, 1893–96), the most impressive of the five Budapest market halls built in the 1890s. The huge iron framework covering more than 10,000sq m was originally built as the city's main wholesale market, but for many years now the building has been used primarily for retail purposes.

The market is always a popular attraction with visitors—Margaret Thatcher was photographed buying paprika here in 1984. Following closure and extensive renovations, the market reopened with its original splendour beautifully restored in 1994. It is well worth a look inside. (Open Mon 06.00–17.00; Tues–Fri 06.00–18.00; Sat 06.00–16.00.)

The large building next door (Fővám tér 8) facing the river

The Central Market in Pest (Pipa u. façade shown here) has been beautifully restored to its original glory

today houses the **Budapest University of Economics**. It was designed by Miklós Ybl in an Eclectic, neo-Renaissance style and built between 1871 and 1874 as the Main Customs Office; a series of tunnels connected the building to the Danube embankment. The 170m façade overlooking the river has ten allegorical statues by the Viennese sculptor, August Sommer.

The building was reconstructed after 1945 and opened as a university in 1951. Then from 1980 to 1990 it was faithfully restored to its original form. The interior is certainly worth inspecting; access is via the main entrance facing the river. Through here, then left and right brings you to a grand, neo-Renaissance customs hall (now an atrium) which, perhaps surprisingly, still has a large bronze seated statue of Karl Marx, whose name used to grace the university. Beyond is a warehouse-type section with cast-iron pillars.

The plain, limestone memorial in the middle of Fővám tér is to Hungary's First Honvéd Infantry Regiment of World War I. Unusually for a Great War monument, it was erected in 1949 in the 'communist' period. Yet this explains the inscription: 'To those who lost their lives in the interests of imperialism.'

The Little Boulevard ends at **Liberty Bridge** (Szabadság híd). The bridge (the city's shortest) was opened on 4 October 1896 by Emperor Franz Josef and bore his name until 1945. Destroyed in World War II, it was the first Budapest bridge to be rebuilt. Even so, the work took until August 1946.

Two original customs houses still stand at the Pest end of the bridge, while at the top of the iron structure there are two Turul birds, the legendary, mythical birds of the ancient Magyars. The structure itself has more tragic connections. Over the years hundreds of Hungarians have climbed to the top to commit, or threaten to commit suicide by jumping off.

BELGRÁD RAKPART runs to the north on the Pest side of the Danube. **No. 2** is the former home of the Hungarian Marxist philosopher György Lukács. His fifth-floor flat today houses a library and research archive belonging to the philosophy department of the Hungarian Academy of Sciences.

A maverick survivor

Perhaps the most surprising thing about György Lukács (1885–1971) is that this maverick Marxist managed to survive all the twists and turns of the international Communist movement and die a natural death in his own country at the age of 86.

The son of a bank manager he had a conventional upbringing attending grammar school and university. In 1906–11 he pursued his studies of literature and philosophy in Berlin. During the First World War, back in Hungary, he began to mix in radical intellectual circles and turned towards Marxism, a shift which was encouraged by the outbreak of the Russian Revolution in 1917. He joined the Communist Party in December 1918 and a few months later worked as a People's Commissar for Education and Culture during the short-lived Council Republic of 1919.

While in exile in Vienna in the 1920s he continued writing, producing *History and Class Consciousness* in 1923—a work which was to inspire many Western New Left radicals over four decades later. His unorthodox Marxist approach, not limited to purely economic concepts, has often been compared to the work of other critical Marxists of the time, notably the Italian Antonio Gramsci and the German Karl Korsch, though there are differences between all three.

A dispute over strategy in 1929 in the Comintern led Lukács to withdraw into purely theoretical work. He moved to Moscow in 1933 and stayed in the Soviet Union until the end of the Second World War. Devoting himself primarily to Marxist aesthetics he managed to escape the purges to which many of his Hungarian colleagues in Moscow fell victim, including Béla Kun the leader of the Hungarian Party.

Returning to Budapest in 1945 he took up a university post and actively encouraged intellectuals to work for a new Hungary. In 1949–50 he was strongly criticised in a campaign of cultural dogmatism and he once again withdrew into theoretical work. He reappeared on the political scene in 1956, becoming Minister of Culture in Imre Nagy's short-lived government. Although he spent time with Nagy in exile in Romania, he was allowed to return to Hungary unharmed in April 1957. He spent the rest of his life studying and writing about aesthetics, philosophy and questions of socialism and democracy.

Lukács is one of the few Eastern European Marxists to have gained a degree of respect in the West, both in academic and political circles. Yet he always retained an orthodox attachment to the Party and often displayed elements of dogmatic simplicity: 'Even the worst socialism is better than the best capitalism,' he said in 1967.

8 · The Old Jewish Quarter

The old Jewish quarter of Pest was bounded by Károly krt, Erzsébet krt, Dohány u. and Király u. in today's District VII. It was not a ghetto as such—at least until 1944—simply the area where there was a high concentration of Jews living and working. Jews flooded here in the second half of the 19C, after liberalisation of laws regarding the rights of Jewish people to buy property in the capital (formal emancipation came after 1867).

At the beginning of the 20C there were about 170,000 Jews in Budapest, many of them living in this area. Here could be found Jewish clubs, Jewish restaurants, Jewish workshops, kosher shops and several synagogues and prayer rooms. Jewish people represented almost a quarter of the entire population of Budapest. Socially it was a relatively assimilated community, and although anti-semitism certainly existed, many Jewish people were able to contribute a great deal to Hungary's cultural life and its business development.

By 1939 there were about 200,000 Jews in Budapest, but, as a result of the holocaust, today there are only 80,000; nevertheless, they constitute the largest Jewish community in central Europe. (The Jews of provincial Hungary fared even worse than those in the capital. Ninety per cent of Jews in the provinces fell victim to the holocaust. The total death toll reached almost 600,000.) Budapest's Jewish population is no longer concentrated in one area, yet some of the atmosphere of the old Jewish quarter still remains.

The city's main synagogue, the **Dohány utca Synagogue,** faces Herzl tér, at the junction of Károly krt and Dohány u. Seating 3000, it is not only the largest synagogue in Europe, but the second largest in the world (after Temple Emmanuel in New York). It was designed by the Viennese (Gentile) architect Lajos Förster with the assistance of Frigyes Feszl, and was built between 1854 and 1859. Like Förster's earlier synagogue in Vienna, the style is Romantic with a mixture of

The richly decorated Dohány utca Synagogue is one of the most visually stimulating buildings in Hungary–both inside and out

Byzantine and strong Moorish elements, which makes it one of Budapest's most striking and impressive buildings, both inside and out.

The synagogue is 'Neolog', a Hungarian denomination combining elements of both reform and orthodox Judaism. For example, the Bimah is at one end with a large organ (reform), but men and women sit separately (orthodox). The basilica-like interior, where Feszl's 'Eastern' decoration is clear, can be viewed during the middle of the day in the summer months. In the winter however, due to the lack of heating, it is closed and not even used for services.

Restoration of the synagogue began in 1989 and was due to be completed in 1996. The total cost of over 40 million US dollars was covered by the Hungarian state and donations mainly from Jewish associations in North America, in particular the Emmanuel Foundation, spearheaded by film star Tony Curtis, the stage name of Bernard Schwartz, whose father Manuel was a Hungarian emigrant.

To the left of the synagogue, through the arches, a section of the brick wall of the ghetto, erected around the Jewish quarter in 1944, can be seen. The ghetto, one of the last to be established in Europe, existed from November 1944 until it was liberated by the Soviet Red Army on 18 January 1945. A plaque on the wall commemorates the liberation.

The building to the left of the arches, on the corner of Wesselényi u. (László Vágó, 1931) stands on the site of the birthplace of Theodor Herzl (1860–1904), the founder of modern Zionism. Inside is the **National Jewish Museum** (Országos Zsidó Múzeum) which exhibits items from Jewish history in Hungary and has a small exhibition of photographs of the ghetto and the war years (tel: 342–8941; open Mon–Fri 10.00–15.00; Sun 10.00–13.00).

Behind the museum there are many gravestones, which mark the site of a mass grave of thousands of people who died in the freezing winter in the ghetto or while crammed in the synagogue.

Beyond the gravestones, set sideways to Wesselényi u., is the **Heroes' Temple** (Hősök temploma) erected in memory of the Jewish soldiers who died fighting for Hungary in World War I (Lajos Deli and Ferenc Faragó, 1929-31). This synagogue is used all year round, but there is no public access for visitors.

The courtyard beyond the Heroes' Temple contains a striking **Holocaust Memorial** (Imre Varga, 1991) in the form of a weeping willow, which takes the shape of an inverted menora. The metal leaves bear the names of families massacred by the Nazis. The inscription is from the Talmud and reads: 'Whose pain can be greater than mine'. The broken marble slab in front is inscribed simply with the word 'Remember'.

Kazinczy u. is 200m along Wesselényi u. To the right at No. 16 is the Ritual Bath of the orthodox community, while to the left, past the kosher bakery at No. 28 and the Electrical Engineering Museum at No. 21, stands Pest's **Orthodox Synagogue** (Béla and Sándor Löffler, 1912). The synagogue, which serves Budapest's small community of just over 3000 orthodox Jews, is not normally open to visitors, but it may be possible to catch a glimpse of the interior through the side door, access to which is either through the large gates at the side of the synagogue or round the corner in Dob u. and through the courtyard leading in by the kosher butcher's at No. 35. The strictly kosher *Hannah* restaurant can be found in this courtyard, as can the building of the former orthodox school. Note the wedding baldachin at the rear of the synagogue.

Klauzál tér is 100m to the north along Dob u. This largish square was at the centre of the ghetto in 1944–45. Raoul Wallenberg once complained to the Germans that over 50,000 were crammed here, in buildings intended for only 15,000, and that due to lack of proper food, several thousand were seriously ill.

In the crumbling courtyard of Kazinczy u. 41, which crosses Dob u., there is an old-established, still-functioning **kosher butcher's**. Inside you can still see the sausages being made. There has been a butcher's here since 1914. The shop was never nationalised, but always operated under the supervision of the Rabbinical authorities.

Returning towards Károly krt along Dob u., you pass a kosher pastry shop at No. 22, while at Dob u. 16 there is the entrance to the unique **Gozsdu Courtyard**, a series of seven large connected courtyards and apartment blocks built in the early years of the 20C. The 200m passageway emerges at the far end in Király u. Gozsdu Courtyard used to be thriving with Jewish workshops and retailers in the old days, yet it is named after an ethnic Romanian who became Hungary's High Court Judge, and it was built from money he left to a foundation for the education of Greek Orthodox Youth.

Opposite Dob u. 11 stands the **memorial to Carl Lutz**, the Swiss diplomat who helped many Jews to escape deportation in 1944. It was placed here in 1991, in the heart of the former ghetto, unlike the memorial to his renowned Swedish diplomat colleague Raoul Wallenberg, which is some distance from the centre on the Buda side (see p 180).

Rumbach Sebestyén u. crosses Dob u. nearby. The **Rumbach Sebestyén u. Synagogue** is to the north, at No. 11. This Romantic, Moorish-style synagogue was built in 1872 for a section of the Jewish community who were not altogether happy with assimilationist tendencies. It is an early work (and the only one in Hungary) of the noted Viennese architect Otto Wagner, who later gained fame for his Art Nouveau creations.

9 · Leopold Town (Lipótváros)—from the Basilica to Parliament via Szabadság tér

This route begins at SZENT ISTVÁN TÉR (nearest metro station: blue—Arany János u.).

ST STEPHEN'S BASILICA

In Szent István tér stands **St Stephen's Basilica** (Szent István Bazilika), Budapest's largest church, which covers an area of over 4000sq m; the dome is 96m high. However, due to the surrounding buildings, this massive structure is not easy to view from a distance.

History

Construction of the church was envisaged in the early 19C when this district, named after Habsburg Leopold II, was being planned. It was only in 1851, however, that building work really got underway to the neo-Classical designs of József Hild. Hild died in 1867 and Miklós Ybl took over, contributing neo-Renaissance elements. A disaster occurred in January 1868 when the dome collapsed during a storm. The incomplete building had to be demolished and work started afresh. By 1891 Ybl himself had died and a third architect, József Kauser finished the interior. The church was consecrated in 1905 and dedicated to St Stephen, Hungary's first monarch.

The **exterior** statues are all by Leó Fessler. The twelve apostles stand on the upper rim of the apse at the back of the church. The four Evangelists are in the outer niches of the dome, and in niches in the front towers are statues of SS Ambrose, Gregory, Jerome and Augustine.

The statue group in the tympanum above the porch shows the Virgin Mary, Patroness of Hungary, surrounded by Hungarian saints. The bust above the main entrance is of King (St) Stephen and above it is a mosaic of the Resurrection. The relief to the left of the porch, depicting Stephen's coronation, was erected in 1938, the 900th anniversary of his death, and the year that Budapest hosted a Eucharistic Congress. It was in 1938, too, that Pius XI granted the title of Basilica Minor to the church.

To the right of the main entrance is a small **treasury** displaying mainly 19C Hungarian, Austrian and German chalices, ciboria and monstrances. To the left is the entrance to the north tower, from the top of which there is a panoramic view of the city (open Apr–Oct).

The **interior** contains many statues, mosaics and works of art by a variety of leading 19C Hungarian artists (see plan). Neglected for many years, these and the building itself are currently undergoing long-term renovation.

On the second altar on the right is Gyula Benczúr's painting of Stephen offering his crown to the Virgin Mary. Stephen, left without a successor when Imre died young in a hunting accident, preferred to symbolically offer his crown to the Virgin rather than to either the Pope or the Holy Roman Emperor. Ever since, Mary has been regarded as the Patroness of Hungary, and this image of her with Stephen offering the crown appears frequently in Hungarian iconography.

The basilica houses what is believed to be St Stephen's right hand. The relic can be inspected in the **Chapel of the Holy Right Hand** (Szent Jobb Kápolna) behind the main altar (through the swing doors to the left of the chancel and across the

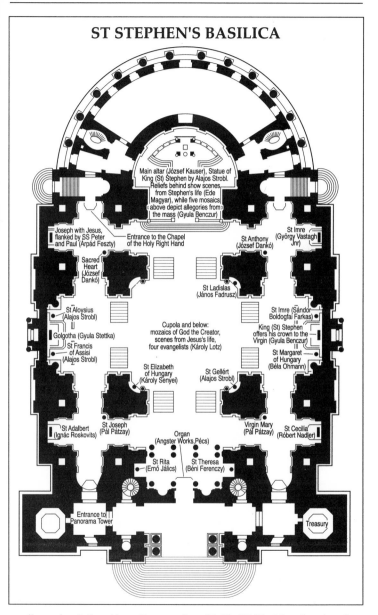

ST STEPHEN'S BASILICA

Main altar (József Kauser), Statue of King (St) Stephen by Alajos Strobl. Reliefs behind show scenes from Stephen's life (Ede Magyar), while five mosaics above depict allegories from the mass (Gyula Benczur)

Joseph with Jesus, flanked by SS Peter and Paul (Árpád Feszty)

Entrance to the Chapel of the Holy Right Hand

St Imre (György Vastagh Jnr)

St Anthony (József Dankó)

Sacred Heart (József Dankó)

St Ladislas (János Fadrusz)

St Aloysius (Alajos Strobl)

Golgotha (Gyula Stettka)

St Francis of Assisi (Alajos Strobl)

Cupola and below: mozaics of God the Creator, scenes from Jesus's life, four evangelists (Károly Lotz)

St Imre (Sándor Boldogfai Farkas)

King (St) Stephen offers his crown to the Virgin (Gyula Benczur)

St Margaret of Hungary (Béla Ohmann)

St Elizabeth of Hungary (Károly Senyei)

St Gellért (Alajos Strobl)

St Adalbert (Ignác Roskovits)

St Joseph (Pál Pátzay)

Organ (Angster Works, Pécs)

Virgin Mary (Pál Pátzay)

St Cecilia (Róbert Nadler)

St Rita (Ernő Jálics)

St Theresa (Béni Ferenczy)

Entrance to Panorama Tower

Treasury

small porch of the side exit; open Sun 13.00–17.00, Mon–Sat Apr–Sept 09.00–17.00; Oct–Mar 10.00–16.00). On 20 August, the anniversary of Stephen's canonisation in 1083, the hand has traditionally been paraded through the streets in a religious procession—a practice which has recently been revived.

On 20 August 1988 (i.e. before the political changes) the square in front of the basilica was packed with 50,000 people attending an open-air mass to commemorate the 950th anniversary of Stephen's death. The square was decked out in both Hungarian and Papal colours. The mass was the culmination of a year-long nationwide commemoration and was the biggest public religious ceremony in Hungary for many decades. Three years later, Pope John Paul II himself celebrated mass in the basilica.

The corner building to the north of the basilica at **No. 9** Hercegprimás u. is one of the few in Hungary clearly inspired by Venetian Gothic (Ferenc Wieser, 1853–57). The architect not only travelled widely, he had also studied extensively in England and was married to an Englishwoman. This building indicates he was probably familiar with John Ruskin's influential work, *The Stones of Venice*.

There are two choices of route through to Szabadság tér. You can walk due north along Hercegprimás utca, where No. 21 at the far end houses the small **Zrínyi Pharmacy**. The furnishings are original and date from 1850 when it was known as the Virgin Mary Mother of God Pharmacy.

The alternative is to walk along the parallel OKTÓBER 6 UTCA, two blocks to the west. (The name recalls the date in 1849 when 13 high-ranking officers were executed by the Austrians at Arad at the end of the War of Independence.) **No. 7**, at the corner of Zrínyi u., is one of the area's most representative neo-Classical buildings (József Hild, 1830–32). Neo-Classical styles were greatly favoured when this area of the city was originally built in the first half of the 19C. Bestsellers English-language bookshop is at No. 11.

No. 22 to the north is in neo-Classical style and has an attractive gateway and courtyard (Fidél Kasselik, 1812). Through the doorway of No. 19 opposite, a **fountain statue of Flora**, the Roman goddess of flowers, can be seen in the courtyard (Lőrinc Dunaisky, 1840s). It is known as the 'suicide fountain', as legend has it that a gentleman once shot himself in the head here over his unrequited love for the Budapest beauty who had served as a model for the statue.

SZABADSÁG TÉR opens out at the northern end of Október 6 u. Immediately on the right at **No. 5–6** is an eight-storey Modern building designed in 1937 by István Nyíri and László Lauber. The large relief facing the square at ground-floor level is entitled Grape Pickers (Ferenc Medgyessy, 1940). The building was originally intended as a Financial Institutions Centre and its design generated heated controversy. One commentator noted that it looked more like a tobacco factory, or a prison, or '…at best, a dreary block of flats'.

The new, massive Post-Modern **International Bank Centre** has been built next door (József Finta, 1995). It is unlikely that anyone will mistake the function of this building.

In the small playground in front of No. 5–6 stands the modest **Széchenyi Fountain** (Ede Telcs, 1930) with the inscription *Virulj!* (Bloom!). It commemorates the planting of trees in Pest in 1846. The relief shows Crestentia Seilern, István Széchenyi's wife, planting a sapling.

The huge **former Stock Exchange**, which occupies the entire eastern side of Szabadság tér, is one of the most imposing structures in the whole of Budapest. Designed by Ignác Alpár, who here employed elements of both Greek and Assyrian temples, it was built in 1905 to house the stock and commodity exchanges, and it functioned as such until both were closed down in 1948. Since the mid 1950s, it has been the headquarters of Hungarian TV (though there are plans for it to move).

Much of the interior was drastically reconstructed to produce a maze of corridors, cutting rooms and studios, but a glimpse of the original grandeur can be had from the small public waiting area just inside and to the left of the main entrance. From here you can see the massive entrance hall with its dramatic stairway.

On 15 March 1989 tens of thousands gathered on the steps of the TV building to hear the popular actor György Cserhalmi read out the 15 points of the newly formed opposition parties. It was one of the relatively few mass actions in Hungary prefiguring the political changes.

In the small park area immediately in front of the TV building is the simple **Memorial to the Martyrs of the New Building** (András Dózsa Farkas, 1934). The New Building (Újépület) was a huge, 90,000sq m barracks built in 1785 on the site of today's Szabadság tér. Representing Habsburg absolutism, it was an object of hatred to Hungarians, many of whom were imprisoned and executed within its walls, particularly after the failed 1848–49 War of Independence. The building was demolished in 1897. From this derives the name of the square (Liberty Square).

Across the park, opposite the martyrs' monument, stands a **statue of Harry Hill Bandholtz** (Miklós Ligeti, 1936). Bandholtz, a US general, was present in Budapest in 1919 after the suppression of the Hungarian Council Republic by Allied-supported Romanian and Czech troops. On his own initiative he intervened to prevent the looting of treasures in the Hungarian National Museum. The statue itself was removed after 1945 and was kept in the garden of the US ambassador's residence. It reappeared here in July 1989 just before US President George Bush visited Budapest.

The large, Eclectic **National Bank of Hungary** (Magyar Nemzeti Bank) stands behind the statue at No. 9 in the square. The bank was completed in 1905 to the designs of Ignác Alpár originally as the Austro-Hungarian Bank. For the tender competition eight prominent architects from Hungary and Austria each were invited. The Hungarian press treated it like a football match and acclaimed the commissioning of Alpár as a national victory.

High up, in front of the tympanum, are two large bronze statues symbolising agriculture and industry. A series of vivid limestone reliefs stretches around three sides of the building on the first-floor level. These show a variety of scenes illustrating the history of money, commerce and industry, as well as the arts and sciences.

Inside (via the Bank u. entrance) there is a small **Museum of Banknotes and Coins** (open Thur only 09.00–14.00). The display includes 'Kossuth' banknotes issued in America during his exile there and notes in denominations of billions from 1946, a year when Hungary experienced the world's worst ever hyperinflation.

The large, white obelisk towards the northern end of Szabadság tér is the **Soviet Army Memorial** (Károly Antal, 1945). The relief at the base depicts Red Army soldiers in the vicinity of (the old) Elizabeth Bridge during the siege of Budapest in 1944–45. Another at the rear shows Soviet soldiers near the Parliament building. There used to be several Red Army monuments in Budapest; in the early 1990s the city council decided to remove them all except this one.

LIPÓTVÁROS (Northern Inner City)

0   100   200m

Politics in stone

Another, quite different, symbol used to stand here from 1928 to 1945—a flag permanently at half-mast mounted on a pedestal inscribed, curiously, with a quotation from the British press baron, Lord Rothermere. Rothermere had befriended Hungary and used his *Daily Mail* to campaign for revision of the 1920 Trianon Treaty, whereby Hungary had lost much territory after the Great War. Rothermere even contributed a statue for the square entitled Monument of Hungarian Grief (see also p 102).

In the same connection, 50,000 people had gathered here in January 1921 to witness the unveiling of four statues called North, South, East and West, symbolising the lost territories. After World War II the statues were removed, as was the flagpole, remnants of its base being used to form the Red Army memorial.

Another statue which stood in the square up to 1956 had quite different symbolism. Entitled Gratitude, it depicted a 'typical' proletarian family and was erected in 1949 to mark Joseph Stalin's 70th birthday. In the same year the first trolley bus ran in Budapest. Inevitably it was given the number 70, and to this day the trolley bus numbers are still in the 70s.

The Soviet memorial stands in front of the **US Embassy** (the irony of which has been lost somewhat in the post-Cold War era). The embassy building (No. 12) was designed by Aladár Kálmán and Gyula Ullmann, and built in 1899–1901 along with the neighbouring Nos 11 and 10, on which the Vienna-style Secessionist decoration is more prominent.

The embassy used to be well known throughout the world, though not for architectural reasons. It was here that Hungary's Catholic Primate, Cardinal Mindszenty, spent 15 years in 'internal exile' following the 1956 Uprising. Mindszenty was badly mistreated in prison during and after a show-trial in 1949. Released in 1956, his subsequent presence in the embassy, publicised around the world, and his uncompromising attitude were a problem in church-state relations until the Vatican persuaded him to leave for Austria in 1971. Mindszenty died in 1975 and was buried in the ancient pilgrimage centre of Mariazell in Austria. In 1991 his remains were brought back to Hungary and reburied in the crypt of Esztergom Cathedral.

Immediately behind the US Embassy stands one of the most unusual buildings in Hungary, perhaps even in Europe—the **former Post Office Savings Bank,** designed by Ödön Lechner and built in 1900. The building, with its colourful, extravagant shapes and ornamentation, almost defies description. Perhaps pure 'Lechnerese' would be best, exemplifying as it does Lechner's individualistic attempt to fuse Art Nouveau and Hungarian features. Note the bees crawling up the walls to beehives on the roof, symbolising savers accumulating pennies. Lechner once asked why the birds should not also enjoy his buildings, and in fact the roof is the most astounding part of the whole.

Today the building belongs to the National Bank. Part of the more sober but nevertheless interesting interior can be seen via the public entrance in Hold (Moon) utca. From 1953 to 1990 this street was named after the Rosenbergs, the American couple executed as Communist spies in the early 1950s amidst much controversy. The authorities at the time presumably thought it a pointed reminder for the diplomats in the embassy nearby.

The Post-Modern **No. 7** Hold u. houses the National Bank Computer Centre (Ágnes Benkő, 1992). At No. 13, facing Perczel u., there is **Market Hall V**, one of several, still-functioning covered markets built in Budapest in the 1890s.

No. 13 Szabadság tér has striking neo-Romanesque forms (László Gyalus, 1901); the statues on the façade are of General Mór Perczel (1811–99) and Lajos Aulich (1793–1849). The latter was Hungary's defence minister and one of the martyrs of Arad executed by the Austrians. Interestingly, Aulich u. at the side has been thus named since 1900, 18 years before the end of Austrian rule over Hungary.

No. 3 Aulich u. appears today like so many rundown buildings in Budapest, hardly worth a look. Close examination of the façade, however, reveals that this was once one of the most highly decorated buildings of its day (Albert Kőrössy, 1901). Note the brightly coloured Art Nouveau mosaic at the top.

At the end of Aulich u. is a little square in the middle of which is a limestone plinth and ornate bronze lamp. This is the **Batthyány Eternal Flame**, erected in 1926 to the memory of Count Lajos Batthyány, Prime Minister of the 1848 independent Hungarian government, who was executed by the Austrians on 6 October 1849 on this spot (then within the walls of the Újépület barracks).

Lajos Batthyány

Count Lajos Batthyány (1806–49) was a landowner and liberal politician, and before 1848 one of the leading opposition aristocrats in the Hungarian Diet. As head of the Hungarian government in 1848 he aimed at compromise with Austria, but finding this impossible he resigned. After heading an unsuccessful peace delegation he was arrested in Pest in January 1849.

Honvéd u. leaves Szabadság tér at its north end. Like the above-mentioned building in Aulich u., **No. 3** here has seen better times, although the various striking Art Nouveau forms are clearly visible (Emil Vidor, 1903). Despite its present condition, you can detect it was once a gem of turn-of-the-century architecture.

No. 15 Szabadság tér, behind the Soviet memorial and to the left, has a large relief in the tympanum at the top showing Lajos Kossuth with Sándor Petőfi and Mihály Vörösmarty (Károly Flerschl, c 1901). This is perhaps the oldest representation of Kossuth in Budapest.

PARLIAMENT

Vécsey u. on the left of this building leads towards KOSSUTH LAJOS TÉR, where stands one of the landmark symbols of Budapest, the massive, neo-Gothic **Parliament Building** (Országház).

The Parliament building can only be visited in guided tours and only then when MPs are not sitting. When they are, however, some of the interior richness can be seen on television, as the sessions are usually broadcast live. (A number of travel agents organise tours of Parliament, but you can also turn up individually to join an English-speaking tour organised by Parliament itself. Information available at gate X of Parliament.)

History

For centuries the Hungarian parliamentary assemblies had no permanent home. In 1843 a resolution was passed at the Pozsony (Bratislava) Diet to erect a permanent building in Pest, though the plans were delayed by the events of 1848–49. From 1861 the Lower House met in what is today the Italian Cultural Centre in Bródy Sándor u. and the Upper House in the National Museum nearby. In 1880 a law was passed approving the present site and work began in 1884 to the designs of Imre Steindl. The building was completed in 1902.

The building has nearly 700 rooms, is 268m long, 118m wide at its maximum and over 90m high at the top of the dome. There are dozens of statues on the exterior. On the Danube side are the Hungarian rulers from the seven conquering chiefs to Ferdinand V (died 1848). On the Kossuth tér side are the princes of Transylvania and several noted commanders. Above the ground-floor windows are coats of arms of kings and princes.

The main entrance from Kossuth Lajos tér leads to a ceremonial staircase with ceiling frescoes by Károly Lotz. From here there opens a 16-sided hall below the dome, used for official receptions and ceremonies. The MPs' debating chamber is in the south wing. The chamber of the former Upper House in the north wing is today used for conferences. All the interior rooms and passageways are ornamented in a rich neo-Gothic style. Many paintings adorn the walls, including Mihály Munkácsy's large canvas 'The Magyar Conquest' (1893).

The pomp and grandeur of this building, one of the largest parliamentary buildings in the world, appealed greatly to official national sentiment at the time of its construction. Yet at that time less than ten per cent of the population actually had the right to vote, and Hungary's non-Magyar nationalities (Serbs, Slovaks, Croats, Romanians et al.), who constituted over 50 per cent of the total, were drastically under-represented in terms of allocation of seats.

The struggle for the right to vote, including female suffrage, was a hallmark of Hungarian politics in the pre-1914 era. In 1918 the franchise was extended, but then reduced during the Horthy era. Universal adult suffrage was first implemented only in 1945. After a period of relatively free parliamentary democracy, one-party rule set in after 1948. Following creeping political liberalisation in the 1980s, a multi-party, parliamentary system was finally introduced in 1990.

The **Library of Parliament**, a designated UN Library, collects foreign and Hungarian books on political science, law and history, and is open to the public. The entrance is via gate XXV on the Danube side (open Mon–Thur 09.00–20.00, Fri 09.00–14.00, Sat 09.00–18.00). A Council of Europe Information and Documentation Centre is also based here (Mon–Thur 10.00-16.00, Fri 10.00–14.00).

Parliament is surrounded by statues and buildings, all of which speak volumes about the country's history.

In front of Parliament at the north end of Kossuth tér is a group of statues whose central figure is **Lajos Kossuth** making a call to arms during the 1848–49 War of Independence.

Kossuth—the standard bearer of independence

Lajos Kossuth (1802–94) is the most celebrated political leader of the struggle for Hungarian national independence in the 1830s and 1840s. He was Minister of Finance in the first independent Hungarian government in 1848 and shortly afterwards was elected Governing President of Hungary. During the war with Austria, he travelled the country rousing the people to arms, which activity is depicted in this group of statues.

Forced to flee the country after defeat, he spent many years abroad, several of them in England and the United States, defending the cause of Hungary. He first arrived in England in October 1851. Landing at Southampton, he surprised his audience with an extempore speech in English. Although popular in England, he refused an invitation from the Chartists to speak at a working men's dinner, an attitude which prompted Karl Marx to write that Kossuth was '...all things to all men. In Marseilles he shouts: Vive la République! In Southampton: God Save the Queen!'

Following his death in Turin in 1894, the city council decided to organise a ceremonial burial in Budapest and to erect a statue in his honour. The funeral was a tremendous affair—about half a million people took part. Two thousand citizens of Cegléd, the town where Kossuth had first called the nation to arms in 1848, walked the 70km to Budapest to participate.

The statue took longer to organise; fund-raising problems, bureaucratic delays and World War I meant that it was not until 1927 that a statue by János Horvay finally appeared here. However, that is not what you see today. The original was removed in 1952 and replaced by the present statue, which is primarily the work of Zsigmond Kisfaludy Stróbl. 1952 was the high point of Hungary's Stalinist period and presumably the reason for the change was entirely political.

The earlier work depicted Kossuth flanked by his aristocratic ministers of 1848—counts and landlords such as Batthyány, Széchenyi, Eszterházy and Deák—all looking rather downcast, reflecting the gloom of the 1849 defeat.

The replacement work is much more 'heroic' in the socialist-realist tradition, albeit the theme is entirely nationalistic. Kossuth is shown proudly calling the nation to arms. He is flanked by 'the people', all enthusiastically responding. They are all here—peasants with children, a soldier, an armed worker, a student with a sword and even a traditional horseman with weapon.

Towards the southern end of Kossuth Lajos tér is a bronze **statue of Ferenc Rákóczi II** sitting proudly on horseback (János Pásztor, 1937). Rákóczi (1676–1735), Prince of Transylvania, led the 1703–11 struggle for independence against Austria. Latin inscriptions on the plinth read 'For Country and Liberty' and 'The wounds of the noble Hungarian nation burst open', the latter being the opening lines of Rákóczi's anti-Habsburg declaration.

Ferenc Rákóczi—the rebel prince

After a Jesuit education in Bohemia and studies in both Prague and Italy, Rákóczi originally grew up as a young aristocrat loyal to the Habsburgs. Contact with disaffected Hungarian nobles resulted in a changed attitude, and for conspiring against the Habsburgs he was imprisoned in 1701. After escaping, he sought refuge in Poland from where he eventually launched the freedom struggle of 1703–11.

Due to both the lack of outside help and internal division, Rákóczi and his 'kuruc' fighters, although brave, were defeated in every major set battle. In the end a peace treaty was signed behind Rákóczi's back while he was away soliciting support from Peter the Great. Forced into exile, Rákóczi eventually settled in Turkey, where he died in Rodosto (today Tekirdag) in 1735. His house there is a place of pilgrimage for Hungarians on their way to Istanbul. His remains, however, were brought back to Hungary in 1909, passing through Budapest in a massive reburial ceremony on their way to rest in the cathedral at Kassa (today Košice, Slovakia).

The Rákóczi War of Independence, as it is called, has gone down in Hungarian history as one of the heroic periods in the country's past, and its leader is extolled as a great national figure. Both Liszt and Berlioz composed variations of the popular 'Rákóczi March'.

On the ground some way in front of the Rákóczi statue there is a **memorial stone** placed here in 1991 to commemorate the shootings of 25 October 1956 (see below). Across the parade ground stands the white ceremonial flagpole on which Hungary's State Flag is raised on festive and other occasions.

There are two large buildings overlooking Kossuth Lajos tér opposite Parliament. The **Ministry of Agriculture** is on the right at No. 11 (Gyula Bukovics, 1885–87). To the right of the entrance stands a statue of István Nagyatádi Szabó (István Szentgyörgyi, 1932). Nagyatádi Szabó (1863–1924) was a peasant small-holders' representative and eventual agriculture minister in the early years of the Horthy regime. The statue was removed in 1945, but reappeared in 1990.

The two statues on the other side of the entrance are both by Árpád Somogyi and are called The Reaper Lad (1956) and Female Agronomist (1954). The busts in the archways on each side of the entrance are of noted agricultural scientists. On the far left of the façade is a small replica of The Seed, a vast bronze relief by Amerigo Tot on a wall of the University of Agriculture in Gödöllő.

A point of protest

It was from the roof of the Ministry of Agriculture that, on 25 October 1956, shots were fired, probably by secret police, into a peaceful crowd actually fraternising with Soviet tank crews in Kossuth tér below. This was not the only time during the 1956 Uprising that Kossuth tér witnessed massed crowds. On the first day, 23 October, Imre Nagy had dramatically returned from the political wilderness when he addressed a huge crowd from the far left balcony of Parliament.

In fact, Kossuth tér has been the scene of many noted political demonstrations, particularly in the pre-1914 era when the Social Democrats persistently agitated for universal suffrage and the secret ballot. 'Red Friday' in September 1905 saw 100,000 gather here. Violent clashes often ensued, such as during the mass demonstration of 23 May 1912, known thereafter as 'Bloody Thursday'.

During the 1918–19 period, with the collapse of the Habsburg empire, and the short-lived Democratic Republic and then Council Republic, Kossuth tér was also the scene of numerous mass gatherings.

The tradition was revived on 24 September 1992 when 50,000 swelled the square to demonstrate for democracy and against extreme nationalism. It was the largest public protest seen in the years following the multi-party elections of 1990.

The other imposing building in Kossuth tér (No. 12) today houses the **ETHNOGRAPHICAL MUSEUM** (Néprajzi Múzeum; tel: 132–6340; open 10.00–18.00 except Mon; free on Tues; auto-guide in English; snack bar; assisance for w/a; free folk music concerts often on Sun mornings).

History

The building was originally constructed for the Supreme Court and was known as the Palace of Justice (Alajos Hauszmann, 1893–96). The inauguration of the Supreme Court by Emperor Franz Josef was seen as a great symbolic event for Hungary, emphasising the country's special role in the empire. Hauszmann's classical façade, tinged with elements of his favourite Renaissance style, emphasised the pomp and importance of this legal institution, and, no doubt, intimidated the ordinary citizen who might have had to pass through its portals. Today the Ethnographical Museum fits rather uncomfortably amidst these surroundings, which bear little resemblance to the folk traditions providing the backbone of the exhibitions inside.

The museum has been based here since 1973, though the actual collection dates back over a century. It was founded in 1872 by the archaeologist and ethnographical researcher János Xantus, who had led quite a colourful life. He had been imprisoned for his participation in the 1848–49 uprising against Austria. He later travelled to England and then the United States where he worked as a labourer and later joined a scientific expedition to Texas. He travelled to China and elsewhere on research projects commissioned by the US government, and at one point was even US consul in Mexico. He returned to Hungary in the 1860s and became instrumental in establishing the collection which eventually became the Ethnographical Museum.

The building's origin as the Palace of Justice is demonstrated in the tympanum above the columns of the large portico, where there is a sculptural representation by György Zala of a court in session. Above it on a chariot drawn by three horses is Justitia, the Goddess of Justice, flanked by statues symbolising The Legislator and The Magistrate. The large hall—through the entrance and up the steps—is particularly impressive. The ceiling fresco here, depicting an enthroned Justitia surrounded by allegories of Justice, Peace, Sin and Revenge, is the work of Károly Lotz.

The museum's permanent exhibition on 19C Hungarian folk traditions is attractive and very well displayed (it has texts in English). There are also lively temporary exhibitions on folk, peasant and ethnographical themes. Free concerts of folk music often take place on Sunday mornings.

There are two further statues in Kossuth Lajos tér; both are of important 20C figures.

In the garden on the south side of the Parliament building there is a statue of a forlorn-looking man, sitting bent forward on some steps, cap in hand, eyeing the Danube. This rather undramatic statue (László Marton, 1980) portrays one of Hungary's most dramatic and most popular 20C poets, **Attila József**. Although a committed left-winger, his passionate verses about ordinary people and everyday life captured an audience irrespective of party affiliation. Indeed, the Communist Party, during his lifetime, found the poet a bit too hot to handle.

The working class poet Attila József sits forlornly by the Danube

An uncompromising poet

Attila József was born in the Budapest working-class district of Ferencváros in 1905. Despite the poverty of his background (his mother was a washerwoman), he managed to win a place at Szeged university, but he was expelled in 1924 after an uproar following the publication of his poem *With a Pure Heart*. It opened with the lines 'I have no father and no mother, I have no country and no god,' and later continues 'with a pure heart, I'll burn and loot, and if I have to, I'll even shoot.' Such sentiments did not go down too well in the early years of the conservative Horthy regime.

After his expulsion he left for Vienna and later Paris where he mixed with anarchist and avant-garde circles. Back in Budapest in 1930 he joined the illegal Communist Party, but was denounced three years later by the emigré party leadership in Moscow. Like Wilhelm Reich in Germany and George Orwell in Britain, he was too much of a libertarian and too interested in the wider, socio-psychological aspects of politics to fit neatly into the communist orthodoxies of the 1930s. Political estrangement, personal problems and constant difficulties with publishers led to depression and schizophrenic tendencies. He was only 32 when he committed suicide under the wheels of a train near Lake Balaton in December 1937.

The inscription by the side of the statue is taken from one of József's best-known poems, *A Dunánál* (By the Danube) and reads: '...as if it flowed from my own heart in a spate...wise was the Danube, turbulent and great.'

In front of the statue by the railings is a Kossuth Bridge memorial stone. The bridge, which stood here from 1946 to 1960, was built in eight months and was the first proper bridge (as opposed to temporary crossing) built after the Second World War.

On the north side of the Parliament building there is a small playground where stands a statue of a rather sad and lonely-looking gentleman with a walking stick. The statue depicts **Mihály Károlyi**, who became known as the 'Red Baron'. The composition, with its arched frame, is the work of Imre Varga (1975).

The Red Baron

Mihály Károlyi (1875–1955) came from one of Hungary's wealthiest landowning families. Although a fine horseman and reckless gambler in the tradition of his background, he was also an avid reader and somewhat 'odd' in that he refused to beat servants, or slaughter birds, foxes or stags.

As a radical liberal politician, he was prime minister in Hungary's government formed during the upheavals at the end of the First World War, when, in autumn 1918, the Habsburg empire collapsed and Hungary was declared a republic—the first time since the 1848–49 War of Independence. On 11 January 1919 Károlyi became Hungary's first president. Suffrage by secret ballot was extended, and freedom of the press, assembly and association were proclaimed.

The Károlyi administration faced many problems: hunger and shortages were rife, land reform was a pressing problem and relations with non-Hungarian ethnic groups were tense. The Western powers disliked Károlyi's politics, particularly his sympathy for, and support from, radical circles. Furthermore, they were determined to treat Hungary as a vanquished nation and dismember its territory in line with secret treaties and promises made during the war. Pressure from the unsympathetic Western powers finally led to Károlyi's resignation and, ironically, the subsequent formation in March 1919 of the revolutionary Council Republic under Béla Kun and the Communists.

During the Horthy period Károlyi was forced into exile. Landowners had not appreciated the example he had set in early 1919 when he voluntarily divided up his own estates. Furthermore, the authorities denounced him as a traitor for his revolutionary sympathies and since they believed his weakness had paved the way both for the Communists and for the dismemberment of Hungary after the Great War.

In exile Károlyi was an active organiser of the anti-fascist and democratic Hungarian forces abroad. From 1943 in Britain, for example, he headed the Movement for a Democratic Hungary. He returned home after World War II, and in 1947–49 was Hungarian ambassador in Paris. However, disaffection over the show trial of László Rajk and other illegalities led to a second exile. He died in France in 1955. Originally buried on the Isle of Wight, his body was finally moved to Budapest and reburied in the Kerepesi Cemetery in 1962.

10 · The Great Boulevard (Nagykörút)

The 'Nagykörút' (literally, Great Ring Boulevard) is about 4.5km long and curves around central Pest from Margaret Bridge in the north to Petőfi Bridge in the south. It is divided by name into five parts—(from Margaret Bridge) Szent István krt, Teréz krt, Erzsébet krt, József krt and Ferenc krt. The Great Boulevard has an everyday, bustling, 'ordinary' (as opposed to 'tourist') atmosphere, albeit that the appearance of many western retailers and fast food outlets has changed its appearance somewhat in recent years. Trams 4 and 6 run its entire length.

The Nagykörút, which follows the line of a former backwater of the Danube, was first planned in 1871, though it finally opened to traffic in 1896, on the 1000th anniversary of the Hungarian Conquest. Its long stretches of imposing, multi-storey apartment blocks, all constructed around the same time, make the Great Boulevard as a whole a significant example of late 19C Hungarian Eclecticism.

For convenience this route is divided into two parts. The first involves a walk from Blaha Lujza tér, the central point of the 'körút' (as it is often simply called), north-wards to Margaret Bridge (2.6km). This is the busier part and has more sights. The second section runs in the opposite direction, from Blaha Lujza tér to Petőfi Bridge, and can be covered conveniently by tram. The Museum of Applied Arts is included in this latter section.

A. From Blaha Lujza tér to Margaret Bridge

The triangular BLAHA LUJZA TÉR at the junction of the Great Boulevard and Rákóczi út is one of the busiest spots of Pest (metro station here on 'red' line 2).

Lujza Blaha

Lujza Blaha (1850–1926) was known as the 'nation's nightingale' (a nemzet csalogánya) and was one of the most popular actresses of her day. She frequently appeared at the National Theatre which stood here from 1908 to 1964, when the building was pulled down amidst much controversy. Lack of finance has prevented the building of a new permanent National Theatre else-where in the city, though fresh plans have appeared recently.

The square is often refered to simply as **'EMKE'**, letters standing for Erdélyrészi Magyar Közművelési Egyesület, the Hungarian Transylvanian Association for the Promotion of Learning. From 1894 the *EMKE Café* used to occupy the ground floor of the large corner building on the north side of the square. To every bill was added a small amount which went to support the Association. Apart from a coffee-house, there was also at times a bar, patisserie and a popular cabaret. Although suffering drastic alterations the *EMKE Café* survived until recent times. The name, and with it a piece of history, finally disappeared when the *Chicago* opened as a modernised 'American' bar/restaurant in 1992. Yet not entirely—interestingly, the modern office block on the corner of Akácfa u. (Gonzales Xavier and István Kruppa, 1994) is known as the EMKE-irodaház (Office Centre). The building even has etchings on its façade of the old National Theatre, which stood nearby. The name EMKE also survives in the title of the hotel in Akácfa u. Maxim Varieté in the same building here was, when it opened in 1962, the city's first purpose-built night club since 1945.

Across the square stands the **Corvin Department Store**, one of the largest in the city when originally built in 1926. Today's appearance dates from 1960s' reconstruction. The building to its left houses the editorial offices of several newspapers and magazines. This was where the old 'Party' newspapers were produced for many decades. During the 1956 Uprising the building was a hive of activity as even these official publications blossomed in the heady atmosphere of free speech.

The large, neo-Renaissance building with a façade of red brick and terracotta ornamentation, on the east side of the square at the corner of Népszínház u. (Alajos Hauszmann, 1887) today houses the Institute of Commercial Quality Control.

Next door stands the Eclectic **Nemzeti** (National) **Hotel**. Originally built at the end of the 1890s, its restaurant was popular at the turn of the century. The atmosphere of those days was maintained by restoration work undertaken in 1987.

The attractive ceiling of the gateway at **No. 2** József krt, on the corner of Rákóczi út (István Kiss, 1893–95), was nicely restored in 1994, as was Károly Lotz's coloured fresco above the steps leading down to the metro.

ERZSÉBET KÖRÚT runs from Blaha Lujza tér to the north. The five-storey building at No. 9–11, with its curious blend of neo-Renaissance and Art Nouveau, is commonly known as the **New York Palace**. It was built for an American insurance company in 1891–95 mainly to the designs of the noted architect Alajos Hauszmann. Not surprisingly, he had the assistance of fellow designers, since at the same time he was working on the massive Supreme Court (today the Ethnographical Museum) in Kossuth tér, and on the reconstruction of the Buda Palace.

The **New York Café** on the ground floor is Budapest's last remaining genuine, classic coffee-house from the pre-1945 era. It has one of the most sumptuous interiors in the city and a rich history.

History

The *New York* was one of the central meeting places for writers, poets, painters, sculptors, composers, singers, actors and, later, film directors. It played an outstanding role in the literary, artistic and cultural life of Budapest up to the Second World War. 'Here you could see everybody',' commented the writer Gyula Krúdy. The *Nyugat* (Occident) circle used to meet here and its editor-in-chief for many years, Ernő Osvát (1877–1929), would often work at a reserved table. A memorial tablet commemorates this inside the café and there are also caricatures of various literary figures on the wall of the side balcony. Many of the journalists who frequented the place worked in editorial offices in the building above, such that the latter became popularly known as the 'Press Palace'.

After 1945 the New York was closed and subsequently became a warehouse and then a sports shop. The authorities were not too keen on maintaining such a centre of 'bourgeois' decadence. However, the café reopened in 1954 under the name *Hungária*. The original name crept back into use in the late 1980s. At the time of writing the building is due to be privatised and its future and that of the café is shrouded in uncertainty.

Café society

A century ago there were about 500 cafés in Budapest, many of which, like the *New York*, became the meeting places of writers and artists. It is difficult to overestimate the role they played in the old days. As the writer Dezső Kosztolányi, paraphrasing the famous English saying, once wrote: 'My coffee-house is my castle.'

The café society culture virtually disappeared after World War II and the *New York*, with its rich interior of marble, bronze and Venetian ground glass and its frescoes and paintings, can be said to be the only surviving coffee-house of the traditional type.

The fountain opposite the *New York*, across the road, is entitled Faun and is the work of László Marton (1986).

Barcsay u. is 300m along Erzsébet krt, to the right. No. 5 is the **Madách Imre Gimnázium**, which traces its origins to 1881 when the first state secondary school was established, though it only moved to this building 11 years later. The four coloured frescoes of muses on the façade are the work of Gyula Stetka.

The **Madách Theatre** at Erzsébet krt 29–33 opened in 1961 to the plans of Oszkár Kaufmann. Note the five bronze statues high up on the façade depicting aspects of theatrical art. The theatre stands on the site of the former Royal Orpheum, one of Budapest's largest and most popular variety theatres. Founded in 1908, many stars from all over the world performed here (including Josephine Baker and Little Titch from Britain) before it finally closed in 1953.

The next street is DOB UTCA. 100m to the right stands the Modern-style Transport, Communications and Water Ministry (Gyula Rimanóczy, 1939). On the façade at the corner are statues by Gábor Boda of King Stephen and representative figures from ancient Hungarian history in period garb. The building houses the **Stamp Museum** (Bélyegmúzeum; entrance from Hársfa u.; tel: 142–0960; open 10.00–18.00 except Mon; children/students free). Here are the first editions of all Hungarian stamps, plus almost every stamp of the world, including forgeries—11 million in total! You can find here the largest stamp ever (US, 1865), plus the smallest (Columbia, 1860s), as well as some of the earliest British stamps from the 1840s. Some Hungarian ones from the hyper-inflation of 1946 have denominations in billions!

Further along Dob u. at **No. 85** is a real gem of an Art Nouveau primary school building, particularly in view of its recent restoration (Ármin Hegedus, 1905–06). The façade has colourful folk motifs and a lively frieze showing children at play and study.

The corner apothecary at Dob u. 80 has original turn-of-the-century furnishings inside. From here, along Csengery u., you can see a large, blue, corner building at **No. 2** Jósika u. Closer inspection reveals an attractive Art Nouveau design (Izidor Sterk, 1902–03), with fantastic decoration of devils and gargoyles.

Returning to Erzsébet krt, the passageway at No. 48 on the left leads to a cassette and CD retailers, which probably counts as the smallest shop in Budapest! No. 50

and 54 have attractive inner courtyards, while the latter also has a highly decorated façade and gateway.

The massive **former Royal Hotel** is opposite at No. 43–49. When it opened the Royal was one of the largest hotels in the Austro–Hungarian Monarchy (Rezső Lajos Ray, 1894–96). Burnt out during the 1956 Uprising, it reopened in 1961 after alterations and renewals, but by the 1990s it was standing empty awaiting new owners and further development.

It was in the Royal Hotel in March 1910 when both Béla Bartók and Zoltán Kodály gave well-publicised concerts which helped to launch the 'New Hungarian School' of avant-garde music. However, the subsequently formed UMZE (New Hungarian Musical Association) soon disappeared in the face of official disapproval and lack of funds.

Hungary's most important music teaching institute, the **Ferenc Liszt Academy of Music** (Zeneakadémia), designed by Flóris Korb and Kálmán Giergl and built between 1904 and 1907, stands 50m south of the körút along Király u., in Liszt Ferenc tér. It is also the home of one of Budapest's major concert halls.

Ferenc Liszt (1811–86) was the first president of the Academy when it was originally founded in 1875. There is a seated statue of Liszt by Alajos Stróbl above the entrance on the main façade. The six reliefs on the ledge above the base (by Ede Telcs) represent stages in the development of music.

The Academy has one of the most ornate Art Nouveau interiors in Budapest. Inside, along the walls above the entrances to the main auditorium, is a fresco from 1907 entitled Hungarian Wedding Procession in the 14C. The artist, Aladár Körösfői Kriesch (1863–1920) was one of the leaders of the Hungarian Pre-Raphaelites, known as the Gödöllő School. English Pre-Raphaelite influence is clearly visible, as it is on his large wall painting (The Fountain of Art, 1907) on the first floor. (If the main entrance is closed, access can usually be gained via the side door in Király u.)

> The Academy of Music is noted not only for its teaching traditions (Béla Bartók and Zoltán Kodály both taught here) but also because it has been the venue for significant historical events. For example, the trial of Cardinal Mindszenty took place here in 1949. Then in 1956, on the eve of the Uprising, a packed audience gave a 15-minute ovation to Zoltán Kodály after a rendering of his unaccompanied choral work based on Miklós Zrínyi's Szózat (Appeal). (Zrínyi was a commander in the wars against the Turks. The clapping was accompanied by chants of his line Ne Bántsd a Magyart—Leave the Hungarians Alone!)

After Király u. the boulevard continues as TERÉZ KÖRÚT. The shop called ERMA at No. 4 was founded by Erzsébet Herzman and Mariska Goldberger in 1922. Its name derives from the first two letters of their names. In 1987 it was reopened in the same style as they had commissioned when it moved here in 1935 (though there have been some alterations subsequently).

The Octogon Pharmacy at **No. 7**, on the corner of Szófia u., was originally founded in 1786 in the Tabán district in Buda. It moved here in 1924 which was when the neo-Baroque furnishings were made. The wall painting inside of Hygieia and Asclepios is by Kocsár Bretschneider (1936). A plaque on the same building records that Gustav Mahler lived here when he was director of the Hungrian State Opera from 1888 to 1891.

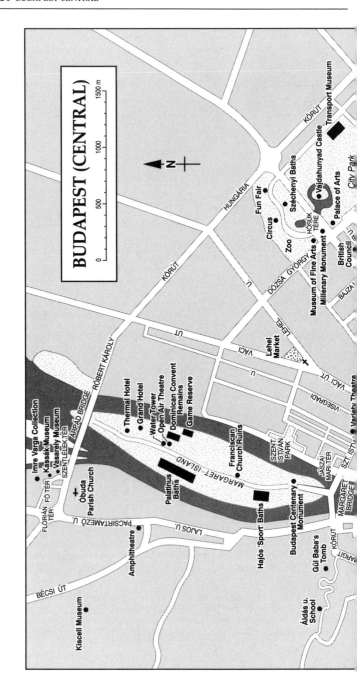

BUDAPEST (CENTRAL)

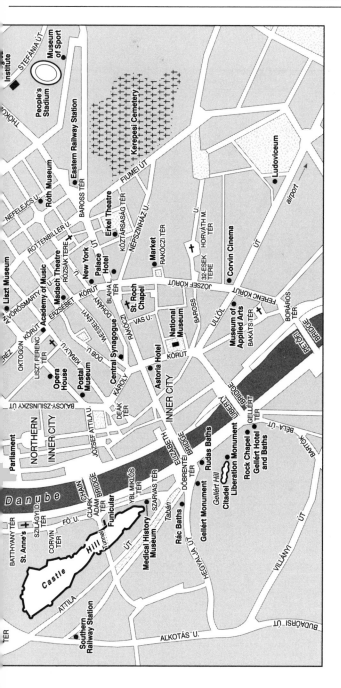

200m along Szófia u. there is the back entrace to the now rather dilapidated **Market Hall IV** (Győző Czigler, 1896).

In contrast with the predominant Eclecticism of the Great Boulevard, **No. 13** Teréz krt looks like an Italian Renaissance mansion. It should do, as it was designed in 1884 by Alajos Hauszmann for one of the Batthyány counts as a replica of the Strozzi Palace in Florence. The intricate gate is by wrought-iron master Gyula Jungfer. The building today houses the Central Marriage Registry Office and (in view of this, perhaps appropriately) the Academy of Sciences Institute of Psychology.

Teréz krt now reaches and crosses the huge junction with Andrássy út known as OKTOGON (see p 144).

400m beyond, at No. 43 on the right, stands the 'Radisson' **Béke Hotel**. Originally built for apartments in 1896, the building was redesigned to open as a hotel in 1913. Henrik Fábri, the owner, had been impressed by hotels he had seen in England and thus it was originally called The Britannia. At the time it was one of Budapest's most up-to-date hotels, its central dust-extraction system and call lights above the room doors attracting particular attention.

History

In the early 1920s the hotel was the base of a notorious right-wing terror group known as the Britannias. In the 1930s the political atmosphere changed and the hotel became noted as a gathering place for the progressive Friends of Nyugat group. They met six days a week here for lectures, discussions and social evenings. The hotel was also a favourite haunt of the writer Ferenc Móra and a special room was furnished for him where many of his works originated.

During World War II the building served as a military hospital and later as a Soviet military base. As a contrast, the present name ('béke' means 'peace') was adopted when the hotel reopened in 1948, ironically at the start of the Cold War. For a further three decades the hotel was renowned for its night life and live performances. Then in the mid 1980s the hotel was completely reconstructed. Only the façade remained as it was.

The coloured mosaic on the exterior corner is of György Szondi (died 1552), a legendary fortress captain at the time of the Turkish wars. The artist was Jenő Haranghy who also decorated much of the original interior. Some of his murals depicting scenes from Shakespeare's plays can be seen today on the walls of the hotel's Shakespeare dining room. The hotel's pleasant *Zsolnay Coffee Shop* uses painted crockery from the famous porcelain factory of the same name in Pécs.

The modern office block across the road from the hotel at **No. 44** (Tibor Szántó and Miklós Dobozi, 1994) shows an interesting blend of Post-Modernism with the surrounding Eclecticism. Further along Teréz krt at **No. 51–53** is a large post office which is open 24 hours a day, every day of the year.

Beyond the post office is the imposing façade of the **Western Railway Station** (Nyugati pályaudvar; August de Serres and Győző Bernardt, 1874–77). The building contractor was the famous Eiffel Company of Paris. The large hall with its iron framework, much of which was cast in Paris, generated great interest throughout Europe. Despite rebuilding, the original framework has been preserved. McDonald's, which occupied a carefully restored part of the station in 1990, can boast of one of the world's finest interiors for a fast-food chain.

The first railway station in Pest was built on the site of the Western Railway Station and the first train left here on 15 July 1846 for Vác, 34km to the north. It covered the journey in 49 minutes and created a sensation. In the previous year a trial run of 8km had been held with Palatine Joseph on board. After that the Town Council requested local priests to warn their parishioners 'not to walk on the rails, nor put anything on or beside the tracks'.

It had taken some persuading on the part of Count István Széchenyi to get the idea of steam trains accepted; before that horse-drawn trains were utilised. Like many of his other initiatives, he had been influenced by his experiences in England. One of his diary entries reads: 'We have inspected the Manchester–Liverpool railway line. It is a staggering sight when the train passes closely by, carrying everything with diabolical force.'

In 1887 the first electric tram in Budapest ran from in front of

The old and the new—fast food at the Western Railway Station, a masterpiece built by the Eiffel Company of Paris

the Western Rail Station along Teréz krt. Originally the current came from below via a third track, since the authorities did not like the idea of unsightly overhead wires. In 1987 the centenary was marked with a small memorial plaque by the tram stop in the middle of the road.

Inside the station hall, to the left as you enter from the street, there is a small **Budapest Tourist Information Office** (open daily 09.00–18.00).

Teréz krt ends at NYUGATI TÉR (formerly Marx tér), a large traffic junction which was entirely replanned in 1978–81 when the pedestrian subways and the flyover were constructed. The modern dark glass-fronted building on the left (György Kővári, 1984), was originally built for the Skála department store chain, which did much to modernise retailing techniques in the 1980s.

The final section of the Great Boulevard is called SZENT ISTVÁN KÖRÚT and runs for 550m to Margaret Bridge. Though some are spoilt by modern shops and boutiques, almost all the inner courtyards on this stretch are worth viewing, particularly those nearer the bridge.

The impressive, neo-Baroque **Variety Theatre** (Vígszínház) stands at Szent István krt 14. It was designed by two Viennese architects, Ferdinand Fellner and

Imposing, Eclectic-style apartment blocks typify the Great Boulevard. This one is on Szent István körút

Herman Helmer, and the first performance took place on 1 May 1896. Destroyed by fire during World War II, it was restored in 1951 and until 1960 was known as the Hungarian People's Army Theatre. The most recent renovation took place in 1994, after which the attractive exterior was perfectly clean. Readers will thus be able to judge the extent of pollution in Budapest by the present state of the building.

The bronze busts in front of the theatre are of the 19C poet-revolutionary Sándor Petőfi, and Miklós Zrínyi, politician, poet and military leader in the anti-Turkish wars of the 17C.

Falk Miksa u. is the second street to the left after the theatre. In recent years this has fast developed into an 'Antiques Row', having the city's highest concentration of antiques' shops.

Szent István krt, and with it the Great Boulevard, ends at JÁSZAI MARI TÉR at the Pest end of Margaret Bridge. Jászai (1850–1926) was a renowned actress of the National Theatre.

The large building to the south today houses parliamentary offices. For years it was the HQ of the former Party Central Committee and was popularly known as 'The White House'.

The building facing the river on the north side of Jászai Mari tér is the **Palatinus House** (Emil Vidor, 1911). Note the parabolic arch of the corner turrets, echoing the shape of a traditional Hungarian oven in a peasant dwelling. This shape often occurs in Hungary's National Romantic architecture.

On the embankment in front of the building there is a landing stage for river boats to Margaret Island, Óbuda Island and other points north.

Nearer the bridge, on the ground between the park area and the river, there is a coloured **tile mosaic** entitled Sin Crying to Heaven (Anna Stein, 1990). It recalls that during the time of the fascist Arrow Cross rule in late 1944 many Jews and others were shot along this stretch of the Danube, their bodies being left to the mercy of the river.

For details of Margaret Bridge see p 156.

B. From Blaha Lujza tér to Petőfi Bridge

This southern section of the Great Boulevard (about 2km) is not as bustling as the northern part and has fewer significant buildings. A convenient way of experiencing this ordinary, everyday part of central Budapest is by tram 4 or 6, both of which run the entire length. The following route is described tram-stop-by-tram-stop, as it is near these stops that the most important items can be found.

The first stop along JÓZSEF KÖRÚT, the name of this stretch of the Boulevard, is at RÁKÓCZI TÉR. This area has traditionally been one of the centres of prostitution in Budapest and although brothels were officially closed down in 1948, Rákóczi tér has continued to be the hub of a down-market, red-light district.

The business has a long tradition. In the spring of 1810 Vladimir Bronievsky, a visiting Russian navy officer, noted: 'Treacherous sirens in Pest weave dangerous nets in the dimness of the night...they are skilled in taking advantage of men's inclinations and desires. Under the effect of their slim figures, gossamer garments and softly calling voices the last traces of self-restraint disappear unnoticed, but at the same time your purse is emptied.'

The **Joseph Town Market Hall**, designed by the city engineering department and opened in 1897, is on the far side of the square. After reconstruction following severe fire damage in 1988, it reopened as a very attractively modernised traditional market hall.

On the other side of the Boulevard the short Kölcsey u. (English-language bookshop here) leads to GUTENBERG TÉR, a small square in the centre of which is a bronze bust of József Fodor (1843–1901), a health campaigner and the first Professor of Public Health at Budapest University when the post was established in 1874.

The Art Nouveau **No. 4** facing the statue belongs to the printers' union. The building, with its unusual curved façade, was designed by József and László Vágó in 1907. By the door is a small, bronze relief of Johann Gutenberg, the 15C pioneer of printing techniques (Tamás Vigh, 1984).

To the north, on the corner of Bérkocsis u., is the **Anna Frank Gimnázium**, the site of a Jewish secondary school since 1919, though only with this name since 1965. The building also contains the **National Rabbinical Seminary**, the only Jewish seminary in eastern Europe. It has been here since 1877 and has functioned non-stop, apart from a brief interruption in late 1944 at the height of the Hungarian holocaust.

The next tram stop is 350m along József krt at the junction with Baross u., which to the left opens into Harminckettesek tere (Square of the 32nd). Here stands the monument of the former home regiment of Budapest, the 32nd Infantry (István Szentgyörgyi, 1933). One relief shows the regiment's foundation by Maria Theresa, the other depicts troops marching off in the Great War.

The **Joseph Town Parish Church** can be seen 300m along Baross u. (originally József Thallher, 1798). The high altar (1837) was designed by József Hild and the painting here depicting the apotheosis of St Joseph is by the Viennese painter Leopold Kupelwieser.

The statue in front with outstretched hand (Béla Radnai, 1914) is of Péter Pázmány who, in 1635, founded the University of Nagyszombat (today Trnava in Slovakia), the forerunner of Budapest University. Although born a Protestant, Pázmány (1570–1637) became a Jesuit and was Archbishop of Esztergom from 1616. With polemical essays and political activities he won many Protestant aristocrats for the Roman Church and laid the foundations for the Counter-

Reformation. He supported the Habsburgs, but also defended the Hungarian nobility.

The old **Joseph Town Telephone Exchange**, one of the earliest in the city, is to the north of the church at the corner of Német u. (Rezső Vilmos Ray, 1910–12). The façade has a large relief depicting Classical figures welcoming the new technology of long-distance communication.

The bronze relief on the right of the entrance depicts the Puskás brothers, Tivadar (1844–93) and Ferenc (1848–84). The former, an inventor, was a colleague of Edison and both were instrumental in organising the early telephone network in Budapest.

József krt, beyond Baross u., has some interesting inner courtyards—at Nos 63, 71–73 (a double one), 69 (triple), 77–79 and 85 on the right, and at Nos 60, 62, 64 and 66 on the left. The wall plaque at No. 83 is to the memory of the writer Ferenc Molnár (1878–1952). He was actually born at No. 68 nearby, but moved here in 1905. His celebrated novel *A Pál utcai Fiúk* (The Paul Street Boys), published in 1907 and later made into a film, recalls the time of his childhood spent in this area.

The tram next stops at Üllői út, one of Pest's main thoroughfares. The junction here was one of the main scenes of action during the 1956 Uprising. Just before Üllői út on the left there is a small street, Corvin köz, which leads to one of the oldest cinemas in Budapest, the **Corvin Cinema** (Emil Bauer, 1923). The *Corvus* (Latin for raven) was the symbol of King Matthias. There are large reliefs depicting Matthias Corvinus, as he was known, on either side of the entrance, and around the ledge there are several raven statues.

The cinema was a stronghold of armed Hungarian street fighters in 1956, as several wall plaques testify. The enclosed space around the cinema was clearly a strategically defensible position.

The huge corner building, across Üllői út is the **former Killián Barracks**. Designed by Ferenc Kasselik in 1845, it is one of the oldest buildings on the Great Boulevard. The barracks, too, played a major role in the events of 1956. The Hungarian troops here joined the insurgents and, under defence minister Pál Maléter, created a centre of resistance. Some of the fiercest fighting took place in this neighbourhood.

Nearby, at Üllői út 33–37, stands the large, impressive, domed building of the **MUSEUM OF APPLIED ARTS** (Iparművészeti Múzeum), designed by Ödön Lechner and Gyula Pártos, and opened by Emperor Franz Josef in 1896 as part of the Millennium celebrations (tel: 217–5222; open 10.00–18.00 except Mon; free on Tue; snack bar; small shop; w/a possible in part; occasional concerts). There is a seated statue of Lechner (1845–1914) in front of the museum (Béla Farkas, 1936).

The building is one of the most significant examples of Ödön Lechner's individual style in which he combined elements of Hungarian folk art and 'Mogul' motifs with the intention of creating a unique national architecture. (Many contemporary researchers believed the early Magyars originally came from the Indian sub-continent.) The building also displays his typical use of coloured pyrogranite ceramics made in the Zsolnay factory in Pécs.

Some early critics did not like the building which they denounced as too ornamental. It certainly was a major departure from the Eclectic or neo-Classical style usually adopted in those days for major public buildings.

The impressive interior has very much an 'Indian' feel. Today it is plain white, but orginally was highly decorated with colourful Hungarian folk motifs.

The museum's collection was founded in 1872 and was the second of its kind in the world after the Victoria and Albert Museum in London. The permanent exhibition is simply called Arts and Crafts and covers the history of glass, ceramics, porcelain, leather, paper, textiles, furniture, metalwork, etc. Most of the museum, however, is devoted to temporary exhibitions, of which there may be two or three at any one time.

An early exhibition with a British connection took place here in 1900—a display of work by artist Walter Crane, who visited Budapest and gave several lectures. The event had a great impact on Hungary's 'Pre-Raphaelites', folk artists and budding National Romantic architects. Many would be later involved with the artists' colony at Gödöllő, which was very much in tune with the William Morris school of art and politics, of which Walter Crane was a major exponent.

The last stretch of the Great Boulevard, beyond Üllői út, is called FERENC KÖRÚT and was named after Francis I in 1792. Surprisingly, this 'imperial' name, like that of József krt, was retained even during 'communist' times. At Tűzoltó u. 14–16, the first street to the left, there is a large, second-hand furniture warehouse, open to the public.

The Museum of Applied Arts on Üllői út–a characteristic example of Ödön Lechner's unique style

The tram stops 300m along Ferenc krt by Tompa u., which to the right leads to Bakáts tér and the **Francis Town Parish Church**. The original church from 1822 was damaged in the great 1838 Pest flood and was eventually pulled down in 1865. The present neo-Romanesque church was built over the following decade to the design of Miklós Ybl, architect of the Opera House. Most of the painted decoration inside is the work of Károly Lotz and Mór Than.

The small column by the church is a **monument to the un-named heroes** of the district who died during the 1956 Uprisng. Surprisingly, given the political changes of 1989–90, this is a rare example of a '1956' monument in Budapest.

A further, short (300m) tram ride leads to Boráros tér and **Petőfi Bridge** (Pál Álgyay Hubert, 1933–37). The bridge bore the name of Miklós Horthy, Hungary's inter-war, ultra-conservative ruler, up to 1945. Since then it has been named after the young poet-leader of the 1848 revolution.

The pillar standing by the end of the bridge is from the old National Theatre and was placed here in 1910. In the underpass there is a bronze statue entitled Wineseller (Borárus) by Imre Varga (1983).

The name of the '6–3' wine bar on the north side of the square at Lónyai u. 62 recalls the famous victory of Hungary over England at Wembley in 1953. It was the first football defeat for England on home ground ever. The bar was estalished by Nándor Hidegkúti, a member of Hungary's 'Golden Team' as it was known. Photographs inside recall the match and the team.

11 · From Ferenciek tere to the Eastern Railway Station—Kossuth Lajos u. and Rákóczi út

This walk (about 2km) stretches from the central point of old Pest along its ancient axis (today's Kossuth Lajos u.), crosses the Little Boulevard and continues along Rákóczi út to the Eastern Station (Keleti pályaudvar). Buses 7 and 78 run the length of the route.

FERENCIEK TERE is at the heart of the Inner City (metro station here). Its present appearance dates from the 1900s, when the area was rebuilt at the time of the construction of the first Elizabeth Bridge. Two tall, prominent buildings known as the **Klotild Palaces** dominate the west end of the square, providing a 'gateway' to the bridge. Named after the daughter-in-law of Palatine Archduke Joseph, they were designed in 1902 by Flóris Korb and Kálmán Giergl in Secessionist style with Spanish Rococo elements.

The highly decorated building which dominates the north side of the square was

One of the striking Klotild Palaces in Ferenciek tere which serve as a gateway to the Elizabeth Bridge

designed in 1909 for the Inner City Savings Bank by Henrik Schmahl, who used a rich, eclectic mix of Venetian Gothic, Italian Renaissance and Moorish elements. The building, which deserves careful scrutiny, is usually simply referred to as **Párisi Udvar**, the name of the equally highly decorated arcade, with intricate woodwork, which runs through it from the Ferenciek tere side to Petőfi Sándor u. The name derives from a previous, early 19C passage here, which then imitated a Paris-style shopping arcade.

The **Franciscan Church** stands at the east end of the square. The Franciscans (Ferenciek) had a church and monastery here as early as the second half of the 13C. Under the Turkish occupation it was turned into a mosque. Nothing survives today of this original building. The present church was begun in 1727 to the plans of Franciscan masters and consecrated in 1743.

Above the entrance is a stone relief depicting Christ on the road to Calvary. The statue in the central niche of the gable is of St Peter of Alcantara. In the side niches are SS Francis and Anthony. The spire, which stands above the chancel, was constructed in 1758, though the decorative elements appeared in the 1860s.

The church has a nave with three chapels on either side. The statues on the high altar date from 1741 and the pulpit, with statues of the apostles, was made in 1851. The frescoes were painted partly by Károly Lotz in the 1890s and partly by Viktor Tardos Krenner in the 1920s. The stone crucifix outside the church, by the entrance, dates from 1763, but the sculptor is unknown.

The **Nereids Fountain** (Ferenc Uhrl and József Fessl) stands in front of the church. It was originally placed here in 1835 and was Pest's first sculpture to decorate a public well. At first it was called the Well of Naiads, which like nereids are mythological water-nymphs. Yet the sculpture actually appears to depict Danaids, those other mythological characters condemned for ever to carry water in bottomless vessels for murdering their husbands.

KOSSUTH LAJOS UTCA begins at Ferenciek tere and runs to the east. It is the main west–east axis of the inner city and used to be a popular promenade before the days of modern traffic.

The prominent relief on the side wall of the Franciscan Church recalls the **Great Flood of 1838** (Barnabás Holló, 1905). It dramatically depicts Baron Miklós Wesselényi in his boat rescuing people stranded by the water. The flood, Pest's most serious natural disaster, began on the night of 13–14 March 1838. The Danube burst its banks and caused a huge flood which lasted several days. Over 400 people died and 2000 houses were destroyed.

Miklós Wesselényi

Wesselényi (1796–1850) was a Transylvanian landowner, a reform-minded colleague of István Széchenyi, a member of the Academy of Sciences and one of the leaders of the opposition in the Hungarian and Transylvanian Diets. Shortly after the flood, however, his heroism was forgotten by the authorities. In 1839 he was accused of treason and imprisoned because of his political activities, and while in prison he lost his sight.

Not all boat operators were as selfless as Wesselényi during the flood. A British traveller, one Miss Pardoe, was in Hungary at the time and recorded some eyewitness accounts which told of boatmen striking at drowning wretches whose remnants of property were insufficient compensation, while they 'hurried off to rescue some wealthy sufferer who could pay them every inch in gold'.

The **Kígyó** (Serpent) **Chemist's** is across the road at Kossuth Lajos u 2. It is one of the oldest working chemist's in the city, being originally founded in nearby premises in 1784. It moved to this building in 1899. The original interior furnishings, part neo-Rococo and part Secessionist, have been restored.

No. 3 on the right is the former Landerer and Heckenast printing works (Mihály Pollack, 1816, then Ference Wieser, 1851). Crowds came here on 15 March 1848 to witness an important event—the printing, in defiance of the official censor, of Sándor Petőfi's 'National Song' and the 'Twelve Points', the radical demands of the revolutionary movement. A plaque on the corner of Szép u. recalls the event.

No. 6 Szép u. is one of the best surviving examples of early 19C neo-Classical

Pest architecture (Mihály Pollack, 1817). The street at the end here, Reáltanoda u., was the site of the first public hospital in Pest. Robert Townson, a visiting Englishman, was not very impressed, describing it in the 1770s as 'the worst hosital in Europe' for its bad conditions and particularly bad smell.

Kincsem—the 'wonder-filly'

The former 'Kincsem Palace' is at Reáltanoda u. 12. The famous racehorse Kincsem (My Jewel) was kept here in stables built from the money the horse won at races all over the world. Although Kincsem was bred in Hungary, she was of English ancestry. She raced for four seasons and created a world record by winning all her 54 races, including the 1878 Goodwood Cup on her one venture in England. There are items relating to Kincsem in the Agricultural Museum in the City Park and there is a statue of her at the Kincsem Park race course on Albertirsai út.

The English influence on Hungarian horse racing was particularly strong and was encouraged by Count István Széchenyi who saw it as a way of developing good breeds. In 1844 the English jockey Thomas Benson arrived and won many important races. He stayed in Hungary and worked as a trainer for 40 years, encouraging others to come from England.

No. 4 Kossuth Lajos u. houses a bookshop usually well-stocked with English and other foreign language books about Hungary. The passageway at the side, past two enormous atlantes, leads to a small but attractive courtyard with neo-Renaissance balconies.

No. 10 (Flóris Korb and Kálmán Giergl, 1897) used to be a medicinal drugs wholesaler's. Inside are neo-Renaissance carved wooden shelves and cupboards and an original American 'Heating' coke-stove.

Semmelweis u. runs north from farther along Kossuth u. **No. 1–3** here on the corner was designed in 1896 by Győző Czigler and Béla Atzél originally for the National Casino. The luxuriously furnished rooms, libraries, billiard rooms, ballrooms and restaurant provided a central meeting place for the gentry, leading politicians and civil servants. The first women's club opened here in 1899. The National Casino, which was one of several English-style clubs in Budapest, functioned until 1945. A glance at the staircase through the main door gives an idea of the former opulence. After many years as the Soviet Cultural Centre, today the building is occupied by the World Federation of Hungarians.

The **Astoria Hotel** stands at the end of Kossuth Lajos u., at No. 19. (Emil Ágoston and Rezső Hikisch, 1912–14). In October 1918, during the post-war republic upheavals, when the National Council met here and formed an independent Hungarian government under Mihály Károlyi, the hotel was the scene of feverish activity, crammed with soldiers and others wearing a white chrysanthemum, the symbol of the democratic revolution.

The building suffered severe damage during the fighting in 1956, when for a time it functioned as the headquarters of the Soviet forces. Today the renovated interior, in particular the attractive Art Nouveau coffee lounge on the ground floor, recalls the atmosphere of pre-World War II Budapest.

In medieval times the Hatvan Gate, one of the three major gates in the old Pest town walls, used to stand at what is now the junction of Kossuth Lajos u. and the Little Boulevard. It was pulled down at the end of the 18C.

The route now continues along RÁKÓCZI ÚT, which is named after Ferenc Rákóczi II (1676–1735), the Transylvanian prince who led the 1703–11 War of Independence. Taverns and inns lined both sides until redevelopment in the last quarter of the 19C, when the street was broadened to become an important through road to the Eastern Railway Station.

The **East–West Trade Centre** stands on the right (Lajos Zalavári, 1991). The stone monument by its Rákóczi út side was originally erected in 1987 to commemorate the 150th anniversary of the foundation here of the Pest Hungarian Theatre. In 1840 it became the National Theatre, which was instrumental in developing Hungarian cultural life. The building was demolished in 1913.

Across the road, on the side wall of No. 2, there is an old street lamp with a tablet underneath recalling that the first electric street lights in Budapest were placed in this area in 1909.

No. 5 on the right is the former Pannónia Hotel and was originally built in 1876. The ground floor used to be occupied by the Pannonia Coffee-house, where writers and artists from the neighbouring National Theatre used to congregate. There is a plaque and small bust of Ferenc Rákóczi above the middle balcony in commemoration of his reburial procession which passed this way. Rákoczi died in Turkey in 1735, but in 1906 his remains were brought back to Hungary.

No. 7 next door was designed in the early 1890s by Henrik Schmahl in a rich neo-Gothic style. On the third-floor exterior are two small frescoes by Károly Lotz. The interior courtyard is small, but well worth viewing.

József Hild designed the neo-Classical house at **No. 13** in 1837. Originally only one storey, the rest of the building was added by József Diescher in 1852. The architect Ödön Lechner was born here in 1845, as was the violinist Jenő Hubay in 1858. Ferenc and Károly Doppler, both musicians, lived here for a time and their guests included Liszt, Wagner and Erkel. In the second half of the 19C the house was one of the centres of artistic and literary life in Pest.

József Hild also designed **No. 15** in neo-Classical style. As the former White Horse Hotel it was well known in the 19C for its popular dances and balls. The building was renovated in 1987–88 and today houses the Slovak Cultural Centre.

Across the road a few metres along Síp u., on the corner with Dohány u., is the striking Art Nouveau building of the **Metroklub**. Formerly the Árkád-bazár, it was designed in 1909 by the Vágó brothers, László and József.

The **Verseny Áruház**, at the corner of Síp u. and Rákóczi út, is one of the oldest department stores in Budapest (Gyula Wälder, 1936). When the Fókusz Bookshop, at No. 14 on the same side, opened in 1969 it was Hungary's biggest bookshop.

No. 18 today belongs to the

Metroklub—this visual surprise is at the corner of Dohány u. and Síp u.

Municipal Gas Authority but was orginally a bank. The building dates from 1911 and was designed by Béla Lajta, one of the fathers of the Modern school of architecture in Hungary, although on this building you can see elements of folk decoration.

No. 19 on the right, at the corner of Szentkirályi u., has a statue of King Matthias on the first floor (Ede Mayer). It was once the sign of a café which was situated inside the building. The **Urania Cinema** is in this same block at No. 21 (Henrik Schmahl, 1893). The striking, Moorish style of the building is even more emphasised inside, a glimpse of which can be had in the foyer. It was once a music hall, appropriately called the Alhambra, then a lecture theatre, a drama school and finally a cinema.

Vas u. is the next street on the right. **No. 9–11** along here was designed by Béla Lajta in 1912 as a boys' commercial school. It is still a secondary trade school today. Although regarded as a significant example of early modern Hungarian architecture, the unusual brickwork and the folkish decoration on the first floor of the façade and on the metal cladding around the entrances betray traces of National Romanticism.

The small **St Roch** (Rókus) **Chapel** on Rákóczi út is just beyond the next street, Gyulai Pál u. It has its origins in a small chapel built here by the Pest council after the great plague of 1711. The area at the time was uninhabited and an isolation barracks was also set up here. The chapel's present size dates from 1740 and the tower from 1797. The stone crucifix outside to the right of the chapel, by an unknown artist, dates from 1798. The level of the flood waters in 1838 ('vízállás') is clearly visible on the façade of the chapel.

The **Immaculata statue** and column here is the work of Johann Halbig and was originally erected in 1867. It was removed in 1949, but reappeared in 1991, the year when Pope Paul VI visited Hungary.

The large building to the right of the chapel and stretching along Gyulai Pál u. is the Pest County Semmelweis Hospital, usually referred to as the **St Roch Hospital**. It stands on the site of the isolation barracks built at the time of the 1711 plague. The main building was begun by József Jung in 1781 and continued by Tamás Kardetter in 1796–98. The wing overlooking Rákóczi út behind the chapel was designed by Mihály Pollack in 1839.

Just into Gyulai Pál u., facing the hospital, is a marble and limestone **statue of Ignác Semmelweis**, head of the hospital's maternity ward in the 1850s (Alajos Stróbl, 1906).

The saviour of mothers

Ignác Semmelweis (1818–65) is known as the 'saviour of mothers' due to his discovery of the cause of puerperal fever and its prevention by simple asepsis. His ideas were opposed by the leading British surgeon at the time, Sir James Young Simpson, and his contribution to protecting the health of women in childbirth was only widely recognised at the turn of the century following Lister's application of antiseptic techniques. Lister himself recalled that on his visit to Budapest in 1885 nobody even mentioned the name of Semmelweis. By 1906, however, his work was acknowledged and the cost of the statue was raised by international donations from many countries.

A few metres along Nyár u., on the other side of Rákóczi út, there is a small map shop (*térképbolt*) specialising in maps of Budapest, Hungary and elsewhere.

Rákóczi út now opens on to the large, triangular BLAHA LUJZA TÉR (for details of the square see p 120). The Great Boulevard runs along the far side of the square (Erzsébet krt to the left, József krt to the right) and Rákóczi út crosses this to continue on the other side.

No. 41 is the first building on the right (István Kiss, 1893–95). It houses a regional water authority. By the entrance there is a tablet marking the level of the flood waters of 1838. It was placed here on the 150th anniversary of the flood of that year. Note how high the mark is, considering that this spot is over 1.5km from the Danube.

The **former Palace Hotel** at No. 43 on the right was opened at the end of 1910 to the designs of Marcell Komor and Dezső Jakab. It is a good example of Hungarian National Romantic architecture which flourished for a while before World War I and in which Art Nouveau was transformed by traditional peasant themes in an attempt to create a specifically Hungarian architecture.

The neo-Romanesque entrance of the former Slovak Lutheran Church is at **No. 57**. By the middle of the 19C there were more than 5000 Slovaks in Pest and in the following decades they continued to arrive to work on the many buildings being erected in the city. The first pastor of the church was the Slovak writer, Ján Kollár.

The large, corner building opposite at **No. 68**, which has Romanesque-type windowframes and a 'Renaissance' corner tower, today houses the Tisza Cinema. Before the First World War there was a cinema of sorts here, too. Films were projected in the building's *Venice Café* and it was here that a young man called Sándor first saw a film and vowed film-making would be the life for him—he was later to become famous as Sir Alexander Korda. His many films included *The Scarlet Pimpernel*, based on the 1905 novel by Hungarian-born Baroness Orczy, and starring the similarly Hungarian-born László Stainer—better known by his adopted name of Leslie Howard.

Luther u., on the right, leads to the peaceful KÖZTÁRSASÁG TÉR, which at 66,000sq m is the largest square in Budapest. Formerly the site of a market it was converted into a park at the end of the 19C. The present name (Republic Square) recalls a mass, pro-republic demonstration held here on 1 November 1918, just days before the Habsburg Empire collapsed. The name was given after World War II, when Hungary finally became a republic. In the inter-war period, Hungary was officially a monarchy, though it had no monarch!

In the corner of the square by Luther u. stands the large, white building of the **Erkel Theatre** (Géza Márkus, Dezső Jakab and Marcell Komor, 1911). This is the second home of Hungarian opera after the State Opera House on Andrássy út, and with around 3000 seats has the largest auditorium in the country. It is named after the renowned composer Ferenc Erkel (1810–93), whose works include the music of Hungary's national anthem.

The theatre was originally built as the 'Népopera' (People's Opera House) on land donated by the city council on condition that seat prices would be very low for the first three years. When built it looked much more impressive than its present appearance, which dates from the 1950s.

No. 26–27 Köztársaság tér, across from the theatre, was the scene of one of the most violent events of the 1956 Uprising. On 30 October a bitter battle raged in the square as insurgents attacked the building, which then housed the Budapest Party Committee Headquarters (today it is the Hungarian Socialist Party offices). Believing it was occupied by members of the secret police and that there were torture chambers inside, the attackers dragged outside whoever they found there, killing many on the spot. Among them was the Budapest Party Secretary Imre

Mező, by no means a hard-liner and a friend of János Kádár, who was later to rule Hungary for over 30 years. Kádár had originally been sympathetic to the Uprising and even a member of the new government of Imre Nagy. Mező's death is thought to have been influential in his abrupt shifting of allegiance during the events.

On the far side of Köztársaság tér stand three nine-storey apartment blocks. Erected in 1933–34 for the National Insurance Administration, these buildings, the work of several architects, count among the earliest examples of the International Modern style in the capital. With their functionalist design and lack of a traditional inner courtyard, they were considered somewhat experimental at the time of their construction.

The route now returns to Rákóczi út.

The spires of the **Elizabeth Town Parish Church** can be seen along Huszár u., which runs to the north. This double-spired, neo-Gothic church was designed in 1893–97 by Imre Steindl, the architect of the Parliament building. To the left, immediately inside the main door, there is an intricately decorated baptismal font by the wrought-iron craftsman Gyula Jungfer (1900).

In front of the church is a marble **statue of St Elizabeth of Hungary** (József Damkó, 1932).

Elizabeth of Hungary—a friend of the poor

Elizabeth (1207–31), daughter of Hungary's King Andrew II, married the Marquis of Thüringia and lived in Wartburg. In Germany she is known as St Elizabeth of Thüringia. Liszt wrote an oratorio in her praise and Wagner made her a central character in his *Tannhäuser.*

Following her husband's death, Elizabeth lived an ascetic life and gave generously to the poor, which allegedly displeased her relatives. As here, she is often depicted with roses, since legend has it that once, while on her way to visit the poor with an apron full of alms, her relatives stopped her, demanding to know what she was carrying. Forced to reply, a miracle happened—the alms had turned into roses!

Her statue stands in Rózsák tere (Square of the Roses), which has had this name since 1932, the 700th anniversary of her death. In view of her legend, the choice of location was fitting—previously it was known as 'Poorhouse Square'.

Elizabeth is one of only a handful of Hungarian saints, all of whom were members of the House of Árpád, Hungary's first royal dynasty. Their canonisation signalled Rome's desire to consolidate the Christianisation of the formerly pagan Magyars.

Interestingly, the name of the church pre-dates the statue and refers not to the saint but to Empress Elizabeth, the wife of Habsburg Emperor Franz Josef. The many other 'Elizabeth' names you see around the city are usually named after her, rather than the saint.

Rákóczi út ends at BAROSS TÉR, on the far side of which stands the **Eastern Railway Station** (Keleti pályaudvar). The subway system, constructed in 1969, leads to the station and 'red' metro line 2.

The Eclectic, neo-Renaissance station was built in 1881–84 and designed by Gyula Rochlitz and János Feketeházi. The 44m span of its steel framework was considered quite daring at the time, and with its electric lighting and centralised track-switching system was regarded as one of the most up-to-date stations in central Europe.

The main façade has something rare for Budapest—statues of two Britons. On the right is James Watt (1736–1819), Scottish inventor of the steam engine, and on the left George Stephenson (1781–1848), the English engineer who improved the steam locomotive and initiated the first railway in 1825, the famous Stockton–Darlington line.

The wall paintings (today very faded) in the departure hall on the left side are by Károly Lotz and Mór Than. Their dilapidated condition fits well with the rather seedy atmosphere currently surrounding the station (but there are plans for renovation). Some of the former grandeur is detectable in the booking hall to the left.

The Eastern Railway Station was the scene of a curious encounter in 1919 when General Smuts was sent to negotiate over truce lines with Béla Kun, head of the then Council Republic, which was fighting to stave off the encroachment of Czech and Romanian forces. Smuts refused to leave his carriage and so the negotiations took place in a siding of the station.

During a break in the (unsuccessful) talks, Harold Nicolson, then a young diplomat in Smuts's entourage, walked down the platform with Kun, who, unconventionally in protocol terms, offered the stump of his cigarette to a train driver who had asked for a light. 'Béla Kun darts little pink eyes at me to see whether I am impressed by this proletarian scene,' Nicolson later recorded. 'I maintain an impression of noble impassivity.'

On the north side of the station is a **statue of Gábor Baross** (Antal Szécsi, 1898). Baross (1848–92) was a leading liberal politician and one-time Minister of Transport. He was instrumental in developing Hungary's railway system, which involved the nationalisation of six private rail companies and tariff scales to encourage rail usage. The square here was named after him in 1902.

Beyond the statue at the side of the station is a post office which is open 24 hours every day.

The **Róth Memorial Museum** (Róth Miksa Emlékmúzeum) is 300m to the north of the Eastern Railway Station at Nefelejcs u. 26 (tel. 141–6789). This is a new museum on the life and work of Miksa Róth (1865–1944), a prolific craftsman of stained glass work and mosaics. Check with Tourinform for opening times.

12 · Andrássy út

Andrássy út is one of the major thoroughfares of Pest. It stretches for 2.5km from the north-east corner of Erzsébet tér to the City Park (Városliget). It was originally called Sugár út (Radial Avenue) then in 1885 was renamed after the one-time Hungarian Prime Minister and later Foreign Minister of the Austro–Hungarian Monarchy, Count Gyula Andrássy (1823–90). For a time after World War II it was called Stalin Avenue, then in 1957 acquired the rather unwieldy title of Népköztársaság útja (Avenue of the People's Republic). Its present name reappeared on the street signs in 1990. This route runs the length of Andrássy út.

Construction of the avenue followed a deliberate act of law in 1870 and was symptomatic of Budapest's expanding wealth and urban renewal following the 1867 Compromise with Austria and the establishment of the Dual Monarchy. Building of this somewhat pompous and serious-looking avenue started in 1872 and within 12 years most of it was complete.

The perfectly straight Andrássy út can be divided into three, almost equal parts. Up to Oktogon it is 34m wide and lined with closely built neo-Renaissance and Eclectic buildings, housing shops and offices. Then up to Kodály körönd it is still closely built but wider, at 45m, and with tree-lined side roads. Finally, the stretch up to Heroes' Square is similarly tree-lined, but the buildings are mainly detached villas.

Metro Line No. 1 (sometimes called the 'small underground') runs under the length of Andrássy út. It was inaugurated as the **Millenary Underground** in 1896, the 1000th anniversary of the Magyar Conquest. After London's it was the second underground to be constructed in Europe. The original line ran from today's Vörösmarty tér to the City Park. It was extended in 1974 and now terminates at Mexikói út on the far side of the park. Apart from the underground, buses 1 and 4 also run the length of the avenue.

The 'bourgeois seriousness' of Andrássy út is well exemplified by the massive buildings at its start. The neo-Renaissance **No. 3** on the right was built in 1884–86 for the wealthy Saxlehner family to designs by Győző Czigler, a professor at Budapest's Technical University. The playful statuettes of Greek gods above the windows are by Antal Szécsi.

Since 1972 the first floor has housed the small but attractive **Postal Museum** (Postamúzeum), which has life-size models and displays of coaches and equipment from the history of Hungary's postal service. There is some opportunity to 'play' with the machines, e.g. by sending messages through a dispatch-tube or operating an early telegraph tape machine (tel: 342–7938; open 10.00–18.00 except Mon; free on Sun; w/a possible via lift).

The museum is situated in what was the Saxlehner's seven-room apartment, and from the furnishings and style you get a good idea of how wealthy families lived a century ago. Károly Lotz, a famous fresco painter at the time, worked on the stair-case of the building. This has been restored and is an exceptional sight.

The five-storey, Eclectic building at **No. 7**, which today houses a Bulgarian folk art shop, was designed by Zsigmond Quittner in 1882. **No. 9** next door also dates from 1882 and is the work of Mór Kollina. The huge atlantes by the entrance are the work of Leó Feszler. Inside today is a branch of the ING Nederlander Bank, which has reconstructed the interior courtyard, transforming it into an impressive modern atrium. A glimpse can be had by boldly walking in, at least up to the recep-tion desk. Beyond that a wary guard is likely to bar your way.

A pair of very attractive caryatids can be found at **No. 23** further along the avenue. These are the work of master sculptor Alajos Stróbl and depict Flora, the Roman goddess of flowers and spring. The building itself dates from the early 1880s.

On the northern side **No. 2**, the corner building at the start of Andrássy út, is a richly decorated Eclectic structure designed by Adolf Feszty in 1882 for the Foncière insurance company. On the ground floor there is a second-hand bookshop with an English-language section.

No. 8 has murals and frescoes by Feszty in the gateway, although they are rather dilapidated today. The female figure holding a lamp at the bottom of the stairway is by the French sculptor A. Durenné and was brought from Paris. The building was originally commissioned in 1876 by the wealthy owner of a sugar factory. In those days there were even stables in the courtyard. Subsequent occupants up to World War I included a 'Berlitz' language school, one of Budapest's first cinemas, a Daimler car showroom and the Red Cross.

No. 10 (c 1890) was cleaned and renovated in the late 1980s and although a bit worn now it gives some idea of the original splendour of the buildings on this stretch. **No. 12** (Zsigmond Quittner, 1884) has a rich ceiling in the gateway and frescoes on the walls of the interior courtyard. The sculpture above the well against the wall there is by Gyula Donáth, who also designed most of the rich, allegorical statuary on the façade. The building belongs to a branch of the police, but it is possible to get a glimpse inside the doorway.

The **Central Ticket Office** (mainly for theatre performances) can be found at No. 18, and if you are thirsty there is a wine bar specialising in Hungary's famous Tokaj wines at No. 20.

The **HUNGARIAN STATE OPERA HOUSE** (Magyar Állami Operaház) is a short distance along the same side at No. 22. This is the avenue's most sumptuous building and indeed one of the grandest buildings in Hungary. It is worth a visit even for non opera-lovers; it will not cost a fortune either, since by Western standards tickets are still cheap. Apart from during performances, the interior of the Opera House can also be viewed every day in English-language group tours organised by the Friends of the Opera (15.00 and 16.00; meet by the side entrance on the left).

The interior, with its ornamental marble stairway and frescoes by Bertalan Székely and Mór Than, is one of the richest in Budapest—the auditorium is among the most beautiful in Europe. Its large, round ceiling fresco is the work of Károly Lotz, Hungary's most famous master of the genre. The fresco depicts Olympus, so with a seat on the top balcony you really are 'in the gods'!

History

The architect of the neo-Renaissance Opera House was Miklós Ybl, one of Hungary's most prolific and successful 19C architects. Construction began in 1875 on the site of a former flea-market, but was not completed for nine years due to financial problems, even though much of the funding came from Habsburg Emperor Franz Josef. Cash limitations meant that Ybl had to produce ten different sketches for the façade.

In December 1881, during the course of construction, there was a serious fire at Vienna's Ringtheatre, in which over 400 people were killed. This was one of the most serious fire accidents which plagued theatres in those days and it prompted the incorporation in the Budapest Opera of the latest safety designs involving all-metal, hydraulic stage machinery, making it the most modern in the world at the time. The hydraulic equipment lasted for nearly 100 years.

All the materials for the original building were Hungarian except the huge chandelier in the main auditorium, weighing 3000 kilos, which was made in Mainz. Today it needs the work of over a dozen people when it is occasionally let down for cleaning.

The Opera finally opened in September 1884. For the occasion the conductor was Ferenc Erkel, the institution's first musical director and the creator of several operas with Hungarian national themes. Ferenc Liszt had been commissioned to write a work for the opening, but because it included elements of the 'Rákóczi March', the Hungarian rebel melody, it was not performed.

Over the years the Budapest Opera could hold its own among Europe's greatest opera houses. Gustav Mahler was its music director at one time, and later Otto Klemperer. During the siege of Budapest in the winter of 1944–45 thousands of people found shelter in the huge cellars of the building, which miraculously only suffered minor damage. The Opera was therefore able to open very quickly after the war, in March 1945.

In the post-1945 decades the state granted the opera enormous subsidies, both for prestige and to allow access for ordinary people via low prices. The subsidies still continue, though to a relatively lesser extent and prices are slowly rising. Visitors may find that in the tourist, summer season, tickets are much more expensive than at other times of the year.

In 1981 the building was closed for major renovations which involved the use of 300,000 small pieces of 23-carat gold leaf. Glittering in its original brilliance, the Opera House reopened on 27 September 1984, the exact centenary of its original opening.

The façade of the Opera is adorned with many statues. On the balustrade above the second floor are statues of Monteverdi, Scarlatti, Gluck, Mozart, Beethoven, Mussorgsky, Tchaikovsky, Moniusko and Smetana. (These are copies of the originals and were made by Hungarian sculptors in the 1960s.) Below them, in the corner niches of the first-floor projection are Terpsichore, Erato, Thalia and Melpomene, representing dance, love poetry, comedy and tragedy. On the ground floor, on either side of the entrance arcade, are statues of Ferenc Liszt and Ferenc Erkel by Alajos Stróbl.

The attractive, neo-Renaissance building standing opposite and complementing the Opera House today houses the **State Ballet Institute**. It was built as an apartment building for the Hungarian Railways Pension Fund in 1883 to the design of Ödön Lechner and Gyula Pártos, who are better known for their later Hungarian Art Nouveau productions. The inner courtyard and the stairway, with its stained glass windows, can be inspected via the side entrance in Dalszinház u. on the right. At the turn of the century there used to be a popular café, the *Drechsler*, on the

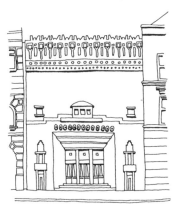

The New Theatre on Paulay Ede u. has one of Budapest's most striking Art Nouveau façades

ground floor. If it were not for today's traffic and pollution, you could almost imagine the locals sipping their coffee on the terrace under the arches, observing the elite arriving for the opera in their carriages.

Immediately behind the Ballet Institute in Paulay Ede u. is one of the most curious-looking buildings in Budapest, the **New Theatre** (Új Szinház), which has undergone many changes, but which today stands with its original splendour restored. Designed by Béla Lajta, it opened in 1909 as a music-hall called the Parisiana. In 1921 it became a theatre and changed to a neo-Empire style. Further alterations occurred in the 1950s and in 1962 it was again 'modernised' and given a steel and glass curtain wall façade. For many years it functioned as Budapest's children's theatre, giving performances by and for young people. In 1988–90 a most unusual reconstruction took place under the direction of Tamás Kőnig, Péter Wagner and art historian Ferenc Dávid. The building was meticulously restored to its original appearance on the basis of photographs and other documentary sources. Lajta's building certainly makes a striking sight today.

Returning to Andrássy út, the building just beyond the Opera House at No. 24 today houses the **Goethe Institute**. As well as a venue for temporary exhibitions, there is a pleasant little café and a German-language library open to the public (Mon 11.00–13.00, 14.30–19.30; Tues–Thur 10.00–13.00, 14.30–17.30). The memorial tablet to the left of the building's main gateway records that here used to be the Three Ravens Restaurant, a favourite haunt of the writer Endre Ady.

The **Opera Pharmacy** next door at No. 26 was founded in 1888. It has original neo-Renaissance furnishings inside.

Across the road at No. 29 is the **Művész Cukrászda**, a well-loved, old-time Budapest patisserie and café, established here before the First World War. Some years ago privatisation prompted fears and protests that the café would either disappear or lose its character; so far it has done neither. The wall plaque to the right of the café records that Jenő Nagy and Vilmos Tartsay, two leaders of the anti-fascist resistance, were arrested in this building in November 1944 and later killed.

In the courtyard of No. 31 next door there is an attractive female statue above an old well. Such decoration was common in old Budapest courtyards, where the water supply for the entire building was often found.

NAGYMEZŐ UTCA crosses Andrássy út a short distance beyond. The street has traditionally been one of the centres of Budapest night life and is sometimes over-enthusiastically described as Pest's Broadway. To the left is the Moulin Rouge night club, the Municipal Operetta Theatre and the Microscope Theatre. To the right is the Miklós Radnóti Theatre. Here also was situated the famous Arizona night club, about which Pál Sándor made the film *Miss Arizona*, starring Hanna Schygulla and Marcello Mastroianni.

> In the inter-war years, the Arizona was one of Budapest's most renowned night spots. Patrick Leigh Fermor in his *Between the Woods and the Water* recalled a visit he made in 1933. The floor seemed to revolve, he remembered, and white horses with feathers careered around it. There were rumours of camels and even elephants. Acrobats flew through the air, then formed massive human pyramids. 'The most glamorous night club I have ever seen,' was his verdict.

To the right along Nagymező u. at No. 8 is the **Ernst Museum**. Founded by art collector and critic Lajos Ernst (1872–1937) in 1912, it is today not a museum as such, but a gallery housing temporary art exhibitions. The Secessionist building also dates from 1912. A particular feature is the colourful stained glass window at the top of the first flight of stairs, the work of József Rippl-Rónai, one of Hungary's most noted Art Nouveau artists. The black marble benches and the bannisters are by the celebrated architect Ödön Lechner.

No. 3 opposite was built for the editorial offices of *Neues Politisches Voklsblatt*, a popular liberal German-language daily (László Gyenes and Andor Vajda, 1913). In the 1930s the 'Hungarian Bauhaus' school was based here, in premises belonging to graphic artist Sándor Bortnyik.

The **Theresa Town Parish Church** stands further along Nagymező u. on the corner of Király u. The original design (1801–11) was by Fidél Kasselik in Louis

XVI style, though the exterior was changed to neo-Baroque in the late 19C. The tower has a balcony which was originally used by fire watchers. Below is a statue of St Theresa (Lőrinc Dunaiszky, 1811). The interior of the church, which is much finer than the exterior suggests, has a high altar in neo-Classical design by Mihály Pollack. The large 1832 chandelier used to hang in the Redoute, the orginal concert hall on the site of today's Vigadó hall by the Danube.

The eye-catching, richly decorated, Romantic-Gothic corner building with pseudo-crenellation and turret-like roof standing diagonally across from the church (Király u. 47) is known as the **Pekáry House**. It was designed in 1848 by Ferenc Brein for Imre Pekáry, a municipal dignitary. In the 1900s the writer Gyula Krúdy lived here and mentioned it in several of his novels. Damaged in World War II, it was restored in 1965.

Returning to Anrássy út, there is a special MÁV (Hungarian Railways) office for advanced booking of rail tickets at No. 35.

The **Polish Institute** is housed across the road in the corner building (Nagymező u. 15). There is a gallery here as well as a shop selling Polish crafts, records, etc.

Andrássy út 39 on the right is the **Divatcsarnok** (literally 'Fashion Hall') department store. It was originally built in 1882 by Austrian architect Gusztáv Petschacher for the Theresa Town Casino, one of the many gentlemen's clubs of 19C Budapest. Its present form dates from 1908–12, following renewals made for the Párisi Nagy Áruház (Grand Parisienne Department Store). However, the main hall from the club, with its rich frescoes by Károly Lotz, survived and this unusual sight as part of a modern shop can be seen at the top of the staircase inside.

In its heyday the Parisienne was one of the city's most fashionable grand stores. Its roof had a restaurant in the summer and a skating rink in the winter! Today, apart from the 'Lotz' hall mentioned above, the interior is nothing special, though the exterior is rather striking. The Art Nouveau façade is probably best viewed from across the road—though only in winter, when the leaves on the trees do not obscure the view!

The so-called **Writers Bookshop** is on the ground floor of the four-storey, Eclectic building at Andrássy út 45. From 1900 to 1945 the famous *Japan Coffee House* operated here. In the inter-war period it was a popular meeting place of writers, poets and artists. Inside the bookshop, in the corner, there are a few archive photographs of the old coffee-house, while elsewhere around the walls are many pictures of Hungarian writers.

LISZT FERENC TÉR follows immediately on the right. Here stands a **statue of Endre Ady** (1867–1919), a polemical journalist and one of the greatest figures in modern Hungarian poetry (Géza Csorga, 1960). The traffic-free section of the square stretches for some way and with its trees and many benches is a pleasant place to relax. Beyond the benches is László Marton's seated, yet dramatic **statue of Ferenc Liszt** (1811–86), placed here on the centenary of the composer's death. The square has been named after Liszt since 1907, when the Academy of Music was built at the far end (see p 123).

JÓKAI TÉR is on the other side of Andrássy út. The bronze statue here (Alajos Stróbl, 1921) is of **Mór Jókai** (1825–1904), the popular Romantic novelist. The Kolibri Puppet Theatre, always a favourite with children of all ages, is at No. 10 at the back of the square.

Another 100m and Andrássy út reaches the large, busy junction with the Great Boulevard known as OKTOGON. This is the original name of the octagonal square, given when its massive Eclectic buildings were erected in 1873–74. From 1945 to

1990 it was known as November 7th Square, recalling the date of the 1917 Bolshevik revolution. For the 16 years prior to 1945, in contrast, it was named after Mussolini.

The plaque on the façade of **No. 2** on the south side of the square recalls that one of the city's famous old coffee-houses, the *Abbázia*, used to be here. It was a meeting place for politicians, among others, and in the old days had one of the richest interiors in Budapest. A sign of the times is that the premises have been remodelled and today house a bank (Antal Puhl and Anikó Z. Havas, 1992).

Beyond Oktogon, on the right-hand side of Andrássy út at **No. 55** is the Exhibition Room of the Ministry of Interior. Temporary exhibitions deal with police work and other activities in the Ministry's field.

No. 52 opposite was the birthplace of the Marxist philospher György Lukács (1885–1971). The wall plaque indicating

Ferenc Liszt's statue in the square named after him is as dramatic as some of his music

that the building, designed by Henrik Schmall, was erected only in 1891 is misleading.

No. 60 is further along the same side. The very words 'Andrássy út 60' send a chill down many spines, for this is the former headquarters of the secret police, the ÁVO (Államvédelmi Osztály—literally, State Security Department) who were particularly active during Hungary's brutal Stalinist period in the early 1950s. They had inherited the building from the pre-war secret police of the Horthy period. Police cars with their victims inside used to drive into the courtyard via the side entrance in Csengery u.

British prisoner

One of those brought to Andrássy út 60 was Edith Bone (1889–1977), a Hungarian-born member of the British Communist Party who came to Budapest in 1949 partly to report for its paper, the *Daily Worker*. On the point of her departure at Budaörs airfield, she was arrested and accused of being a British Secret Service agent. The *Daily Worker* denied she was their special correspondent, although they had printed her articles, and she was sub-sequently sentenced to 15 years in prison. She spent seven years mainly in solitary confinement before being freed during the 1956 Uprising. Her auto-biographical *Seven Years Solitary* was published in 1957. The copy in Budapest's Széchény Library was on the secret, restricted list for over 30 years.

Across the other side of the avenue Csengery u. leads to Hunyadi tér, where there is a small open-air market.

The Eclectic building at **No. 63–65** Andrássy út was built c 1880 by Gusztáv Petschacher (1844–90), a Viennese architect who came to Hungary to participate in the construction of Andrássy út. It was one of the oldest girls' secondary schools in the capital until 1966 when it was transformed into a technical school.

A noteworthy feature of Andrássy út between Oktogon and Heroes' Square, is its long row of attractive lamp-posts, recreated in traditional style in recent years through the efforts of the City Protection Society and with the financial support of various enterprises, whose names appear on little plaques on the posts.

No. 67 on the right was the centre of Hungarian musical life in the late 19C, as it then housed the Academy of Music (Adolf Láng, 1877–70). Above the windows on the second floor are reliefs of Bach, Haydn, Liszt, Erkel, Mozart and Beethoven.

Ferenc Liszt, the Academy's first president from its foundation in 1875, lived here from 1881 to 1886. In 1986 Liszt's former first-floor flat was opened as the **Ferenc Liszt Memorial Museum** (Liszt Ferenc Emlékmúzeum). The collection includes personal memorabilia including Liszt's pianos, one of which is an 1867 American Chickering (entrance round the corner in Vörösmarty u.; tel: 322–9804; open Mon–Sat 10.00–18.00; small snack bar; free concerts held here most Sat mornings).

A composer of controversy—Ferenc Liszt (1811–86)

Though more commonly known by his Germanised name of Franz, Liszt was actually Hungarian. He was born in the small village of Doborján on the Esterházy estate in western Hungary (today, Raiding in Austria) in 1811. At the age of nine he dazzled an audience in the nearby town of Sopron with a virtuoso piano recital and several improvisations. His career took off and he later travelled Europe giving countless performances to rapturous audiences.

The great Pest flood of 1838 touched his conscience and following a series of benefit concerts he then was never far from Hungary, either in body or spirit. His presence in Budapest could draw adoring crowds, even on the street. Yet despite his avowed love for his homeland, he never fully learned Hungarian and in both his writings and compositions, such as his famous Hungarian Rhapsodies, he had a tendency to mix up Hungarian folk themes with traditional gypsy music, an approach which rattled Magyar chauvinists as well as serious music scholars such as Bartók.

He was rather controversial in his personal life, too, generating many scandals. Despite being a novice for the priesthood and wearing clerical garb, he was a great womaniser and fathered illegitimate children with a number of married women.

Like the old Music Academy, **No. 69** was also designed by Adolf Láng (1875–77). This Italianate Renaissance building has a full-length balcony with Corinthian pilasters. Frescoes by Károly Lotz decorate the entrance hall and first-floor corridors. The popular Budapest Puppet Theatre occupies the lower ground floor, while the rest of the building belongs to the **Academy of Fine Arts**. Some glimpses of the interior can be had via access to the Barcsay Gallery located inside.

The Fine Arts Academy also occupies the adjoining premises at **No. 71**, a neo-Renaissance building designed by Lajos Rauscher (1875). The sgraffito on the façade is the work of Róbert Scholtz. (The first Hungarian drawing school was founded under Maria Theresa in the Fortuna Hotel on Castle Hill, Buda, in 1777. The Academy has been here since 1876.)

The **Lukács Cukrászda** at No. 70, across the avenue on the corner of Isabella u., has long been noted for its cakes and coffee. The 1930s' furnishings on the ground floor are literally museum pieces, having been supplied by the Museum of Catering in Buda. At the time of writing the café is closed and its future is uncertain.

The large building at **No. 73–75** Andrássy út, on the right just across Isabella u., belongs to the Hungarian Railways (MÁV) Administration (Gyula Rochlitz, 1876). The near corner has a large bronze relief to the memory of railway workers who fell in the First World War (János Zsákodi Csiszér, 1932). The relief on the far corner, by Rózsa u., was placed there in 1946 on the centenary of the first Hungarian railway (Imre Turáni Kovács). In the hand of the figure is a model of the first Hungarian railway engine, which ran from Pest to Vác in 1846.

The gateway of the building at **No. 83–85** leads to a very impressive, albeit run-down, double courtyard with loggia, well worth viewing (József Kauser, 1890s).

KODÁLY KÖRÖND (Circus) ends the second section of Andrássy út, roughly midway between Oktogon and Heroes' Square. It is regarded by many as one of the most appealing squares in Budapest, with its four large symmetrical buildings describing a circle around its edge, though most of the year these are obscured by the large, leafy plane and horse chestnut trees.

The most attractive building, **No. 3** in the square, is the large neo-Renaissance mansion immediately on the left (also numbered Andrássy út 88–90). It was built for the Railways Pensions Administration in the early 1880s to the designs of Gusztáv Petschacher. The building is noteworthy not only for its size and proportions, but also for the attractive sgraffiti on the exterior (the work of Lajos Rauscher and Bertalan Székely) and for its magnificent gate made by wrought-iron master Gyula Jungfer.

Beneath the trees there are four rather serious statues of military figures. Starting from the one in front of No. 3 and working clockwise, they are: György Szondi (died 1552), a fighter in Hungary's anti-Turkish wars (László Marton, 1958); Bálint Ballassi (1554–94), a lyric poet who died fighting the Turks at the siege of Esztergom in northern Hungary (Pál Pátzay, 1959); Miklós Zrínyi (1508–66), Bán (Duke) of Croatia who died in the defence of Szigetvár in southern Hungary while fighting the Turks (József Róna, 1902); and Vak (Blind) Bottyán (died 1709), a general who died during Prince Rákóczi's War of Independence against Austria (Gyula Kiss Kovács, 1958).

Across the square at No. 1 is the former home of internationally renowned composer, music teacher and researcher Zoltán Kodály (1882–1967), which today houses the **Kodály Memorial Museum** (tel: 322–9647; open Wed 10.00–16.00; Thur–Sat 10.00–18.00; Sun 10.00–14.00). Kodály lived here from 1924 until his death. His former flat is decorated with many textiles, ceramics and other folk items he had acquired over the years. Note the decorated wooden desk from Körösfő in Transylvania.

Zoltán Kodály

Zoltán Kodály, along with Béla Bartók, put the study of Hungarian folk songs and folk music on a systematic basis, travelling around the country recording songs in villages for later analysis. He was also a pioneer of music education and as such gained an international reputation. The so-called Kodály method places great emphasis on choral singing and the enjoyment of song as the basis of musical education. 'An instrument is the privilege of the few,' Kodály wrote in 1941. 'The human voice, an instrument accessible to all, free and still the most beautiful, can be the only soil where a general music culture may grow.'

The 'körönd' has borne Kodály's name since 1971. Before that it was mostly name-less, though from 1939 to 1945 it was actually called Hitler Square.

No. 98 on the left side of the avenue is yet another product of the architect Gusztáv Petschacher (1882). This Italianate neo-Renaissance mansion was built for the Pallavicini family, which was of Italian descent but whose members were prominent in Hungary's political circles before 1945.

Andrássy út crosses Bajza u. 200m beyond the körönd. **No. 101** across the road on the right has housed MUOSZ, the Hungarian Journalists' Federation, since 1945, though the Art Nouveau building itself (by Frigyes Spiegel) dates from 1908. The ground-floor bar and the basement *Silver Pen* restaurant are open to the public.

No. 103 next door houses the small **Ferenc Hopp Museum of East Asian Art** (tel: 322–8476; open 10.00–18.00 except Mon). This is the former home of Ferenc Hopp (1833–1919), a rich businessman and owner of an optical instruments firm, Calderoni and Co., who travelled around the world five times between 1882 and 1914. He left the villa (Gyula Bukovics, 1878) and the works of art he had collected in the East to the Hungarian state. The collection, extended over the years, houses Indian, Mongolian and Indonesian art (Chinese and Japanese material is in the nearby György Ráth Museum at Városligeti fasor 12, see p 180).

The **British Council Library** is not far away in a nicely restored Art Nouveau building at Benczúr u. 26 (Albert Kőrössy and Géza Kiss, 1913). English-language books, magazines, and audio and video cassettes can be borrowed. There is a small café in the basement. (Open Mon–Thurs 11.00–18.00; Fri 11.00–17.00.)

The last 500m stretch of Andrássy út after Bajza u. consists mainly of individual villas built at different times between 1870 and 1914. Since 1945 they have been occupied by a variety of embassies and official offices. Recent years have also seen a number of Western businesses move into this exclusive neighbourhood.

A number of places of (mainly architectural) interest can be found by taking a diversion along the northern section of BAJZA UTCA. **No. 42**, for example, has very large, impressive frescoes under the top ledge by Károly Kernstok, one of Hungary's leading Art Nouveau artists. The mansion was designed in 1902 by Zoltán Bálint and Lajos Jámbor, who had also designed the neighbouring building four years previously.

The **Epreskert** (Strawberry Garden) is 200m along Bajzu u., at the corner of Kmety György u. There used to be a grove of wild strawberry trees here, but for over 100 years the grounds and its building have belonged to the Academy of Fine Arts' sculpture department. Although not open to the public, a stroll around the fence may reveal something of interest, including sculpting in progress. The grounds are also a repository of old statues. From the Bajza u. side, for example, you can see a copy of the noted 14C St George and the Dragon statue by the Kolozsvári brothers.

Szondi u. leads along the far side of the garden to MUNKÁCSY MIHÁLY UTCA, where there are two fine examples of the work of Hungarian Art Nouveau archi-tect, Albert Kőrössy. His 1904 **Sonnenberg Mansion** stands by the corner of the garden at No. 23 (though the addition of a floor in the 1960s rather spoiled the whole effect). A short distance to the left at No. 26 is the massive **Kölcsey Grammar School**, which he designed in 1906–08 as part of an ambitious school building programme initiated by the liberal mayor of Budapest, István Bárczy , who took an interest in and encouraged the Art Nouveau and progressive artists of the time. The influence of Ödön Lechner in the school's form and decoration is clearly visible.

The **Schiffer Villa**, one of the most interesting products of Hungarian Art Nouveau, stands in a garden at Munkácsy Mihály u. 19/b, back in the direction of Andrássy út. It was built in 1910–12 to the designs of József Vágo for one of the owners of Schiffer & Grünwald, a large construction company. Schiffer, a businessman with taste, commissioned several noted artists of the day to decorate the interior. Károly Kernstok designed stained glass windows, while painters István Csók, Béla Iványi-Grünwald and József Rippl-Rónai produced colourful interior panels. Attempts have been made to restore the building and its interior. At the time of writing further renovations are underway and it is not clear whether there will finally be any access for the public.

Munkácsy u. leads back to Andrássy u., from which junction it is 300m to the end of the avenue and Heroes' Square.

13 · Heroes' Square and the City Park

HEROES' SQUARE
With its statues and colonnades, and flanked by the massive buildings of the Museum of Fine Arts and the Palace of Arts, HEROES' SQUARE (Hősök tere) is one of the largest and most impressive spaces in Budapest. The equivalent in a way to London's Trafalgar Square (although not so central) it has, over the years, been the scene of many historic events, demonstrations, celebrations and popular gatherings. Originally it was more like a small park with trees and bushes, the ornamental paving being laid out in 1938 for the 34th International Eucharistic Congress.

On the square stands a complex of statues and sculptures known as the **Millenary Monument**, the work of architect Albert Schickedanz and sculptor György Zala. Construction began in 1896, to mark the 1000th anniversary of the Magyar Conquest of the Carpathian Basin, but it was not completed until 1929, and even after that political considerations resulted in alterations in the composition of the statues.

In the centre rises a 36m stone **column with the Archangel Gabriel** at the top and equestrian statues of Árpád and the other six conquering Magyar chiefs at the base.

Gabriel is depicted standing on a globe holding aloft the Hungarian crown and an Apostolic cross, representing the unity of the Hungarian state and Christian culture. Legend has it that the archangel had appeared in a dream to Stephen, Hungary's first monarch, charging him to convert the then pagan Magyars to Christianity.

> The column has its own peculiar history. An initial problem was that nobody was quite sure when the anniversary of the Magyar Conquest actually fell. A committee of the Academy of Sciences could only confirm that the original Hungarians arrived some time between 888 and 900. The government arbitrarily selected 1895 as the millenary anniversary year. Work on the

momument and other related projects took longer than expected, and even though the official date was changed to 1896 the central column and statue were only ready in 1897.However, city engineers declared that the statue would be swept away in the first major storm. Thus a new, reinforced column was commissioned, but this was only ready in 1901. In the meantime the statue was sent to Paris for the 1900 World Exhibition, where it won the Grand Prix.

The block of stone on the ground in front of the column is the **Heroes' Monument**, the traditional spot for wreath-laying ceremonies. The inscription reads: 'To the memory of the heroes who have sacrificed their lives for the freedom of our people and national independence'. The original memorial, placed here in 1929, was dedicated to the unknown soldiers who lost their lives in World War I, and had inscriptions on it referring to that war and the territories lost at the Treaty of Trianon.

Behind the column is a two-part **colonnade**. The four groups of symbolic figures on the top represent, from left to right, Work and Wealth, War, Peace, and Knowledge and Glory. These, like the statues at the base of the stone column, are the work of György Zala.

Between the columns of the colonnade are **statues of Hungarian rulers and princes**. From left to right (with dates of rule) they are: King Stephen (1000–38); King László (1077–95); King Kálmán (1095–1116); King Andrew II (1205–35); King Béla IV (1235–70); King Charles Robert (1308–42); King Louis the Great (1342–82); and on the right-hand side Regent János Hunyadi (1446–52); King Matthias Corvinus (1458–90); István Bocskay, Prince of Transylvania (1604–06); Gábor Bethlen, Prince of Transylvania (1613–29); Imre Thököly, Prince of Upper Hungary and Transylvania (1682–85 and 1690); Ferenc Rákóczi II, Prince of Transylvania (1704–11) and of Hungary (1705–11); and Lajos Kossuth, Regent of Hungary (1849).

Below each statue is a relief. All but one show some significant scene from the life of the person represented above. For example, below King Stephen the scene depicts him receiving the crown from the Pope; King Matthias is shown among his scholars; and Lajos Kossuth is portrayed calling people of the Alföld to arms in the 1848–49 War of Independence.

The statues of the Transylvanian princes on the right-hand colonnade were all added after World War II in place of statues of Habsburg rulers. The Habsburgs had also been removed, though later replaced, during the 1919 Council Republic period. For May Day of that year the whole square was decked out with red, and the central column covered by a huge red obelisk—it was a time when avant-garde painters and sculptors were encouraged to decorate the streets and public squares with 'uplifting' images and slogans, as had occured in Russia after the 1917 Revolution.

The massive neo-Classical façade of the **MUSEUM OF FINE ARTS** (Szépművészeti Múzeum), one of the major art galleries of central Europe, dominates the north side of Heroes' Square. Inside is Hungary's main collection of non-Hungarian works of art (tel: 343–6755; open 10.00–17.30 except Mon; bookshop and pleasant café on lower ground floor. Excellent free tour in English by members of the Budapest International Women's Association, Tues–Fri 10.30; confirmation advisable, tel: 342–9759).

Designed by Albert Schickedanz and Fülöp Herzog and completed in 1906, the huge building displays all the Historicist elements deemed appropriate at the time for a temple of the arts—Classical, Romanesque, Renaissance and Baroque revival can all be found.

Full-scale renovation of the museum is under way and is expected to continue until at least the end of the 1990s. This is causing some disruption to the layout of the collections, but at least the building is slowly being restored to its original grandeur.

The most important collection of the museum is the **Old Masters Gallery** on the first floor, the core of which came from Count Miklós Esterházy's private gallery, which he sold to the state in 1871. The collection covers 13–18C European painting and includes a rich selection of Italian works such as Corregio's Virgin and Child with Angel (1520s), Titian's Portrait of the Doge Loredan (1553), Bronzino's Venus, Cupid and Jealousy (c 1550), Raphael's Esterházy Madonna (1508) and Portrait of Pietro Bembo (c 1504) and Tiepelo's St James Conquers the Moors (1759).

The Spanish section comprises 70 works and is one of the largest Spanish collections outside Spain itself. There are seven El Greco's in all, including his Mary Magdelene in Penitence (c 1580), Study of a Man (1590s) and Agony in the Garden (c 1614). The museum has five works of Goya, including The Water Seller and The Knife Grinder (both c 1810). Velázquez's Peasants' Repast (c 1618) can also be found here, as can works by Murillo, Zurbaran and Ribera.

In the Flemish and Dutch sections there are paintings by Rubens, Van Dyck, Jordaens, Pieter Bruegel the Elder (St John the Baptist Preaching, 1566), Frans Hals (Portrait of a Man, 1634), Jan Steen and Rembrandt. The German collection includes works by Dürer and Altdorfer.

The **Collection of 19C Art** can be found on the ground floor to the left. Although not extensive, there are a number of good quality French Impressionist and other works here by such painters as Cézanne (Sideboard, c 1875), Monet (Fishing Boats, 1886), Gaugin (Black Pigs, 1891) and Pissaro (Pont-Neuf, 1902). Works by Delacroix, Courbet and Manet can also be found.

The **Collection of 20C Art,** on the lower ground floor to the rear and left, is even smaller but does contain works by a number of significant painters including Kokoshka, Chagall, Picasso and Vasarely. A small **Egyptian Collection** is also on the lower ground floor (at the front, to the right). Down here, too, there is a book-shop and a café.

The **Ancient Greek and Roman Collection** is on the ground floor to the right, while also on the gound floor at the rear there is the **Prints and Drawings Room**. This houses rotating displays from the museum's extensive collection, which includes drawings by Raphael, Tiepolo, Rembrandt, Rubens, Dürer, Poussin, Picasso and Chagall.

The **Palace of Arts** (Műcsarnok) stands opposite the Fine Arts Museum on the south side of Heroes' Square. Major (temporary) exhibitions of mainly contem-porary works are held here. The neo-Classical red-brick building was designed by Albert Schickedanz and Fülöp Herzog in 1895 and completed the following year, in time for the Millenary Celebrations.

Behind the portico's six Corinthian columns there is a three-part fresco by Lajos Deák Ébner depicting The Beginning of Sculpture, with figures of Vulcan and Athene; the Source of Arts, with Apollo and the Muses; and The Origins of Painting, with images from the mythology of antiquity. The two smaller ones in between show allegorical figures of Painting and Sculpture. For the ceramic ornamentation around the cornice, frost-proof pyrogranite, newly invented by the Zsolnay factory in Pécs, was applied.

Originally the tympanum was plain. The present design (by Jenő Haranghy), depicting St Stephen as patron of the arts, was added between 1938 and 1941.

The steps of the Palace of Arts have been the scene of a number of remarkable events going all the way back to 1900 and the massive ceremonial burial of Mihály Munkácsy (1844–1900), the only 19C Hungarian painter who gained an international reputation.

The most recent significant event took place on the morning of 16 June 1989 and attracted world attention. The façade of the building was decorated in black and white and over 100,000 people packed Heroes' Square to witness a ceremony marking the public reburial of Imre Nagy, the Prime Minister during the 1956 Uprising who was secretly executed on 16 June 1958.

Nagy's coffin was flanked by five others. Four belonged to colleagues with whom he had been executed after 1956 (including Pál Maléter, his Minister of Defence) and one was empty, representing the unknown victims of the period. In the afternoon the coffins were taken to plot 301 in a far corner of Budapest's Új köztemető cemetery where Nagy and over 200 others had lain in unmarked graves for three decades.

The reburial with the concurrent political 'rehabilitation' of Nagy was the most public, symbolic event of Hungary's political changes of 1989–90.

Imre Nagy (1896–1958)

During World War I Imre Nagy was a prisoner of war in Russia, where he joined the revolutionary movement. He returned to Hungary in 1921 but seven years later went into exile first to Vienna, then to Moscow. After returning to Hungary in 1945 he held a number of ministerial posts but always maintained an interest in agriculture. In July 1953 he was Prime Minister during Hungary's mini thaw following the death of Stalin, but two years later was divested of his party and government offices. During the events of 1956 he was hurled back into office as Prime Minister between 24 October and 4 November.

After the crushing of the Uprising, Nagy and his colleagues found refuge in the Yugoslav Embassy by Heroes' Square (at the corner of Andrássy út opposite the Palace of Arts). Tricked by false assurances given to the Yugoslav government, they emerged on 23 November only to be arrested and taken to Romania. Nagy was finally executed after a secret trial in Budapest in June 1958, the victim of a system he had helped to create, but which he had also tried to reform.

The broad section of DÓZSA GYÖRGY ÚT, which runs from the side of the Palace of Arts for almost 1km to the south, was formerly used as a huge parade ground on 1 May and other festive or political occasions in the manner of Red Square in Moscow, and was thus often known as 'Demonstration Square'.

Along here there was a huge statue of Joseph Stalin, erected in 1951. The 25m statue stood on a plinth 30m high. On the evening of 23 October 1956, the first day of the Hungarian Uprising, massed crowds pulled the statue down. It was the most symbolic event of the entire Uprising, though not without a touch of humour. Despite obtaining wires, pulling vehicles and cutting equipment, the crowds only managed to topple the top three-quarters of the statue, leaving Stalin's massive footwear in place. Thus the area was known as 'Boots Square' for some time after. The statue was smashed to bits, but some years ago its enormous hand reappeared after being kept in a private garden for decades. It is held today by the National Museum.

CITY PARK (Városliget)

The City Park stretches beyond Heroes' Square and Dózsa György út. Covering 1 sq km it is one of the biggest parks in Budapest and has been a popular recreation spot for many decades.

History

Originally marshland, the site was presented to Pest in the mid 18C by Leopold I. Later Maria Theresa ordered the systematic planting of the area, and this began in 1751. New plans were drawn up in the 1810s by Henrik Nebbien, a landscape gardener of French descent, but the present layout mostly dates from the end of the 19C when English-style gardens were popular. There were nearly 200 'English' gardens in Hungary at that time.

The City Park was the site of the main exhibition during the six months of the 1896 Millenary celebrations, which marked the 1000th anniversary of the Magyar conquest of the Carpathian basin. Over 200 halls and pavilions were erected to display the agricultural, industrial and commercial life of the country. Hungary's first museum village was built to represent peasant life and 'real' peasants were on hand to demonstrate authenticity. A great attraction was the balloon that rose 500m providing its passengers with a panoramic view of the city. The balloon was unfortunately ripped to pieces by a storm during the celebratory year.

The City Park has also been a traditional focal point for the labour movement. In the pre-1914 era a number of restaurants with large gardens on the far side of the park became known as workers' meeting places and even strike centres during disputes. On 1 September 1930, with demands for work and bread, the largest workers' demonstration of the inter-war, Horthy period headed along Andrássy út and assembled in the park.

The park has also seen many May Day labour movement celebrations, which date back well beyond 1945. The first great May Day demonstration was in 1890, when up to 40,000 marched in the park. The tradition continues today with festivities every 1 May, though without the orchestrated demonstrations of the post-1945 decades.

The City Park can be approached across the bridge immediately behind Heroes' Square. To the right of the bridge is the open-air **Skating Rink** (open Nov–Mar only; Mon–Fri 09.00–13.00; weekends 10.00–14.00; and 16.00–20.00 daily). When floodlit at night, the skaters and their setting provide a grand spectacle.

The Pest Skating Club was founded in the 1860s. Originally skaters used the frozen surface of the lake but an artificial rink has operated since 1926. The club house on the right was designed in 1893 by Ödön Lechner.

Beyond the skating rink on an island in the lake stands a most unusual building, the fairy-tale-like **Vajdahunyad Castle**. It was originally designed by Ignác Alpár as a temporary structure for the Millenary Exhibition which opened in the park in May 1896. The idea was to present in one building the different architectural styles which could be found in Hungary. Due to its popularity Alpár was later commissioned to rebuild the structure in a permanent form; hence the present building actually dates from 1907. There is a statue of Alpár (1855–1928) dressed as a medieval guild master by the road leading to the castle.

The section facing the lake is a copy of part of the original Vajdahunyad Castle in Transylvania (today Hunedoara, Romania) from which the whole complex of buildings takes its name. Work started on the original castle c 1450 under the direction of Erzsébet Szilágyi, the mother of King Matthias who continued the building until its completion at the end of the 15C.

To the left of the main gate are copies of towers of former castles in Upper Hungary (Slovakia) while to the right is a copy of the tower of Segesvár (in Romania today).

In the courtyard on the left is the Romanesque wing and the **Chapel of Ják,** a copy of the still-standing 13C Benedictine church at Ják in western Hungary, one of the country's oldest monuments. In fact only the doorway decorated with the 12 apostles is a copy; the rest is both smaller and different from the original church. To the left of the chapel is a cloister, with elements copying 11–13C Hungarian architecture.

Opposite, around a small courtyard, is the façade of the so-called Palace section, containing a mixture of Romanesque and Gothic styles (on the right) and the 'Vajdahunyad' section. Further to the left Renaissance style appears in a small building with a balcony copied from Sárospatak Castle in eastern Hungary. Beyond that, the large sprawling 'Baroque' building is based on details of various 18C mansions.

Inside here is the **Museum of Agriculture** (Mezőgazdasági Múzeum), which traces the history of agriculture in Hungary including the development of tools and machines (tel: 343–0573; 10.00–17.00 except Mon; free on Tue; small snack bar; limited w/a). On the ground floor is a steam engine built in 1852 by the Clayton–Shuttleworth company of Lincoln, England, which was brought to Hungary and used for nearly 50 years for driving threshing machines.

The museum has sections on sheep, horse and cattle breeding, hunting and fishing, and wine-making. There are many models of animals and much equipment both large and small. Texts are in Hungarian but the displays speak for themselves.

Facing the entrance of the Agricultural Museum is Miklós Ligeti's 1903 **statue of 'Anonymus'**, the unknown and thus named author of a late 12C or early 13C chronicle of the Magyars. A popular statue, many bronze or ceramic copies of it ranging from mantlepiece decorations to inkpots adorned pre-1945 apartments.

Just to the south of the museum stands the first **statue of George Washington** to be erected in Europe (Gyula Bezerédi, 1906). In the period 1871–1913 over three million people emigrated from Hungary to the United States. The statue was paid for by donations colleced by various Hungarian–American societies in the USA.

Many of the City Park's popular attractions are located on ÁLLATKERTI KÖRÚT, which runs from the side of the Fine Arts Museum around the north side of the park. Immediately behind the museum at No. 2 is **Gundel's**, one of the most famous restaurants of Central Europe between the two World Wars, catering to royalty and heads of state from around the globe.

The popular Wampetic's restaurant was here from the late 19C. Károly Gundel (1883–1956), the son of János Gundel (1844–1915), a pioneer of the

Hungarian catering industry, acquired the business in 1910. Through exhibitions he popularised and developed Hungarian specialities.

In 1991, after four decades of being in state ownership, *Gundel's* was purchased by Ronald S. Lauder and George Lang, the noted Hungarian–American restaurateur. The building was completely renovated and restored. The dining room walls hold paintings by 19C Hungarian masters and inside there is also a collection of Gundel memorabilia.

The **Budapest Zoo** (Állatkert) is just beyond the restaurant (open all year round, but many animals hidden away inside in the winter. Trolleybus 72 from Arany János u. metro station brings you right here, and to the other attractions mentioned below).

The Municipal Zoological and Botanical Gardens opened in 1866 on the initiative of the Academy of Sciences and in particular of János Xantus (1825–94), a natural scientist who spent much of his life in the United States. Taken over by the city council in 1907 it has been modernised several times. Some of the architecture of the zoo represents significant examples of Hungarian Art Nouveau, such as Kornél Neuschloss-Knüsli's main gate (1912) and elephant house (1910). The bird house near the south-west corner of the zoo, designed by Károly Kós, is in National Romantic style.

All zoo regulars are found here—elephants, giraffes, hippos, bears, tigers, lions, monkeys, seals, polar bears, etc. The palm house (a product of the Eiffel workshop) has snakes and crocodiles. One of the bird houses has creatures walking and flying around you, though most animals are in cages.

Next to the zoo is the **Municipal Circus** (Fővárosi Nagycirkusz). The first circus in Pest, the Hetz Theatre, was opened in 1783 on the site of today's Lutheran church in Deák tér, but because of fire danger it moved several times. The first permanent circus was built on the present site in 1891 by a German entrepreneur, Ede Wulff. It operated until 1966; today's building dates from 1971. (Open throughout the year. Tickets available on the spot, but booking recommended. Be advised that the idea that animals should not be exploited for circus entertainment has not yet caught on in Hungary.)

The **Széchenyi Baths** (Széchenyi Gyógyfürdő) stands opposite the circus. Designed in 1909–13 by Győző Cziegler and Ede Dvorzsák it was extended in 1926. The baths have an open-air pool (open throughout the year!) and medicinal pools fed by some of Europe's hottest thermal springs. The building is undergoing major renovation throughout the 1990s (see p 43).

The **Fun Fair** (Vidám Park) is at Állatkerti körút 14–16 beyond the circus. Before the war it was called the Angol (English) Park. The traditional merry-go-round through the entrance and immediately on the left, and the wooden switchback at the rear of the fairground, are original and date from before the Second World War. (Open all year, but with limited operation in the winter.)

Between the circus and the Fun Fair there is a **small children's fairground** (Kis Vidám Park) particularly suitable for toddlers (open spring to autumn).

Across the City Park, in the corner near the junction of Ajtósi Dürer sor and Hermina út, stands the large **Transport Museum** (Közlekedési Múzeum). The exhibitions cover the history of shipping, road and rail transport. There are many models on display, both large and small, as well as Hungarian veteran vehicles. Some of these are actually right-hand drive—prior to World War II Hungarians drove on the left! (Tel: 343–0561; open 10.00–18.00 except Mon; free on Wed; snack bar.)

The Transport Museum's Exhibition of Air and Space Travel is in a separate building, the Petőfi Csarnok (Hall) a short way to the west (open Apr–mid-Oct 10.00–18.00 except Mon). Part of this complex regularly functions as a popular venue for pop and rock music concerts.

Behind the Transport Museum at Hermina út 23 stands the small, neo-Gothic **Hermina Chapel** (József Hild, 1842–46), erected in memory of Palatine József's daughter Hermina Amália, who died in 1842 aged 25. For the consecration Liszt's *Mass for Male Choir* was performed in the presence of the composer.

The following four large buildings are not in the City Park proper, but are of architectural interest. At Nos. 37 and 39 Ajtósi Dürer sor, 100m from the museum at the end of Hermina út, stand, respectively, the **Blanka Teleki Grammar School** (1901–02) and the **Institute for the Blind** (1899–1904). Both were designed in Hungarian Art Nouveau style by Sándor Baumgarten and Zsigmond Herczegh.

Directly across Hungária körút, and through the pedestrian tunnel under the railway line, is Mexikói út. **No. 60** to the left is by Béla Lajta (1905–08) and was also built originally as an institute for the blind. Note the copper plate to the left of the entrance—one remaining of several which Lajta designed containing literary quotes in Braille.

More impressive is his massive 1909–11 **Jewish Hospital for the Long-Term Sick** not far away (via Korong u.) at Amerikai út 57 (today the National Institute for Neurological Surgery). Note the typical Lajta application of folk motifs in stone on the side door.

14 · Margaret Island

Margaret Island, which lies on the Danube between Margaret Bridge and Árpád Bridge, is one of Budapest's most attractive parks and a popular recreation spots, full of life and activity in the summer and calm and peaceful in the winter.

This route starts from the middle of Margaret Bridge at the south end of Margaret Island and crosses the island from south to north (approximately 2.5km).

Trams 4 and 6, which run the length of the Great Boulevard, cross Margaret Bridge and stop in the middle, by the island. Bus 26 runs from Nyugati tér, by the side of the Western Railway Station, to the island itself and then crosses it on the main road to the north end. Private cars are only allowed on the island at the north end from Árpád Bridge and then only as far as the car park to the north of the Thermal Hotel.

Margaret Bridge (Margit híd) links Szent István krt at the northern end of the Great Boulevard with Margit krt on the Buda side. Over 600m long and 25m wide, it was designed by French engineer Ernest Gouin following an international competition and built in 1872–76 by the Société des Bettignoles company of France. The statues on the pillars are the work of the Thabard studio in Paris.

Unusually, the bridge is bent. Its two arms meet in the middle at an angle of 150° such that each is at right angles with the current of the river. The view to the south from the middle of the bridge is quite spectacular. To the left by the Danube is the neo-Gothic Parliament building, while straight ahead are Gellért Hill and the former Royal Palace on Castle Hill. The spire of the Matthias Church on Castle Hill is also clearly visible.

The large **lion statue** at the Buda end of the bridge (Szilárd Sződy, 1932) was raised to the memory of those who fell in World War I at Przemysl Castle in Poland, which at the time stood in a part of the Austro–Hungarian Empire. An inscription on the plinth reads in part: 'They fought like lions'.

Early in the afternoon of Saturday 4 November 1944, during World War II, an error caused Margaret Bridge to blow up, resulting in one of the worst tragedies of the war. Several hundred people were killed including German engineers who were planting explosives in preparation for the destruction of the bridge. (Photographs in the underpass at the Pest end of the bridge show the extent of the damage.) What remained of the bridge was destroyed by the Germans in January 1945. It was rebuilt after the war in 1947–48, though prior to this there was a temporary pontoon bridge, affectionately knicknamed 'Manci' (a diminutive of 'Margit').

A small connecting bridge leads to **MARGARET ISLAND** (Margit-sziget).

History

Margaret Island used to be known as The Island of Hares—it was a royal game reserve at the time of the Árpád dynasty. Frivolity gave way to piety and from the 12C it was the home of the Premonstratensians and, from the 13C, the Franciscans. The Order of St John had a monastery at the south end and the Archbishop of Esztergom a castle at the north end, though all traces of these have disappeared. Béla IV had a convent built on the island for Dominican nuns in the 13C and for a while under his patronage the nuns became the largest ecclesiastical landowners in the country.

According to tradition, Béla vowed during the Mongol invasion of 1242–44 that if Hungary were victorious his daughter Margaret would be brought up as a nun. History has not recorded what she thought of that at the time, nevertheless in 1252, when she was aged nine, Margaret was brought to the island where she lived until her death in 1271. The island was named after her at the end of the 19C.

After the victory of the Turks over the Hungarians at the battle of Mohács in 1526, the island became depopulated and during the Turkish occupation many of its buildings were destroyed. After the Turks the island became the home of the St Clare nuns, but when the order was suppressed it passed into the hands of Archduke Palatine Alexander. Palatine Joseph took over the island in 1795 and in line with his zeal for renewal had vines and rare trees planted. Many European dignitaries participated in vintage festivals here in the first half of the 19C.

An English traveller, a certain Miss Pardoe, visited the island in the late 1840s and recorded an amusing observation indicating that vandalism has not simply been a 20C phenomenon: '(the island) was for some time appropriated by the Palatine as a public promenade; but the destruction among the trees and vines was so great that he was compelled to deny admission to the island from the Pest side, and to limit the permission of ingress on the other shore to such individuals as, from the respectability of their appearance, might be presumed not to indulge in wanton mischief.'

The island-park was opened to the public in 1869, but until 1900, when the connecting link with Margaret Bridge was built, the only access was by boat. Baths were built at the end of the 19C to exploit the natural waters of the island, but these were destroyed in World War II.

The city bought the island in 1908 and placed it under the management of the Budapest Council of Public Works. Visitors were charged an entrance fee which doubled on Sundays and holidays. This rather exclusive system lasted, apart from the brief period of the 1919 Council Republic, until 1945 when the island was declared a free public park for all citizens. Since then it has been one of the most popular recreational areas in Budapest, attracting locals and visitors alike.

To the left of the bridge-island link are the stadium and 14,000sq m grounds of the **Athletics Centre** (Tibor Hübner, 1949). The site used to be the sports field of the Hungarian Athletics Club which, when it was founded in 1875, was one of the first such clubs in Europe. The club was suppressed in 1946 after being labelled a fascist organisation and for decades the grounds were known as the Pioneers (Communist Youth) Stadium and were used mainly by school pupils.

At the end of the link road, on the roundabout, stands the 10m bronze **Centenary Monument**, erected in 1973 to mark the 100th anniversary of the unification of Buda, Pest and Óbuda. The sculptor, István Kiss, placed inside the monument various mementoes of the city's previous 100 years. The tall fountain behind has become one of the symbols of the island, though it has only been here since 1962.

Beyond the fountain is the so-called **casino**, which functions as a restaurant and terrace-bar in the summer. It was originally designed by Miklós Ybl and built in 1869, though it has changed a lot. In the inter-war period it was one of the most popular spots on the island.

To the left of the main road which runs the length of the island is the **Alfréd Hajós Swimming Baths**, named after the winner of the 100m and 1200m swimming races at the first modern Olympics held in Athens in 1896. Hajós (1878–1955) was not only a swimmer but also a professional architect and he actually designed the building. When it opened in 1935 it was Hungary's first competition-standard indoor swimming pool. Since then two open-air pools, a diving pool and children's pools have been added (see p 42). The baths are also known as the National Sports Pool (Nemzeti Sport Uszoda), the official name up to 1975.

The **ruins of the Franciscan church** are 500m along the island to the right of the main road. These date from the late 13C and early 14C. Part of the west façade and some parts of the tower are still standing; an original window with Gothic tracery can be seen high up. The north wall of the church is also clearly visible. The statue of the girl with pipe on the far side of the wall is by Jenő Kerényi (1965).

The huge, 70,000sq m, open-air **Palatinus Baths** complex (István Janáky and György Masirevich, 1937) is about 300m farther along the main road, on the left. The open-air pools are fed by the island's thermal springs. The main pool is enormous—over 100m in length! (see p 42).

To the east of the baths, in the middle of the island, is the **Rose Garden** at the south end of which is Tibor Vilt's 1973 bronze seated statue of Imre Madách (1823–64), whose play, *The Tragedy of Man*, is one of the most famous Hungarian dramas and has frequently been translated into other languages.

To the east of the statue, on the Pest side of the island, is a **small game reserve** which has colourful peacocks, pheasants and other small birds and animals.

About two-thirds of the way along the island, on the east side, are the **ruins of the Dominican church and convent**. The originally 13C convent stood for nearly 300 years and its copying workshop played an important part in Hungarian culture. It was here that Béla IV's daughter, Margaret, lived for most of her life in the mid 13C.

The legend of St Margaret was first written down by Lea Ráskai, a nun who lived here in the 16C. During the Turkish occupation the nuns fled and the buildings fell into ruin. They were not discovered until the mid 19C. The convent used to stand to the south of the church and the foundations of the cloister court, well-house, chapter hall, kitchen and refectory can be seen. A marble tablet marks the original burial place of Margaret and there is a shrine to her in the modern brick construction nearby. Many legends and miracles are associated with the name of Margaret, who appears to have lived a life of extreme asceticism bordering on masochism. She was beatified after her death at the age of 29 in 1271 but was not canonised until nearly 600 years later in 1943.

The 200m stretch north of the ruins contains many busts and statues of Hungarian writers, poets, painters, sculptors, musicians and actors which were mostly erected after 1945. To the left is the large **Open-Air Theatre** (Péter Kaffka, 1938). Concerts and performances are given here during the summer months.

The 57m **Water Tower** nearby was built in 1911 to the designs of engineer Szilárd Zielinszky and architect Vilmos Ray Rezső. A pioneering structure, it was one of the first in Hungary where reinforced concrete was used. No longer functioning as a water tower, it occasionally houses exhibitions in the summer.

A **Premonstratensian Chapel** stands a few metres to the north-east of the tower. Built in the 12C in Romanesque style on the site of an even earlier chapel it was largely destroyed in the Turkish wars of the 16C. Excavated in the 1920s it was reconstructed in 1930–31. In the tower hangs one of the oldest bells in Hungary. The work of the 15C master Hans Strous, it was found nearby in 1914 in the roots of a walnut tree torn out during a storm.

The nearby 'Ramada' **Grand Hotel** is one of Budapest's classic hotels (Miklós Ybl, 1873). It originally functioned as a sanatorium attached to medicinal baths built at the end of the 19C, though destroyed during the Second World War. The building was restored to its original style in the mid 1980s.

The neighbouring **Thermal Hotel** was built on the site of the former baths (Gyula Kéry, 1978). To the left of the hotel there is a small **rock garden** which is also a botanical garden with exotic plants, streams, waterfall and ponds. Tropical water lilies and small fish thrive in the warm-water ponds.

Towards the northern end of the island near the roadway is a replica of Péter Bodor's **Musical Fountain** built in 1820 in the centre of Marosvásárhely in Transylvania. Originally the musical mechanism played by the force of water. Today it is driven by electricity and, when working, plays for about five minutes on the hour.

Árpád Bridge (Árpád híd), named after the 9C Magyar chieftain, cuts across the north end of Margaret Island and is a relatively 'young' city bridge. Construction began in 1939, after it was deemed necessary for workers from Óbuda to be able to cross more easily to factories in the Angyalföld district on the

Pest side. However work was held up by the war and the bridge was not completed until 1950, when it was named Stalin Bridge, a title it kept until 1956.

This is the city's longest bridge, stretching with its flyovers for nearly 2km in total. In the first half of the 1980s the bridge was widened to twice its original width, such that today it carries two tram lines and six lanes of traffic.

15 · Óbuda

Óbuda is the area on the right bank of the Danube by Árpád Bridge. In the Middle Ages Óbuda was the first significant settlement in the territory of today's Budapest. At that time it was called simply Buda ('Ó' is an ancient form meaning 'old') and was an area of royal residences. After the Mongol invasion in the mid 13C, Béla IV had the royal residence moved to Castle Hill and the area declined in importance.

Following the Turkish occupation, Óbuda revived as a market town and up to the end of the 19C was also well known for its local wines. The cosy nostalgic atmosphere portrayed in many pictures and described in many accounts of pre-1945 Óbuda has survived in a few small pockets up to the present day, but much of the old area has been demolished to make way for modern tower blocks and housing estates.

The modern centre of Óbuda is the large, unattractive junction of Flórián tér, with its shopping precinct. Most visitors, however, head for FŐ TÉR (Main Square), a short distance away on the north side of the Buda end of Árpád Bridge. This was the focal point of Óbuda in the 18C. Today it has been renovated and often at weekends in the summer months there are live music performances and other festivities. There are a number of museums and several restaurants in the vicinity.

Before exploring Fő tér, however, this route begins on the south side of the bridge abutment with the Baroque **Óbuda Parish Church**, designed by János György Paur in 1744–49 for the Zichy family, which owned much of Óbuda in the 18C.

Above the door is a relief of St Rosalie. On the façade are statues of SS Sebastian (left) and Roch, and on the sides of the tower are SS Peter and Paul after whom the church is officially named. All the statues are the work of Károly Bebó who also made the richly carved Rococo pulpit inside on the left and the frame of the picture of St Charles Borromeo on the other side of the triumphal arch.

At the back of the church, on the external wall, there is a memorial relief to the 'heroes of Óbuda' who died in World War I (István Toth, 1928).

The **statues of SS Flórián and John of Nepomuk** 100m in front of the parish church are also the work of Károly Bebó. These are two of the oldest statues in Budapest (1753–54). On the bases are the coats of arms of Count Miklós Zichy and his wife.

St John of Nepomuk

Statues of St John of Nepomuk (died 1393) are very common in Hungary. This 14C priest was born in southern Bohemia and became the confessor of the wife of Wenceslas IV. Because he refused to reveal her confessional secrets (or, according to others, due to internal church power politics), the king had him thrown into the river Moldva. He was canonised in 1729, became a patron saint of Bohemia and today rests in the St Vitus Cathedral in Prague Castle. In view of the way he was martyred, he is also regarded as the patron saint of bridges. Thus his statue, unlike here, usually appears on bridges and at river crossings.

A short distance to the south stands the neo-Classical **former Óbuda Synagogue**, designed by András Landherer and built in 1820–21. The six-columned portico supports a tympanum and at the top are the Tablets of the Commandments. The Jewish Museum used to be here in the 1930s. Since 1986 the building has been used as studios by Hungarian Television.

Opposite, at Lajos u. 158, is the **Budapest Gallery Exhibition House** (Budapest Galéria Kiállítóháza). There is a permanent exhibition of the work of sculptor Pál Pátzay (1896–1979) and temporary exhibitions are also held here. (Open 10.00-18.00 except Mon).

In the area behind the gallery and the parish church there are a number of renovated, one-storey houses characteristic of the old Óbuda. In Kálvin köz, which is at the rear and to the right of the first modern block of flats behind the church, stands the small **Óbuda Calvinist Church**, which was built in 1785–88. The church house next door was built in National Romantic style in 1908 to the design of Károly Kós and Dezső Zrumeczky. It represents a rare, albeit small, example of Kós's work found in the capital.

The route now passes through the subway under Árpád Bridge to Szentlélek tér. There are some old photographs of Óbuda on the walls of the underpass.

Facing the exit of the subway across Szentlélek tér is the two-storey, white building of the **Vasarely Museum** (tel: 250–1540; open 10.00–18.00 except Mon; w/a good). In 1982 the 'father of Op Art', Victor Vasarely, who was born Győző Vásárhelyi in the southern Hungarian town of Pécs in 1908 and who emigrated to Paris in 1930, donated 400 of his works to the Hungarian state. The museum, which was opened in May 1987, contains a large selection of his paintings spanning his life's work.

FŐ TÉR is reached via the cobbled area to the left of the museum. A bronze bust of the novelist Gyula Krúdy (1878–1933) stands at the rear of the museum's side wall (Tamás Gyenes, 1958). Krúdy once described Óbuda as an 'antique town' where the streets were 'as bent as old people, huddling like tramps in the merciless wind on the high road'.

The gateway on the right at Fő tér 1 leads to the former **Zichy Mansion**, built in Baroque style for Miklós Zichy in 1746–57 to the design of János Henrik Jäger. The building today is a cultural centre and houses the Óbuda local history collection and the small **Kassák Memorial Museum** (Kassák Emlékmúzeum; tel: 168–7021; open 10.00–18.00 except Mon). Lajos Kassák (1887–1967) is one of the most unusual and interesting figures in Hungarian 20C arts. He was an avant-garde poet, writer and artist, editor of the *Ma* (Today) journal and the leading representative of Hungarian 'constructivism' in design.

Lajos Kassák—unorthodox artist

The son of a Slovak pharmacist's assistant and a Hungarian washerwoman, Kassák failed his primary school exams and became a blacksmith's apprentice. Before World War I he wandered through Austria, Germany, Belgium and France experiencing life at the bottom, which he wrote about after his return. Politically he was always an internationalist and being on the margins (some would say at the forefront) of cultural trends he inevitably had clashes both with progressive cultural circles and with left-wing political leaders. Although seriously at odds with its dogmatism, he was a supporter of the 1919 Council Republic, after the suppression of which he spent several years in Vienna.

He returned to Hungary in 1926 and continued his publishing activities. In the 1930s he launched a leftist politico-cultural journal and movement called simply *Munka* (Work), criticising both orthodox communism and social democracy.

For a while in the post-1945 period he held prominent positions in the arts world, but after 1949 and the growth of local Stalinism, his anti-authoritarian unorthodoxy inevitably led to a form of internal exile. Unlike some of his colleagues, however, he never renounced his radical constructivism, and before his death in 1967 he even received a certain amount of official recognition.

The two-storey, Copf-style building on the west side of Fő tér at No. 4 was built c 1780 and today houses the **Zsigmond Kun Folk Art Collection** of pottery, textiles, carvings and furniture (open Tues–Fri 14.00–18.00; weekends 10.00–18.00). Zsigmond Kun, born in Mezőtúr on Hungary's Great Plain in 1893, was a connoisseur and collector of ceramics and folk art. His former home here has been preserved as a museum. Items include dishes, brandy flasks, a dowry chest, kitchen utensils and jugs collected from all over greater (i.e. pre-1920) Hungary.

The neo-Baroque, three-storey building with two large atlantes at **No. 3** Fő tér was built in 1906 and today houses the Third District (Óbuda) Council.

Hajógyár u. is at the north-east corner of Fő tér. The statue composition of three women with umbrellas here is the work of Imre Varga (born 1923), one of the most prolific of contemporary Hungarian sculptors. There is a collection of his characteristically striking, metallic work in the **Imre Varga Gallery** nearby at Laktanya u. 7, to the left from Hajógyár u. (tel: 250–0274; open 10.00–18.00 except Mon). The collection includes copies of his statue of St Stephen and composition of Our Lady of Hungary which stand in the Hungarian Chapel of St Peter's in Rome.

Óbuda contains the majority of Budapest's Roman remains, the subject of the following route.

16 · Roman Budapest

The Romans arrived in the territory of present-day Hungary around the time of Christ, but it was not until the 2C that people started to arrive from all parts of the empire to settle. The Romans called their province in the western part of the Carpathian Basin *Pannonia*. The Danube was its border and along the river bank they built a string of fortifications as defences against the barbarians beyond (see Contra-Aquincum p 80).

A thriving Roman settlement was created on the banks of the Danube in the area of today's Óbuda. Known as *Aquincum*, it had a population of 40,000 at its height. Military and civilian public baths were built as well as workshops, market halls, inns, gymnasiums, religious shrines and two amphitheatres. At the end of the 4C decline set in and when the Huns arrived the Romans evacuated Aquincum.

The ruins of the large **Military Town Amphitheatre** can be seen at the junction of Nagyszombat u. and Pacsirtamező u., 2km north of Margaret Bridge on the Buda side (five stops on tram 17 from the bridge). Built in the 2C, it could seat 13,000–15,000 spectators. The arena was larger than that of the Colosseum in Rome and it was used until the end of the 4C. It was probably utilised as a fortress following the Magyar conquest but was built over in subsequent centuries. Excavations of the foundations and some reconstruction took place in the late 1930s.

A number of Roman sites are within striking distance of FLÓRIÁN TÉR, the large juncion at the Buda end of Árpád Bridge, 1km north of the amphitheatre along Pacsirtamező u. (buses 84 and 86 from the amphitheatre).

This area used to be the centre of the Roman military camp, where 6000 soldiers were garrisoned in the 2C and 3C. In the 1970s, during construction work on the junction, remains of the camp were found and today the whole of the underpass network beneath the surface has been turned into a **Roman Settlement Museum**, with display cabinets and stone relics lining the walls. The large baths of the Roman legion were originally discovered in the late 18C and became the subject of the first excavations in Hungary made on a scientific basis. The entrance to the **Roman Baths Museum** (Fürdő Múzeum) which constitutes a separate section is in the underpass. (Access May–Aug with prior arrangement. Tel: 250–1650.)

The small **Roman Camp Museum** (Táborvárosi Múzeum) is at Pacsirtamező u. 63, 150m to the south of Flórián tér (for access tel: 250–1650). Remains of Roman buildings and graves were discovered when the foundations of the present building were being laid in 1950. The remains were of a 2C dwelling house which was transformed into a bathing establishment in the 3C or 4C. In addition to the architectural finds, some Roman tools and items of glass and earthenware are also on display.

Two sites are nearby to the north of Flórián tér. The first street to the right off Szentendrei út (the major road running north) is Kórház u. Along here and on the left are the ruins of the Acquincum Praetorian Gate, which was built at the end of the 3C.

The **Hercules Villa** is at Meggyfa u. 19–21 (west off Szentendrei út along Raktár u., then north along Szél u. or Vihar u., or cut through between the blocks of flats). The name refers to the 3C mosaic floors representing the Herculean myth which were unearthed here in the late 1950s, and which are preserved in situ under a protective covering, albeit almost hidden by the surrounding high-rise dwellings. Hercules is shown shooting an arrow into the centaur Nessos who abducted Deianeira. The mosaics probably originated abroad and were brought here 'ready-made', but the surrounding framework, which is coarser work, is in all likelihood of local origin. The mosaics are considered to be one of the most highly artistic Roman relics found in Hungary. (For access tel: 250–1650, though a glimpse of the mosaics can be had through the window).

Approximately 3km north of Flórián tér, alongside Szentendrei út, are the ruins of the Roman civilian town and the **Aquincum Museum** (tel: 250–1650; open 10.00–18.00 except Mon. Buses 42 and 106 run along Szentendrei út; alternatively the HÉV suburban railway stops nearby at 'Aquincum'. The HÉV starts from Batthyány tér and can be picked up at Árpád híd station by Szentlélek tér, 400m to the east of Flórián tér).

The neo-Classical Aquincum Museum was built in 1894 to exhibit Roman relics found locally. Apart from the statues, pottery, tools, utensils, coins, mosaics and jewellery, there is a rare, albeit reconstructed example of a 3C Roman water organ.

The excavated areas of part of the civilian town lie around the museum in the open air. They include the remains of large public baths, a market place, dwelling houses and an old Christian church and a shrine of the Persian Sun-god Mithras.

By the side of the HÉV station (across the road and under the bridge) are the ruins of the civilian town amphitheatre. It was much smaller than that of the military town and was built to seat up to 8000 spectators.

17 · The Buda Hills

One of the great things about Budapest is that even within the city boundaries, just a few kilometres west of the centre, there are many easy-to-reach, attractive woods and hills. Throughout the year the Buda Hills are a favourite place for relaxation and walking for both visitors and locals alike. The air is much cleaner and fresher than in the city, and splendid views can be had from many vantage points.

A convenient and pleasant way of sampling the hills by public transport is via the Cog-Wheel Railway and the Children's Railway. There is also a chair-lift to one of the hills, and buses to different spots run from various points in the city.

Pathways through the hills are usually clearly signposted and give the distance in kilometres and/or the approximate time the walk takes (ó = hour, p = minute). 'Hill' in Hungarian is *hegy*.

Cog-Wheel Railway
The lower terminus of the **Cog-Wheel Railway** (Fogaskerekű Vasút) is on Szilágyi Erzsébet fasor, opposite the 17-storey, circular Budapest Hotel (György Szrogh, 1967). The hotel is two stops from Moszkva tér on tram 56 or 18.

The railway, the third of its kind in the world, was originally built in 1873 by a Swiss firm on commission from the mayor of Buda, Ferenc Házmán. The first train ran on 24 July 1874 and was driven by steam power. Electrification was implemented in 1929. For the best view, sit on the right-hand side by the window in a seat facing backwards. There are nine stops in all and the total journey is about 20–25 minutes.

The grounds of the Szent János (St John) Hospital, one of the oldest in the city, stretch out by the side of the first stop. As the train climbs you can see behind it the modern 'Kútvölgyi' Hospital, which used to be an exclusive hospital for top Party personnel. To its left is the smaller, modern building of the International András Pető Institute, which has become renowned worldwide in recent years due to its unique and successful methods of teaching children with motor disabilities to walk. International interest in Conductive Education, as the Pető method is known, mushroomed following *Standing Up For Joe*, a 1986 BBC documentary about Joseph Horsley, a British boy attending the Budapest institute.

The train slowly climbs **Sváb Hill** (420m). The name derives from the many German-speaking Swabians who settled here after the Turks had left Hungary. Up to the 19C the hillside was covered mainly with vineyards. The construction of the Cog-Wheel Railway opened up the hill and it became a popular place of residence for many writers and artists. One summer villa belonged to the romantic novelist Mór Jókai (1825-1904). The actual building no longer stands, but a small **Jókai Memorial Room** (Jókai Emlékszoba) can be found in its former grounds at Költő u. 21, a short distance from the Városkút station (open Wed–Sun 10.00–14.00).

The **Széchenyi Look-Out** is 300m south-east of the Művész út station, along

Széchenyi-emlék út; a good view can be had from here. The gloriette, designed by Miklós Ybl, used to stand in what is now Heroes' Square. It was moved here when the square was being planned in the 1890s. The bust of István Széchenyi is by Alajos Stróbl (1891).

The upper terminus of the Cog-Wheel Railway is on **Széchenyi Hill** (427m). The Panorama Hotel near the sation was built in 1938 as the Golf Hotel in the style of an alpine hunting lodge.

Children's Railway

The start of the **Children's Railway** (Gyermek Vasút) is along the road to the left, 200m beyond the kiosks and buffet. This narrow-gauge railway was constructed between 1948 and 1951 as the 'Pioneers' Railway'. The title comes from the political youth movement of that name. All controllers, conductors and booking clerks, but not the driver, are still uniformed children who enthusiastically salute the trains in and out of the stations. The total 11km journey takes about 45 minutes as the train slowly winds through the wooded hills (operates throughout the year except Monday, unless a public holiday).

Normafa is the first stop. This is a very popular open spot in the hills with a beautiful view. In the winter skiing and sledging take place here. The name comes from an occasion in 1840 when a celebrated star of the National Theatre, Rozália Klein, sang the grand aria from Bellini's *Norma* to a company of artists gathered here. A memorial plaque today recalls the event. (Normafa can also be reached on bus red 21 from Moszkva tér; this bus can be picked up at the Sváb-hegy station of the Cog-Wheel Railway. From there, too, bus 190 goes to Normafa at weekends and on public holidays.)

János Hill (529m) is the highest point in Budapest. An 800m path from the fourth stop of the Children's Railway (János-hegy) leads up to the hill. It can also be reached along the 2km road from Normafa by foot (cars are not allowed). On weekdays and holidays bus 190 connects János Hill, via Normafa, with the Cog-Wheel Railway's Sváb-hegy stop.

Another, more dramatic way to reach the hill is via the **chair-lift**, *Libegő* (floater) in Hungarian. Cable-chairs, suspended ski-lift style, ascend János Hill in a journey of only 12 minutes, but which seems longer. The best view is undoubtedly on the way down (open all year; mid-May–mid-Sept 09.00–17.00, otherwise 09.30–16.00, but closed every other Mon). The lower station on Zugligeti út can be reached on bus 158 from Moszkva tér.

The 24m-high **Erzsébet Look-Out Tower** (Erzsébet-kilátó) stands on the peak of János Hill, some way up from the top of the chair-lift. The neo-Romanesque tower was built in 1908–10 to the designs of Frigyes Schulek. From the top there is a spectacular panorama of the surrounding hills and most of the city (opening times erratic, but should be daily May–Sept 10.00–18.00; in winter, often open at weekends).

Szépjuhászné is the fifth stop on the Children's Railway. Alongside Budakeszi út, it can also be reached on bus 22 from Moszkva tér. Nearby are the ruins of the central Pauline monastery which was built in the early years of the 14C. The Paulines were the only monastic order founded in Hungary. Nagy-Hárs Hill is just to the north; you can either climb up or walk round it on the marked path. To the east is Kis-Hárs Hill, which has two look-out towers. Marked paths from here lead to Hűvösvölgy.

Hűvösvölgy (Cool Valley) is the last stop on the Children's Railway (alternatively tram 56 from Moszkva tér). To the east, through the woods, is the Nagy-rét meadow, a grassy clearing popular for picnics, etc. There is a small fairground here with a little ferris wheel. Special festivities often take place here on May Day, perhaps recalling that in the 1930s this was a meeting place for semi-underground political gatherings.

Bus 56 and tram 56 both run from Hűvösvölgy back to Moszkva tér.

LÁTÓ HILL

After taking bus 11 from Batthyány tér to its terminus, there are several possibilities. You can walk straight on down the road, which brings you to a huge forest-park area providing lots of opportunities for walks, picnicking, etc. In the Middle Ages this area used to be a favourite royal hunting ground. Almost all the paths going west (to the left) eventually lead to Hűvösvölgy (see above). The path straight on brings you to the gliders' airfield, a huge open patch where gliders can often be seen taking off and landing.

Alternatively, from the terminus of bus 11 you can climb Látó Hill to the right, through the wood and up the short distance to the Árpád Look-Out (Kilátó), which provides a good view of the city. From here it is 600m through the woods to the east down to Fenyőgyöngye (restaurant here) and bus 65 back to town (though see also next entry).

HÁRMASHATÁR HILL

A very high, grass-covered peak, with a grand view. Like Látó Hill above, this is to the north-west of the centre. There is a restaurant with terrace view, and kiosk at the top. To reach Hármashatár Hill from town, take bus 65 from the bottom of Szépvölgyi út, which in turn is reached on bus 6 (Kolosy tér stop) from Nyugati Station. Alternatively, you can walk up the road (2km) from Fenyőgyöngye (see above), though bus 65 from there is easier.

BUDAKESZI GAME PARK (VADASPARK)

A beautiful wooded, hilly, enclosed park, covering extensive grounds right on the border of Budapest and Budakeszi, about 8km from the centre. Some animals (wild boars, goats, deer, etc.) are in large enclosures, others are free to roam through the grounds. There are various raised vantage points throughout the park for observing the animals undisturbed. This is a place you can spend some time just walking and looking. Paths for walks of 3.5km and 5km are clearly marked, and there is a look-out tower (*kilátó*) which gives an excellent view of the surrounding hills and countryside.

Open all year round from dawn to dusk. Bus 22 from Moszkva tér takes you right there—the express 'red' 22 is a little quicker. Alight just on the boundary of Budakeszi and take the road running away from the bus stop, following signs for 'Vadaspark'.

SAS HILL

This is a very special hill to the east of Gellért Hill. Due to its dolomite rock formations, its rare plants and birds, the hill is a protected area. Access is by conducted group and only at certain times of the year (information from Tourinform: 117–9800).

ORGANISED WALKS

A sure way of not getting lost, a way of seeing the parts many tourists miss and a way of meeting Hungarians! Guided walking tours through the hills are organised throughout the year on different days of the week; some are specifically aimed at young people and families with small children. You can usually just turn up on the day. For further information contact Tourinform, 2 Sütő u., near Deák tér, tel: 117–9800.

18 · Off the Beaten Track

ÁLDÁS UTCA SCHOOL

One of the most attractive school buildings in the city can be found on Áldás utca in District II. The school, called simply the **Áldás utca school**, was designed by Dezső Zrumeczky and built in 1911-12 as part of a major school-building programme initiated by Budapest mayor István Bárczy. The design is virtually 'pure' Hungarian National Romanticism, with sharply sloping, Transylvanian-style roofs and wooden folk-motif carvings on the entrances. Although accommodating over 500 pupils, the building gives off a warm and friendly atmosphere. The school can be reached on bus 91 from Nyugati tér. Alight at the top of Rómer Flóris u., four stops after Margaret Bridge.

The composer and music researcher Zoltán Kodály lived on the second floor of No. 11, half-way up Áldás u. from 1910 to 1924; Béla Bartók and other musicians were regular visitors. At that time the street was rather quiet. It constituted part of the exclusive Rozsadomb area of Buda, and had fewer buildings than today. Kodály must have witnessed the construction of the school at the bottom of the street. Perhaps its Hungarian folkish form and elements gave him inspiration in his composing.

Two more stops on bus 91 takes you to Vérhalom tér (children's playground here), from where it is a short walk up Áfonya u. to the little-known **József-hegy look-out**, which provides a fine view of the Danube and the surrounding hills. From here the Szemlő-hegy Cave (see 'Caves' below) is within walking distance along Józsefhegyi u. and Pusztaszeri út.

BARTÓK BÉLA ÚT

Bartók Béla út is a very busy artery running south-west from the Gellért Hotel into the heart of the XIth District in southern Buda. This area, close to the city centre, was still fields and vineyards only 100 years ago—what we see is virtually all a product of the 20C. In the late 19C there was an ambitious plan to create here a district on a geometrical pattern similar to many cities in the USA. Although this was never fully realised, many elements of such a layout can be seen today.

The older buildings are near the Gellért tér end of Bartók Béla út and in this vicinity there are a number of attractive (albeit today rather run-down) turn-of-the-century Art Nouveau creations. Four can be viewed by starting at Kemenes u., which runs up the south side of the **Gellért Hotel** and from which you have a good view of the rear of the hotel and its ever-popular, open-air pool (see also p 68). The villa at **No. 14** at the top (1908) is by Emil Vidor, one of Hungary's most prolific Secessionist architects. The large **No. 1** Mányoki út, round the corner, was designed in 1902 by the architect and painter Gyula Kosztolányi Kann to serve as artists' studios and apartments. Orlay u. drops down from here back to Bartók Béla út. **No. 9** has seen better days, but the building's original splendour is still detectable (Lajos Schoditsch, 1909).

The bell outside **No. 6** Orlay u. recalls the architecture of ancient Armenian churches. This is because the building behind is today the Armenian Catholic Ministry, the only one in Hungary.

Mészöly u. is the next street leading up from Bartók Béla út. **No. 4** has also seen much better times but there are still clear traces of its rich decoration. It was built in 1910 to plans by László Warga and Jenő Kismarty-Lechner. The latter, who lived here until his death in 1962, was not only a designer, but also a prolific art historian, university teacher and influential public figure. He even managed to produce a highly commended plan in the 1922 architectural competition for Chicago's *Tribune* building.

No. 40 Bartók Béla út was designed by Ödön Lechner—in his own characteristic style (though most of the decoration is missing today)—and built for the accommodation and studio of his writer-painter brother, Gyula, in 1899.

The thoroughfare now reaches the huge junction known as MÓRICZ ZSIGMOND KÖRTÉR. Móricz (1879–1942) was a very popular novelist of social realism. Prior to 1945 the junction bore (along with Bartók Béla út itself) the name of Miklós Horthy, Hungary's ultra-conservative ruler of the inter-war years. This massive square and the wide, straight streets radiating from it, stem from the late 19C 'American' plan for the area.

In the middle is Zsigmond Kisfaludi Strobl's 1930 statue composition featuring Prince (St) Imre. Imre was the son of Stephen, Hungary's first monarch. He died in a hunting accident in 1031 aged 24. Interestingly, this very 'royalist' composition stood here right throughout Hungary's 'communist' period.

VILLÁNYI ÚT is the major road leading west from the junction. The massive, white neo-Baroque building set back and up from the road just along here at No. 5–7 is the **Margit Kaffka Girls' School** (Gáspár Fábián, 1930). Beyond it can be seen the twin spires of the neo-Baroque **Church of St Imre**, built in 1938 for the Cistercians to plans by Gyula Wälder, who had also designed the adjoining boys' school ten years previously. Baroque Revival, as exemplified by the girls' school and the church here, was often employed in Hungary in the 1920s and 1930s. The idea behind this Late Eclecticism was to try to recreate some of the country's architectural glory, much of which had been lost when many ancient towns were severed from Hungary under the peace treaty following the First World War.

The St Imre Church is perhaps best viewed, particularly when lit at night, from KOSZTOLÁNYI DEZSŐ TÉR, 500m further along Bartók Béla út. This is another massive junction with wide radial roads on the 'American' plan. The church can be seen across the park, on the other side of Feneketlen-tó, the 'Bottomless Lake' fashioned from an old clay pit, which despite its name is only a few metres deep.

On the east side of the park, which was laid out in 1960, stands a striking bronze **statue of Béla Bartók** framed by bells (József Somogyi, 1981). Bartók (1881–1945) is one of Hungary's most internationally renowned 20C composers.

BOCSKAI ÚT runs to the west from Kosztolányi tér. The inter-war apartment blocks in Modern style along here and the surrounding area's houses and villas produce a completely different atmosphere from that encountered earlier in the district. One curiosity is the former synagogue at Zsombolyai u. 6, on the corner of Bocskai út. This was the only synagogue in Hungary built in the Modern style (Baráth, Novák and Hamburger, 1936). Another oddity is Bertalan Árkay's red-brick, geometrical Art Deco villa (1928) not far away at Diószegi út 54/b.

BAUHAUS ARCHITECTURE

Bauhaus, functionalist and International Modern styles were rather slow to develop in Hungary. In the atmosphere of the 1920s and 1930s they were often seen as 'too internationalist' by an official culture keen to reassert national values severely undermined by the post-World War I settlement. Commissions for modernist architects, therefore, tended to be for private dwellings, often family villas in District II rather than for large, officially funded projects.

The leading protagonist of Hungarian Bauhaus was Farkas Molnár (1897–1945) who had been a member of the Weimar Bauhaus in the early 1920s, and whose 1929 apartment house at Mihály u. 10, on the west side of Gellért Hill, was one of the first Bauhaus-type constructions in Budapest. (Works mentioned below are also by Molnár unless otherwise stated.)

In 1931 several Bauhaus architects participated in the experimental Napraforgó u. project (see p 177) and in the same neighbourhood other examples of Modernist villas can be found at Pasaréti út 7 (1937) and 97 (Gyula Rimanóczy, 1934), Lotz Károly u. 4/b (1933), Harangvirág u. 11 (1933), Orsó u. 21 (Lajos Kozma, 1930), Csévi köz 7/a (1935) and Hankóczy Jenő u. 3/a (1932).

The nearby Rózsadomb (Hill of Roses) area also contains similar styles— Berkenye u. 19 (Lajos Kozma, 1937), Cserje u. 12 (1932) and József Fischer's Szemlőhegy u. 35 (1936). Fischer's Bajza u. 10 is a rare example of a Bauhaus villa in Pest (1936).

Two good examples of larger buildings in Bauhaus style are the Atrium Cinema building at Margit krt 55 (Lajos Kozma, 1935) and the apartment block not far away at Rómer Flóris u. 1–3 (Béla Hofstätter und Ferenc Domány, 1938).

CAVES

A particular attraction of the Buda Hills are its unique caves, which were formed by thermal waters in the ground and not, as is common elsewhere, by infiltrating rain water. The high temperature and the dissolved salts brought by the thermal waters have resulted in their special beauty. Two caves that are easily accessible and which can be visited in normal clothing are the **Pál-völgy Cave** at II. Szépvölgyi u. 162 (open 09.00–16.00 except Mon) and the **Szemlő-hegy Cave** at II. Pusztaszeri út 35 (open Mar–Oct 09.00–16.00 except Tues). The latter has more varied rock formations and more modern facilities for visitors. Both have guided tours on the hour, every hour.

The starting point to reach both is Kolosy tér, near the Buda embankment between Margaret Bridge and Árpád Bridge (bus 6 from Nyugati tér goes there). Bus 65 runs from Kolosy tér past the Pál-völgyi Cave; bus 29 runs by the Szemlő-hegy Cave (fourth stop).

The lower terminus of both these bus routes is, strictly speaking, not in Kolosy tér but nearby at the bottom of Szépvölgyi út, a few metres to the west of the square. The **Újlak Parish Church** here dates from 1746–59. A tower which originally stood in the centre was pulled down and replaced with the present one in its unusual off-centre position in the 1760s, though the top part was added by Miklós Ybl in 1877. On the main altar (1799) is a copy of Lucas Cranach's Madonna by Ferenc Falkoner. The interior furnishings are mainly from the Baroque period.

CEMETERIES

Cemeteries in Budapest can be, paradoxically, quite lively places, particularly at weekends when crowds of people converge on them bringing, flowers and tending graves. The crowds are particularly large around the 'day of the dead' (All Souls' Day—2 November) when even traffic flows have to be specially regulated in the neighbourhood of cemeteries. On most weekdays, however, the cemeteries are quiet places, offering peace and tranquillity, away from the bustling life and noise of the city.

Several cemeteries are noted for their large mausoleums, which are architectural monuments in themselves, and/or their political and historical connections. Maps showing the layout of who is buried where are usually available by the entrances of the larger cemeteries.

Kerepesi Cemetery (Kerepesi temető, Fiumei út, 600m south-east of Baross tér, which is by the Eastern Railway Station). This is the nearest major cemetery to central Pest and is noted as the official burial place for national heroes. The massive mausoleums of Lajos Kossuth, Ferenc Deák and Count Lajos Batthyány, for example, can be found here. One curiosity, which is still standing at the time of writing, is the large Pantheon of the Working Class Movement (Körner József, 1958) built for the graves of labour and communist movement leaders (to the right from the entrance). The inscription behind the Socialist Realist statues reads: 'They lived for communism and the people'.

This cemetery has witnessed many funerals of historic importance. It was here on 6 October 1956, for example, that the reburial took place of László Rajk. Rajk (1909–49) was an underground communist leader in the 1930s who fought in the Spanish Civil War. After World War II he was Hungary's Minister of the Interior, and later Foreign Minister. Falsely accused of 'Titoism' he was arrested and executed in 1949, becoming the most famous victim of the Hungarian purges. In the thaw following Stalin's death he was posthumously rehabilitated and reinterred in the cemetery here. The reburial in effect became a mass demonstration prefiguring the Uprising which broke out 17 days later.

The neighbouring **Jewish Cemetery** (entrance round the south side, 600m along Salgótarjáni u.) has some very old, impressive, large tombs. It has suffered from neglect for many years, but is currently undergoing restoration.

The Jewish Cemetery can be reached directly on tram 37 from Népszínház u., by Blaha Lujza tér. This, or tram 28 from the same place, can also be taken to reach the Kerepesi Cemetery.

Uj köztemető. This cemetery, one of the largest in Budapest, is situated on Kozma u., on the east side of Pest, about 15km from the centre. Plot 301 in the far north-east corner of the cemetery is where Imre Nagy and others executed after 1956 were buried in secret. For his reburial on 16 June 1989 (see p 152) the plot was transformed by the erection of traditional-style wooden graves posts, and public access was made easier. Today the landscaped area is a place of political pilgrimage and the scene of official commemorations on 23 October, the anniversary of the start of the 1956 Uprising. The stark monument to the martyrs of 1956 near the grave of Imre Nagy is by György Jovánovics. The plot is well-signposted ('300, 301 parcella'), but is a good 2km from the main entrance. There is a minibus service, though, which should run every 20 minutes or so.

The entrance to the adjoining, large **Jewish Cemetery** is 700m to the north along Kozma u. Although most are in a sad state of neglect, there are many still-impressive Art Nouveau tombs here. Note, for example, that of Sándor Schmidl, to the right from the entrance (Béla Lajta and Ödön Lechner, 1903).

Trams 28 and 37 from Népszínház u. by Blaha Lujza tér go all the way to the main cemetery on Kozma u. (At 35 minutes, this is one of the longest tram rides in the city, taking you through the highly industrialised District X and past the large Kőbánya breweries.) Tram 37 goes a bit farther, past the entrance of the Jewish cemetery.

Farkasrét Cemetery (Farkasréti temető). This is one of the largest cemeteries on the Buda side. It has many graves of poets and writers, though curiously also holds that of Mátyás Rákosi (1892–1971), Hungary's one-time Stalinist dictator. Tram 59 from Moszkva tér stops by the main entrance on Németvölgyi út.

CSEPEL

Csepel, Budapest's XXI District, is situated on the northern tip of Csepel Island, which is on the Danube to the south of the centre. This is an industrial and working-class area, of interest to visitors wanting to get a feel of 'ordinary' Budapest. Its centre, Szent Imre tér, is easily accessible—two stops on the HÉV suburban railway from Boráros tér at the Pest end of Petőfi Bridge.

For over a century thousands of locals have found employment in Csepel's huge iron and metal works, which grew from an ammunition works founded here in 1892 by Manfred Weiss. By the First World War, the Hungarian Krupp, as he was known, was employing 30,000 workers in what was Austro–Hungary's most up-to-date armaments factory. Weiss died in 1922, but the family continued the business and diversified, producing everything from munitions to motorbikes. In the 1980s, after three decades of nationalisation, the massive, centralised Csepel Iron and Metal Works was broken down into smaller units to operate more or less independently with a market orientation. Privatisation followed in the 1990s.

At Gyepsor u. 1, near the old main entrance, there is a **Csepel Works Museum** (Csepel Művek Múzeum) devoted to the history of the plant (access by prior arrangement only; tel: 277–6347).

> The traditional militancy of the local labour movement earned the district the epithet of 'Red Csepel'. During the Second World War there was even a prison inside the factory, but it did not stop a massive strike from taking place in September 1943. In addition, one of the few acts of mass resistance to the Germans took place in Csepel in December 1944 when the population was ordered to be evacuated. Women led the passive resistance and the police sided with the people, leaving the Germans and the Hungarian Arrow Cross authorities helpless.
>
> In the post-1945 years Red Csepel was the pride of the 'proletarian state'. The iron and metal works was named after Mátyás Rákosi, Hungary's Stalinist ruler, and the city's first post-war Lenin statue, with characteristic outstretched arm, was erected in front of the main gate. Dissatisfied workers, however, on more than one occasion placed a slice of bread and dripping in its hand. In 1956 the local workers' council was one of the longest to hold out, and when Soviet leader Nikita Khrushchev visited Csepel in 1958, giving a speech over the factory's loudspeakers at the end of a shift, workers walked away not stopping to listen.

Csepel Island itself, although only 5–6km wide, stretches for nearly 50km to the south, and is by no means entirely industrial. Nor is its history. The Romans were once here, the conquering Magyar chief Árpád is believed to have settled in the area, and in medieval times the island was a favourite hunting ground of royalty.

The **Csepel Local History Museum** (Csepel Hélytörténeti Gyűtemény) at Szent Imre tér 3 traces the general history of Csepel from early times to the present day. The Csepel Gallery in the same building holds exhibitions of contemporary works (tel: 276–7343; open 10.00–18.00 except Mon; closed in July and August).

KISPEST

Kispest, a district south-east of the centre, is for the most part unattractive, with high-rise, tower-block estates dominating the area. In one corner of the district, however, there is one of the architectural peculiarities of Budapest, the **Wekerle Estate** (Wekerletelep), named after Sándor Wekerle, the prime minister at the time of its planning. (To reach the estate, take blue metro line 3 to Határ út—near its northern corner, from where buses 99 and 194 run to Kós Károly tér.)

> The estate was built between 1908 and 1925 as a public housing project, though most of it was completed by the First World War. The houses were primarily intended for civil servants, office workers and public officials who worked in Budapest (at the time Kispest was a separate township). Of the 1000 houses on the geometrically patterned streets, 70 per cent are single storyed. Many are detached or semi-detached with their own plots, which makes the whole area very much akin to an English 'garden city' along the lines of the theories of Ebenezer Howard. The idea was to provide all the necessary services—kindergartens, schools, shops, churches, etc—amidst healthy and green surroundings. Letchworth, Britain's first garden city, was started in 1903. The Kispest estate was begun just five years later and this fact alone makes it of European significance. Dereliction and modern-day traffic have inevitably transformed the local environment, but you can still get a feel of what the area must have been like when it was first built.

Of particular interest is the ensemble of buildings surrounding KÓS KÁROLY TÉR, a large park area at the centre of the estate. These were constructed in Hungarian National Romantic style under the direction of the architect Károly Kós. Although Kós (1883–1977) studied in Budapest, for the most part he lived in Transylvania, and these buildings are among the few of his works to be found in the capital.

Kós believed that the true roots of a genuine Hungarian architecture were to be found in the folk and peasant styles of ancient times, particularly in the Transylvania region. The characteristic high-pitched roofs and use of wood can be seen here in massive gateways on two sides of the central square. They give the appearance of entering a medieval castle area, which was presumably the intention, and one expects to see a knight in armour ride though on horseback at any moment. No. 2–3 in the square is the work of Kós himself, No. 10–11 that of his colleague Dezső Zrumeczky. A statue of Károly Kós stands in the square (László Péterfy, 1987).

The police station on the edge of the estate at Ady Endre út 29 was built at the same time (Lajos Schoditsch and Béla Eberling, 1912–13) and is an attractive example of the more sober Hungarian Art Nouveau style rather than of Kós-type Romanticism. In recent years there has been a revival of the National Romantic tradition, though today it tends to go under the name of 'organic' architecture. Its most prominent representative is the architect Imre Makovecz.

KŐBÁNYA

Kőbánya, District X, is to the east of the centre, on the Pest side. The name means stone quarry and refers to the local quarries that provided stone for construction work in the city from the 17C to the 19C. The stone was quarried in underground passages which stretched for more than 30km. These were later used by the several breweries which were established in the late 19C and which utilised the spring waters found here.

Kőbánya is an ordinary, industrial district, worth visiting if only to get a feel of the Budapest not normally featured in tourist brochures. Tram 28 from Népszinház u., by Blaha Lujza tér, progresses along the main road of the district, Kőbánya út, to the modern centre of Liget tér, as does bus 9 from near Deák tér.

There are, however, some special sights and places of interest in Kőbánya. In Szent László tér, a short distance to the north of Liget tér along Kőrösi Csoma út (one stop on tram 13 or 28), there is the beautiful little **St László Church** (Ödön Lechner and Gyula Pártos, 1894–98). The style is a mixture of neo-Gothic and Hungarian Art Nouveau and bears the characteristic marks of Lechner's designs. The interior brickwork, altars and pulpit, decorated with Zsolnay ceramic ornamentation, were designed by Ottó Tándor. The church was badly damaged in the Second World War but was rebuilt. Restoration work in recent years has made this church a gem amidst rather dreary surroundings. The Pataky Cultural and Community Centre across the road (Dezső Tóth, 1975) contains a cinema and a local history collection.

The **Fire Service Museum** (Tűzoltó Múzeum), situated at Martinovics tér 12, 300m east of Liget tér, has an exhibition of fire-fighting equipment and documents relating to the great fires of the past (tel: 157–2190; open Tues–Sat 09.00–16.00; Sun 09.00–13.00; limited w/a). Nearby, at the far end of Kápolna tér, stands Kobánya's oldest historic monument, the Baroque Greek Catholic **Holy Trinity Chapel**, built in 1739–40. The Art Nouveau **former synagogue** in Cserkesz u., also near the museum, has been nicely restored (Richard Schöntheil, 1909–12).

In Mázsa tér, 100m to the south of Liget tér (under the railway bridge and to the left) there is a small, characteristic local open-air market. Saturday morning is the liveliest time.

Kőbánya also has one of Budapest's most unusual buildings, the **Watch-Tower** at Harmat u. 43, on the corner of Gitár u. Designed by Ferenc Brein, it was built in 1844 to overlook the vineyards which then occupied the area. Above the watchman's small house is a tower with an exterior corkscrew stair. The neo-Gothic elements combine a utilitarian functionalism and fanciful Romanticism (bus 185 from Kőbánya centre runs along Harmat u.).

THE LUDOVICEUM

This massive neo-Classical building was constructed in 1830–39 to plans by Mihály Pollack, architect of the (later) National Museum, for the Ludovika Akadémia, a military academy which functioned here until 1945. At the time of its construction it was well outside the urban limits. Foundation of the academy had been mooted at the end of the 18C, but it was a delicate matter, given that Hungary was ruled by Austria, and indeed the 1848–49 War of Independence meant that the academy did not officially open until 1872. Today the building belongs to the University Natural Sciences Faculty. There are plans to house the Natural History Museum here in the second half of the 1990s, following extensive renovations.

The Ludoviceum stands in LUDOVIKA TÉR, a triangular park alongside Üllői út, 300m east of Klinikák (blue line) metro station. As that name implies, this area contains many clinics and departments of the Semmelweis Medical University. In front of the Radiology Clinic (gate XIII, just before Ludovika tér) stands a copy of the original Wallenberg Memorial (see 'The Wallenberg Memorial' below).

Nearby, at the corner of the park, is János Horvay's 1942 limestone memorial to doctors who fell in World War I. Nearer the Ludoviceum is another Great War monument, also by Horvay. This one is a memorial to un-named heroes (1924). At the rear is a bronze relief in memory of Hungary's 'soldier heroes' of World War II. This is quite a rarity for Budapest, as the authorities in the post-1945 decades were not keen on memorials to those who had died fighting against the Soviet Union. This relief was erected in 1993.

Ludovika tér has seen several monuments which have come and gone for political reasons. Here have stood at different times memorials to the 1919 counter-revolutionary forces of Miklós Horthy and to leading members of the Council Republic which Horthy suppressed. Both have disappeared.

The park behind the Ludoviceum is known as the **Orczy-kert**. When it was laid out in the 1790s it was one of the largest 'English' gardens in the Pest area. Once a military sports ground, today it is often the scene of open-air concerts. Here stands a statue of Maria Ludovika, the wife of Emperor Franz I (Viktor Vass, 1929, after a 1901 original). She helped found the academy, thus named after her, and is depicted here flanked by uniformed officers.

Immediately to the north of the Ludoviceum, by the former manège, is the **Illés Well,** one of the oldest springs of Pest, dating back to medieval times. The well-house was constructed in 1990 following several years of excavations by enthusiasts in search of the long-lost water source.

The University's **Botannical Gardens** (Botanikus kert) are across Korányi Sándor u. (entrance round the corner at Illés u. 25). Hundreds of specimens of plants and trees grow here and can be viewed by the public (open Mon–Thur, Sat 09.00–16.00; Sun 09.00–13.00; closed Fri). The administrative offices are based in the former Festetics Villa, a noted example of early neo-Classicism dating from 1803.

NÉPLIGET AND ÓBUDA ISLAND

These are two large, quiet parks on the outskirts of the city centre, though both are easily reached.

Népliget (Peoples' Park), one of Budapest's largest parks, is about 5km south-east of the centre. There is a metro station, bearing the name of the park, on the blue No. 3 line. The exit takes you to the **Planetárium** at the corner of the park. This is not strictly a museum but temporary exhibitions dealing with physics, space research and related matters are often organised here.

Built in 1977 by the Jena Zeiss works in the then GDR, the mechanism inside the planetarium projects the planets and their movents as seen from the Earth on to a 23m-diameter dome. However, the building is more popularly visited for its regular laser light shows, accompanied by pop or classical music.

The park has no other major attractions, but is a quiet place of relaxation with many open spaces and a great variety of trees.

Óbuda Island (Óbudai-sziget) is the large island on the Danube which stretches northwards from Árpád Bridge. Its northern half is like a huge park and has one area which is basically a large playground with several sections. Here you can find what are probably the biggest slides in Budapest (though beware in hot weather—the plastic can burn your legs and hands as you slide down).

A fun way to reach the island in the summer is by boat. The BKV river boat service can be picked up on the Pest embankment, by the northern side of Margaret Bridge. The boat calls at several points, including the east side of Óbuda Island, not far from the playgrounds. Alternatively, the HÉV railway from Batthyány tér stops at Filatorigát near the island.

For the past few years, Óbuda Island has been the scene of a regular, Woodstock-type pop festival, lasting several days in August.

The southern part of the island, nearer Árpád Bridge, is occupied by the Óbuda shipyard. The Danube Steamship Company, founded in Vienna in 1830 and later based here, employed 2000 people a century ago.

Count István Széchenyi laid the foundations of steam navigation in Hungary in the 19C. He entered into partnership with the British ship-building company, Andrews and Richard, and as a result the steamer *Franz I* made its trial run between Vienna and Buda on 4 September 1830. The development of steam navigation on the Danube was a stimulus to Anglo–Hungarian connections. British engineers came to Hungary to supervise the construction of ships and the installation of engines, many of which were made by the British firm Boulton and Watt. In the early years many of the ships' captains were also British.

OPEN AIR MARKETS

The city's food and vegetable markets are lively, colourful places, with a mixture of established traders and elderly peasant women selling their home-grown produce. They are a traditional aspect of 'everyday' Budapest, but given that their buildings are ramshackle and none too clean, they are likely to disappear in the near future to be replaced by something more modern and functional—though no doubt lacking the old atmosphere.

They are worth a visit before they do disappear, as there is always something to see, not to mention that produce is likely to be fresher and cheaper here than elsewhere. The markets are fully operational and at their busiest in the morning and early afternoon hours, particularly towards the end of the week. (For the central, covered market see p 103).

Lehel Market (Lehel Piac) in Pest is the city's largest open-air market (open every day, including Sun morning). There is a wide variety of fruit and vegetable stalls, plus butchers, fishmongers and pickle sellers, as well as traders hawking cigarettes, alcohol, leather goods and clothes. Situated at Lehel tér, it is easily reached on blue metro line 3, one stop north of Nyugati tér.

The large **Church of St Margaret** in Lehel tér is actually not as old as it looks. It was built in 1931–33 as a copy of one of Hungary's most important monuments of Romanesque architecture, the 13C church at Zsámbék, 34km west of Budapest. The original, constructed for the Premonstratensian order, was severely damaged by an earthquake in 1763, although the ruins are still impressive. The church here has stained glass windows by master-craftsman Miksa Róth.

Fény utca Market is one of the busiest markets in Buda (open Mon–Sat). On two levels, the atmosphere is similar to Lehel market, though it is smaller. Both markets have stalls selling hot soups and stews, as well as Hungary's own traditional 'fast food', *lángos*—a fried dough, somewhat of a cross between a pizza base and a Yorkshire pudding, and eaten with or without various toppings.

The market is 100m from the north side of **Moszkva tér**, Buda's busiest public transport interchange and the traditional 'gateway' to the hills (metro station and various bus and tram termini here). A century ago there was an athletic field here, and a skating rink in winter, but today the junction is noisy, polluted and unattractive. The large building overlooking the square, with its castle-like corner tower, is a post office and mail sorting centre (Gyula Sándy, 1925).

The **Flea Market**, commonly known as the 'Ecseri' market from a previous location, is about 8km south-east of the centre on Nagykőrösi út, near the start of the M5 motorway (bus 54 from Boráros tér by Petőfi Bridge). Items of all description can be found here, from junk to genuine antiques (open Mon–Fri 08.00–16.00; Sat 07.00–15.00).

PASARÉT

Pasarét is the short valley running alongside Szilágyi Erzsébet fasor in Buda, below the south-west slopes of Rózsadomb. The name derives from 'Pasa' in Serbian and 'Ried' in German, names found on old maps and meaning 'pasture', which essentially was what the area was in the 19C. The district was built up in the three decades after 1900, mainly with family houses and villas for the well-to-do, and so presents a picture of what such an area was like in the pre-World War II period. The main thoroughfare is Pasaréti út, which starts just beyond the Budapest Hotel. Bus 5 from Március 15 tér in Pest runs here and along its length; the bus can also be picked up in Moszkva tér.

The terminus of bus 5 is in Pasaréti tér, where stands the area's most well-known building and a symbol of Budapest's inter-war architecture—the Franciscan **Church of St Anthony of Padua** (Gyula Rimanóczy, 1931–34). The nave is a simple prism, while the equally simple bell-tower stands slightly apart. A tall arcaded portico stresses the entrance, which is flanked by Tibor Vilt's statues of SS Francis and Anthony. The interior height is emphasised by reinforced concrete arches. The decoration on the side altars is by Lili Sztehló. To the right of the church is a monastery building with an enclosed garden.

Walking about 600m (up the hill and then left along Csévi u.) you arrive at a bend in Csalán u. Here at No. 29 is the **Béla Bartók Memorial House** (Bartók Emlékház; tel: 176–2100; open 10.00–18.00 except Mon; free on Sat; shop; no w/a). The internationally renowned composer and musicologist Béla Bartók (1881–1945) moved into this villa in 1932 and lived here until he left for America in 1940. The building dates from 1924, but was substantially altered when it opened as a museum in 1981 on the centenary of the composer's birth.

The small permanent exhibition has photographs and texts (in English) about Bartók's life and work, and also displays his furniture and equipment. Note his desk from Kalotaszeg, a famous folk-art region in Transylvania, and the phonograph, the type of which Bartók used to record and transcribe thousands of authentic folk songs in the early decades of the 20C. Throughout the year, usually on Fridays, intimate concerts are given in the first-floor room, the ceiling of which is decorated with painted wooden panels originally made in 1740 for the Calvinist church of Tök, a small village 20km west of Budapest. In the summer the concerts sometimes take place in the courtyard outside. The statue of Bartók here is the work of Imre Varga (1981).

Pasaréti út itself continues by the side of the Franciscan church. About 600m along here it approaches a brook. A small bridge leads to **Napraforgó utca**. This short street of just 22 houses was built in 1931–32 as an experimental showcase for modern building design. A dozen or so architects produced the plans, including Lajos Kozma, József Fischer and Farkas Molnár, Hungary's leading Bauhaus specialists. Trends of the International Modern movement are decipherable here, even though some of the buildings have undergone reconstruction over the years. That the municipality supported the project ran against the general tendencies of the time—Hungarian authorities usually regarded Bauhaus-inspired ideas as rather too 'internationalist'. Commissions for large public buildings in the 1930s rarely went to Modernists, though a number of white-cube, private dwellings were constructed in the Buda Hills (see Bauhaus Architecture, above).

THE STATUE PARK (SZOBORPARK)

'A unique collection in Eastern Europe' is how the Statue Park was described when it opened in late 1993. After the multi-party municipal elections of 1990, the new city council decided to remove over 40 political statues erected during the Kádár era and place them in a specially designed, open-air statue park on the southern outskirts of the city.

Huge statues of Marx and Engels, and Lenin greet you on either side of Ákos Eleőd's massive neo-Classical entrance gate, which recalls both a temple and a mausoleum. Inside, dramatic statues, such as the memorial to the 1919 Council Republic, mix with small wall plaques. There are statues familiar to all in Budapest, such as the one of Soviet plenipotentiary Ostapenko which used to stand at the beginning of the Balaton motorway, and others of little-known communists whose images are familiar only to a few. There are some whose removal caused much controversy, such as the memorial to the International Brigades who fought against Franco in the Spanish Civil War, or another to the Budapest volunteers who battled with the retreating Germans in 1944–45.

A historical peculiarity is that the overwhelming majority of these mainly Socialist–Realist statues were erected not in Hungary's Stalinist period of the early 1950s, but in the late 1960s, the 1970s and even the 1980s, the more liberal years of the Kádár era.

One infamous, massive statue, however, is not here—that of Joseph Stalin, which used to stand near the City Park. He was pulled down and smashed to bits by angry demonstrators on 23 October 1956, the first day of the fateful Uprising.

The Statue Park is located about 15km from the city centre on Balatoni út (Road 70 towards Érd) by the junction with Szabadkai út. A yellow bus from stand 6 at Kosztolányi Dezső tér takes about 20 minutes to get there. (Open daily 10.00–18.00; weekends only in winter.)

SZÁZADOS ÚT ARTISTS' COLONY

The Százados út artists' colony comprises a group of single and two-storey, attractive, folkish-style houses, specially built by the municipality in 1909–11 for artists and their studios. The first of its kind in Budapest, the colony accommodated (as it still does today) mainly sculptors and painters, whose built-in studios were provided with extra-large windows for natural lighting.

Among the sculptors, Zsigmond Kisfaludi Strobl worked here from 1911 until 1944, and Ferenc Medyessy also had a studio here from 1912 to 1958 (memorial plaque on block 8). The painter Bertalan Pór (1880–1964) was one of the colony's founders and on the wall of his former studio in block 9 by the main entrance you can still see etched the political slogan: 'Let the form of art be national, its content socialist'. At the time of writing there is still a 1967 plaque praising Bertalan as a founder of Hungarian revolutionary art and recalling that he was the secretary of the Artists' Directory during the 1919 Council Republic.

The large school building at Százados út 6, on the corner of Szörényi u., was designed by László Gyalus and built in 1913, at the same time as the colony. Although a victim of reconstruction, its original Hungarian Art Nouveau appearance is still detectable.

Százados út runs south from Kerepesi út, 150m from the latter's junction with Hungária krt (Népstadion metro station here, red line 2). The colony's entrance is opposite the school, 100m along Százados út.

STEFÁNIA ÚT
Stefánia út (1.5km) is a broad, tree-lined avenue to the south of the City Park. In the old days it extended into the park and was popular with the gentry for horse-drawn carriage riding. 'It's my desire to ride along Stefánia út; in a fine carriage with a pretty flower in my lapel' went the words of a popular music hall song.

The southern end of the avenue is easily reached from the Népstadion station on red metro line 2. This area is dominated by the huge, circular **Budapest Sports Hall** (Sportcsarnok), the scene of a variety of sporting events, as well as pop concerts and conferences (István Kiss, 1982).

From here Stefánia út runs for about 300m alongside the grounds of Hungary's largest sports facility, the massive **People's Stadium** (Népstadion). Designed by Károly Dávid, it was completed in 1953 after five years of construction. This was perhaps the most symbolic building project of Hungary's Stalinist era. No expense was spared, even though work began at a time when building resources were still being absorbed by post-war reconstruction.

'Sport for the people' was a serious matter throughout Eastern Europe in those days. The ideological atmosphere is detectable in the series of statues leading up to the stadium and visible through the railings from Stefánia út. The work of various sculptors in the 1950s, they depict, in classic Socialist Realist style, heroic-looking proletarians mostly engaged enthusiatically in a variety of healthy sports.

From 1946 to 1962 Stefánia út was named after the Soviet military and political leader Marshal Voroshilov. Surprisingly, you can still see this old street name on a small plaque just before the large gate at the far end of the railings.

Walking alongside the railings you have a good view of the striking blue roof of the **Hungarian State Geological Institute** (Stefánia út 14). Designed in his own characteristic Hungarian Secessionist style, this is one of Ödön Lechner's most impressive buildings (1898–99). Colourfully decorated, it is certainly a unique sight. Inside there is a small museum with a collection of rocks, minerals and geological rarities (access by appointment only, tel: 251–0999).

No. 20 nearby was built as a studio and living quarters for the sculptor Miklós Ligeti (Zoltán Bálint and Lajos Jámbor, 1900). The building is sadly in need of repair, unlike the Slovak Embassy next door which has had its façade restored.

There are more embassies along the following stretch of Stefánia út, mostly occupying former villas and mansions. This is the section of the avenue noted in the old days as a 'society promenade'.

Thököly út crosses Stefánia út 300m beyond the Geological Institute. Izsó u. is 100m to the left. **No. 5** here is an attractive example of Hungarian National Romanticism by the noted architect Béla Lajta. It was built in 1907 for Dezső

Malonyay, an art historian who specialised in Hungarian folk art. The building today houses the Romanian Cultural Centre and has been nicely restored.

No. 34–36 Stefánia út is the neo-Baroque former Park Club, an exclusive social centre for the well to do (Artúr Meinig, 1895). There was a terrace outside where the gentry would sip their wine as they watched the carriages go by. Today the building functions as a cultural centre and concerts take place in the adjoining building, added in an incongruous modern style in 1979.

The Art Nouveau mansion at the end of Stefánia út, on the corner of Ajtósi Dürer sor, was specially designed in 1901 by Bálint and Jámbor for György Zala, the sculptor of the Heroes' Square statues. Zala himself did the striking relief on the façade facing the the City Park. The building today houses the Libyan People's Bureau.

SZENT ISTVÁN PARK

Situated on the Pest bank of the Danube, opposite Margaret Island, the park and its surrounding buildings constitute one of the most attractive examples of 1930s urban planning in Budapest. (Two stops on trolley bus 76 or 79 from Budai Nagy Antal u., near Margaret Bridge, or on foot from the bridge—600m.)

The most representative building (Béla Hofstätter and Ferenc Domány, 1936) stands on the north side of the playground area, between Pozsonyi út and the riverside park. This luxury apartment block, with its larger-than-average, spacious rooms, was built with all the latest conveniences, including push-button flush toilets and even roof gardens with showers. The Dunapark café used to be on the ground floor. Its Modern-style, split-level interior is still visible.

A bronze statue of the Hungarian Marxist philosopher György Lukács (1885–1971) stands in the middle of the park, by the pool (Imre Varga, 1985).

The riverside section of the park stretches for 400m by the Danube. This is a quiet, attractive place to walk or sit and admire the surrounding view. The limestone monument at the south end is a memorial to the 'Szír' partisan group (Ferenc Kovács, 1971). This was one of the most active of the Hungarian resistance groups which sprang up in 1944 to oppose the Germans and the puppet Nazi regime of Ferenc Szálasi. There were about 30 such groups in Budapest, with up to 50 members each. They comprised a mixture of Communists, Social Democrats, Christians and independents, and included both factory workers and academics.

At the far, north end of the park is Zoltán Borbereki Kovács's 1937 'Zsákhordó' (Sack heaver) statue. It used to stand by one of the large wholesale markets before it was moved here in 1948.

On the building immediately behind are two wall plaques commemorating Giorgio Perlasca and Angel Sanz Briz, two foreign diplomats who, like Raoul Wallenberg, helped many Jews to escape deportation in 1944. There were several Jewish 'safe houses' under diplomatic protection in this area.

VÁROSLIGETI FASOR

Városligeti fasor (City Park Avenue) is a short tree-lined road running parallel with Andrássy út from Lövölde tér to the City Park (trolleybuses 70 and 78 go to Lövölde tér). In the 19C this area was outside the city boundary, but towards the turn of the century it started to be built up with high-class villas. Some of its atmosphere of quiet exclusivity still remains.

The striking **Calvinist Church** stands at No. 7 (Aladár Árkay, 1912–13). The style is a mixture of English, Finnish and even American National Romanticism, touched with Magyar folk elements, notably the abstract ceramic tiles on the façade. The decorative interior has an Art Nouveau character.

The **György Ráth Museum** (Ráth György Múzeum) stands across the avenue at No. 12 (open 10.00–18.00 except Mon; free on Tue; texts in English). Ráth (1829–1905), a collector and art critic, was the first director of the Museum of Applied Arts. His widow donated his collection to the nation after his death. His villa here was badly damaged in World War II, but was restored in 1955. The small museum specialises in Chinese and Japanese art.

The avenue's thin-spired **Lutheran Church** is at the junction with Bajza u. Construction began in 1903 to the neo-Gothic designs of Samu Pecz, who also designed all the details of the interior and furnishings. The church was consecrated in 1905. The stained glass windows were all destroyed in World War II, except for a picture of Christ from the workshop of the celebrated master Miksa Róth. The Adoration of the Magi on the high altar was painted by Gyula Benczúr.

Budapest's famous **Lutheran Grammar School** stands next to the church. It was taken over by the state in 1951, but resumed as a denominational school in 1989. Former pupils include many outstanding scientists and scholars, such as the mathematician János (John) Neumann (1903–57), the 'father of the computer'.

Across the avenue at **No. 24** stands a striking Art Nouveau villa, built in 1901 and restored in 1989, though with some original decoration missing. It is the work of Emil Vidor (1867–1952), one of Hungary's most prolific and creative turn-of-the-century architects. One could re-name the avenue after him, since it contains much of his work. There is, for example, his 1905 villa opposite at **No. 23**, though it is sadly dilapidated today. Further along, **No. 33** is one of his masterpieces, designed for his father at the beginning of the 20C. The whole building, today a music students' residence, is visually quite remarkable— note all the details around the exterior walls and side doorway. It is possible to walk along the drive to view the fantastic wooden terraces at the rear. The plaque on the façade records that the noted nuclear scientist Leo Szilárd (1898–1964) was brought up here.

Another of Vidor's buildings, dating from c 1907, stands towards the end of the avenue at **No. 47**. However, he was not the only turn-of-the-century architect to fashion the avenue. Sámuel Révész and József Kollár, for example, designed the villa at **No. 40** in 1911 both as living quarters and their own office, as well as the attractive **No. 44** in 1912, though the latter has changed much over the years.

The avenue ends at Dózsa György út, the long broad road that used to be the site of May Day parades. Just here stood the notorious Stalin statue, which was pulled down by the crowds on 23 October 1956.

No. 84/a Dózsa György út, on the corner of Városligeti fasor, is the Building Workers' Union HQ, though today it also houses many different offices. It was built in the early 1950s in Hungary's 'heroic socialist' age of post-war architecture, and was one of the few large buildings which actually got off the drawing board in those days. Interestingly, rather than rigid, unimaginative neo-Classical 'Stalinism', an airy Modernism was applied, and with its open spaces and circular glass lifts the building has retained its appeal.

THE WALLENBERG MEMORIAL

Raoul Wallenberg (1912–?) was the Secretary of the Swedish Legation in Budapest who, after his arrival in July 1944, boldly and heroically saved thousands of Jews from the hands of the German Nazis and Hungarian fascists. Wallenberg, a gentile himself, not only issued them with Swedish documents, he intervened personally, standing up to the authorities whenever he could.

Wallenberg disappeared in January 1945 during the siege of Budapest. Probably on the paranoid grounds that he was some kind of spy, he had been arrested by the Red Army and taken to Russia. After years of official silence, Soviet Deputy Foreign Minister Andrei Gromyko announced in February 1957 that Wallenberg had died in Moscow's Lubianka Prison ten years previously. However, despite denials, many continued to believe for years that he could still be alive somewhere in the Soviet prison network.

In Hungary the authorities were equally wary of the Wallenberg case. In April 1949 a memorial to Raoul Wallenberg, commissioned from the sculptor Pál Pátzay, mysteriously disappeared on the eve of its unveiling in Szent István Park in Pest. Pátzay had depicted a male figure struggling with the snake of evil. The statue curiously turned up later in front of a pharmaceuticals factory in Debrecen in eastern Hungary—only this time symbolising the fight against disease. A copy also appeared, and can still be seen, in front of the Radiology Clinic on Ülloi út, though it was not until 1989 that a plaque was added acknowledging it as the Wallenberg monument.

For years the only official recognition of Wallenberg in Budapest was a street in District XIII which bore his name. Then in 1987 a new bronze statue of Wallenberg by Imre Varga (originally commissioned by US Ambassador Nicholas Salgó) was erected on Szilágyi Erzsébet fasor. Although one of the main arteries of Buda, the fact that this is far from the former Jewish ghetto and from the area of Wallenberg's Pest operations indicates the sensitivity that still persisted. The statue is flanked by granite blocks, on which is etched an outline of Pátzay's original statue.

The Wallenberg Memorial is at the junction of Szilágyi Erzsébet fasor and Nagyajtai u., four stops on tram 56 from Moszkva tér.

HUNGARIAN LANGUAGE

In Budapest English is spoken in hotels, and often at places frequented by tourists such as city-centre shops and restaurants. The first language of tourism, however, is German and visitors may often find themselves being addressed in this language rather than either Hungarian or English.

Hungarian belongs to the Finno–Ugric group of languages, which includes Finnish, Estonian and some languages spoken in northern areas of Russia. It is unrelated to the Indo–European languages and thus there are relatively few words with which visitors will feel familiar—knowledge of French, German, Italian, Spanish, Greek or even Latin are unfortunately of little help. Learning a few words or phrases in Hungarian, therefore, can be very useful.

Hungarian is also quite different from English grammatically. Suffixes abound. With 'to our house', for example, the possessive and directional suffixes are added to the word for house (*ház*) making one word—*házunkba*. This can make some words confusingly long. Verbs are also difficult having different endings depending on whether there is a definite or indefinte object.

On the positive side the Roman script is familiar and pronunciation, once learned, is simplified by the fact that letters and combinations of letters are always pronounced in the same way. There is also a regular stress pattern, with a slight emphasis on the first syllable of a word and each following syllable being clearly and evenly pronounced.

Interestingly, Hungarian is a 'non-sexist' language in that words have no grammatical gender, and in that there is no distiction in the terms for 'he' and 'she'.

Pronunciation
Vowels

a	like the *o* in 'hot'
á	like the *a* in 'car'
e	as in 'ten'
é	like the *a* in 'day'
i	as in 'hit'
í	lengthens the above, as the double *e* in 'feet'
o	as in 'open'
ó	lengthens the above
ö	like the *e* in 'bitter'
ő	lengthens the above, like the *u* in 'fur'
u	short as in 'put'
ú	long as in 'rule'
ü	short as in the French 'tu'
ű	lengthens the above

Consonants

Consonants are pronounced much as they are in English except for the following:

c	like the *ts* in 'cats'
cs	like the *ch* in 'chapel'
g	is always hard, as in 'gun'
gy	like the soft *d* of 'during'
j	like the *y* in 'yes'

ly	also like the *y* in 'yes'
ny	like the *gn* in 'cognac'
s	like the *sh* in 'ship'
sz	like the *s* in 'sit'
ty	like the soft *t* of 'tube'
zs	like the *s* in 'pleasure'

Some basic phrases and vocabulary

Good day/hello	Jó napot kivánok
Good morning (early)	Jó reggelt (kivánok)
Good evening	Jó estét
Good night	Jó éjszakát
Goodbye	Viszontlátásra

The above phrases are used continuously on meeting and parting, even in situations where you would not necessarily use them in English (e.g. in shops or before buying a ticket, or with strangers in a lift).

Szia and *Szervusz* (in plural *sziasztok* and *szervusztok*) are familiar forms both of which are used among friends on meeting and parting. Both can mean either 'hello' or 'goodbye' depending on the situation. It is not as confusing as it sounds and is easily picked up. But it explains why Hungarians, when leaving you, will often wave and say 'hello'!

Yes	Igen
No	Nem
Thank you	Köszönöm
Good; OK!	Jó!
Very good	Nagyon jó
Thank you very much	Köszönöm szépen
Thank you very much indeed	Nagyon szépen köszönöm
Please	Kérem
Excuse me	Bocsánat
Do you seak English/German?	Beszél angolul/németül?
Sorry, I don't understand	Elnézést, nem értem
I am English/American	Angol/amerikai vagyok

Numbers are quite straightforward:

One	Egy
Two	Két/kettő
Three	Három
Four	Négy
Five	Öt
Six	Hat
Seven	Hét (hét also means 'week')
Eight	Nyolc
Nine	Kilenc
Ten	Tíz
Eleven	Tízenegy
Twelve	Tízenkettő
Thirteen	Tízenhárom etc.

Twenty	Húsz
Twenty one	Húszonegy
Twenty two	Húszonkettő
Thirty	Harminc
Thirty one	Harmincegy
Forty	Negyven
Fifty	Ötven
Sixty	Hatvan
Seventy	Hetven
Eighty	Nyolcvan
Ninety	Kilencven
One hundred	Száz
One hundred and twenty	Százhúsz
One hundred and twenty one	Százhúszonegy
Two hundred	Kétszáz
Two hundred and twenty one	Kétszázhúszonegy
One thousand	Ezer.
One thousand two hundred	Kétezerkétszáz etc.

One Hundred Basic Words (see also the 'Food and Drink' section, pp 31–35 and post office and shops/shopping words on pp 29 and 30 respectively.)

ajándék	gift
állomás	station
amerikai	American
angol	English
angolul	in English
ár	price
asztal	table
balra	to the left
bejárat	entrance
benzinkút	petrol station
bocsánat	excuse me!
bolt	shop
busz	bus
cigaretta	cigarette
cím	address
délben	at noon
délelőtt	(in the) morning
délután	(in the) afternoon
drága	expensive
éjszaka	night
emelet	floor
emlékmű	monument
eső	rain
este	(in the) evening
fagylalt	ice cream
falu	village
fehér	white
fekete	black
feleség(em)	(my) wife
férj(em)	(my) husband

filmszinház	cinema
fürdő	bath
fürdőszoba	bathroom
gyufa	matches
hajó	boat, ship
ház	house
híd	bridge
hideg	cold
hol van a ..?	where is the ..?
holnap	tomorrow
hónap	month
időjárás	weather
itt	here
jobbra	to the right
kastély	mansion
kerékpár	bicycle
kép	picture
kevés	little, few
kijárat	exit
kicsi	small, little
kirándulás	excursion
kórház	hospital
könyv	book
kulcs	key
ma	today
magyar	Hungarian
magyarul	in Hungarian
Magyarország	Hungary
megállóhely	(bus, tram, etc.) stop
meleg	warm
messze	far
mosdó/WC	toilets
mozi	cinema
nagy	big
nagykövetség	embassy
nagyon	very
nap	day or sun
népművészet	folk art
név	name
nincs...	there is no...
nyár	summer
olcsó	cheap
orvos	doctor
ott	there
pénz	money
pénztár	booking office, cash office
pénzváltás	exchange
rendőrség	police (station)
repülőtér	airport
ruhatár	cloakroom
segitség	help

sok	many, much
szálló(da)	hotel
szám	number
szép	lovely, beautiful
szivar	cigar
szoba	room
tánc	dance
tegnap	yesterday
templom	church
új	news
újság	newspaper
útlevél	passport
vám	customs
végállomás	terminus
villamos	tram
virág	flower
víz	water
vonat	train
zene	music

In a Nutshell—Important dates and names in Hungary's history

c 896
Conquest of the Carpathian Basin by Magyar tribes arriving from the east led by **Prince Árpád.**

1000
Coronation of **King Stephen** (István) marks the foundation of the Hungarian state. Stephen pushes ahead with the conversion of the hitherto pagan Magyars to Christianity.

1241–42
Mongol invasion lays the country to waste.

1458–1490
Reign of **King Matthias** sees the golden age of Buda as a centre of European Renaissance culture.

1526
Disastrous defeat of Hungarian forces by the Turks at the **battle of Mohács**.

1541–1686
Most of Hungary is under **Ottoman rule**. Transylvania in the east retains some autonomy, while north-western territories are under Austrian influence. The Turks are finally driven out by the combined forces of several Western nations.

1686
Austrian rule over Hungary as a whole begins and is to last for over 200 years. The Austrians bring the Counter-reformation, Baroque architecture and the incorporation of Hungary into the Habsburg Empire.

1703–11
War of Independence against Austria led by Transylvanian Prince **Ferenc Rákóczi II** (1676–1735).

1825–48
The Reform Period. An era of national and cultural revival spearheaded by **Count István Széchenyi** (1791–1860), whose many innovations include the building of the Chain Bridge, the establishment of the Academy of Sciences, the introduction of steam shipping on the Danube and the beginnings of a modern banking system.

1848–49
Revolutionary poet **Sándor Petőfi** (1823–49) leads the uprising for national independence on 15 March 1848. This spills over into the **War of Independence** against Austria led by **Lajos Kossuth** (1802–94). Hungarian forces are eventually defeated, the prime minister of the independent Hungarian government Count

Lajos Batthyány (1806–49) is executed along with many others and a period of harsh reaction sets in.

1867–1914
The 'Compromise' with Austria of 1867 gives Hungary virtual independence in domestic matters. There follows a period of rapid industrial expansion and urban development. Much of central Pest today is a product of this era. 1873 sees the administrative unification of Óbuda, Buda and Pest, and the 'birth' of Budapest. The official national confidence of the times is signalled most prominently by the bombastic **1896 Millenary Celebrations**, marking the 1000th anniversary of the Magyar conquest of the Carpathian Basin. Serious problems with Hungary's nationalities and over the lack of voting rights for most citizens, however, remain unresolved with the outbreak of the First World War and Hungary's participation on the side of Austria and Germany.

1918–19
Collapse of the Austro–Hungarian empire at the end of the First World War sees the formation of a democratic Hungarian republic under **Mihály Károlyi** (1875–1955), followed in 1919 by the short-lived, Soviet-style **Council Republic** under Béla Kun and the communists.

1920–44
The Horthy era. Under Regent **Miklós Horthy** (1868–1957) Hungary becomes an authoritarian, ultra-conservative society characterised as a 'nation of three million beggars'. The key political reference point is the **1920 Trianon Treaty**, under which, after the First World War, about two-thirds of the territory and half the population of the former Kingdom of Hungary was lost to neighbouring countries. Demands for the return of these lost territories and associated nationalistic propaganda is a hallmark of the Horthy era.

1941–45
Hungary enters the Second World War allied to Hitler's Germany and fights primarily on the eastern, Soviet front. Germany nevertheless occupies Hungary in March 1944, following which the extermination of 90 per cent of Hungarian Jewry commences. Regent Horthy is overthrown in October 1944 and the Hungarian fascist Arrow Cross takes over. German forces are finally driven out of Hungary by the Red Army in early 1945. Budapest is left in ruins.

1945–48
Brief period of multi-party democracy and enthusiasm for post-war reconstruction finally engulfed by Communist Party monopoly and Soviet influence.

1948–53
The Rákosi era. Worst years of hard-line Stalinism under political leader **Mátyás Rákosi** (1892–1971). Tight political control, including show trials. Economic emphasis on building heavy industry.

1953–56
Following the death of Stalin, Hungary slowly begins to 'thaw'. Unleashed pressures eventually contribute to the Uprising.

1956

The **Hungarian Uprising** breaks out on 23 October. Demands include national independence, an end to Communist Party domination and a Socialist system based on workers' power. Uprising suppressed by Soviet tanks on 4 November, although resistance continues for some months. Albeit defeated, the Uprising is a historic turning point, for Hungary and eastern Europe, and for the international communist movement.

1957–1989

The Kádár era. Under political leader **János Kádár** (1912–89), following initial years of repression after the 1956 Uprising, Hungary develops into the most liberal member of the Eastern Bloc, epitomised by Kádár's famous phrase: 'Those who are not against us are with us'. 1968 sees the introduction of tentative market reforms, which accelerate dramatically in the late 1980s. The rehabilitation and reburial of 1956 premier **Imre Nagy** (1896–1958) in June 1989 is the most symbolic event of Hungary's political changes, the most peaceful in Eastern Europe.

1990–

Multi-party parliamentary system introduced. In the elections of 1990 a new centre–right coalition government comes into power. The 1994 elections produce a curious centre–left coalition of parties based on former reform communists from the Kádár era and liberal oppositionists from that same period. On the economic front, development of a market economy accelerates. Prominent signs of this in Budapest are an office building boom and a noticeable increase in the number of private cars on the roads, both indicating increased wealth for some, and a perceptible increase in the number of beggars on the streets, reflecting increased poverty for others.

Museums checklist

It may help to avoid disappointment if careful note is made of the following:

- Most museums **close on Monday**, others on another day. Very few are o p e n every day. (ex. Mon below = except Monday).

- Most museums operate shorter hours in the low/winter season (roughly O c t - Mar). the high/summer season. Opening times given below and in the main text are for **summer season** only.

- Last entrance is usually 30 or even 45 minutes before final closing.

- For most of the museums listed here further information about the collection and/or building can be found in the main text (see page refence numbers).

- Exhibition texts in English occur, but are not common. Booklets in English about the displays, however, are often available, but usually have to be requested. (*Van valami a múzeumról angolul?*—Is there something about the museum in English?). Major museums can usually provide an English-speaking guide for a fee, given prior notice.

- There is little provision for people with mobility difficulties. Comments in this list about wheelchair access (w/a) are relative—the general standard is low. However, most major museums and many smaller ones can provide access via various side entrances and/or lifts. It takes organising and may require a helper, but it is worth asking.

The 'big twelve'—major museums

Castle Museum (Vármúzeum). The Budapest History Museum's Castle Museum traces the history of medieval Buda. Building E, former Royal Palace; tel. 175-7533. Castle bus from Moszkva tér, funicular from Clark Ádám tér or bus 16 from Pest. 10.00–18.00 ex. Tues; free on Wed; auto-guides; snack bar; w/a poor; see p 66.

Ethnographical Museum (Néprajzi Múzeum). Hungarian folk history collection. V. Kossuth Lajos tér 12; tel. 132-6340. Tram 2 or red metro to Kossuth tér. 10.00–18.00 ex. Mon; free on Tues; auto-guide in English; snack bar; assistance for w/a; free concerts often on Sunday morning; see p 117.

Hungarian National Gallery (Magyar Nemzeti Galéria). The country's main collection of Hungarian works of art. Buda Royal Palace, buildings B, C and D; tel. 175-7533 ex. 423. Transport as for Castle Museum above. 10.00–18.00 ex. Mon; free on Sat; all titles in English; pleasant café area; bookshop; lifts for w/a; see p 63.

Hungarian National Museum (Magyar Nemzeti Múzeum). The main museum for the political history of Hungary, plus the Hungarian Crown Jewels. V. Múzeum krt 14–16; tel. 138-2122. Blue metro to Kálvin tér. 10.00–18.00 ex. Mon; small café; w/a difficult; free concerts on various days; see p 100.

Kiscell Museum (Kiscelli Múzeum). This former 18C Trinitarian monastery, place of popular pilgrimage and later barracks, today belongs to the Budapest History Museum. The mixed collection includes Baroque sculpture, printing presses, a pharmacy interior, and many paintings and drawings of 18C and 19C Pest-Buda. The gallery in the large, former chapel is particularly impressive. Temporary art exhibitions are held here. III. Kiscelli u. 108; tel. 188-8560. Tram 17 from Margaret Bridge to 'Margit kórház' then up Kiscelli u. on the south side of the hospital. 10.00–18.00 ex. Mon; free on Wed; limited w/a.

Ludwig Museum (Ludwig Múzeum). International contemporary painting. Building A, former Royal Palace; tel. 212-2534. Transport as for Castle Museum above. 10.00–18.00 ex. Mon; free on Tues; snack bar; see p 66.

Military History Museum (Hadtörténeti Múzeum), I. Tóth Árpád sétány 40, in the Castle District; tel. 156-9522. Castle bus from Moszkva tér. Tues–Sat 09.00–17.00, Sun 09.00–18.00; children free; snack bar; w/a difficult; see p 60.

Museum of Applied Arts (Iparművészeti Múzeum). Small permanent exhibition, usually several temporary ones concurrently. IX. Üllői út 33–37; tel. 217-5222. Blue metro to Ferenc körút. 10.00–18.00 ex. Mon; free on Tues; snack bar; small shop; w/a possible in part; occasional concerts; see p 130.

Museum of Fine Arts (Szépművészeti Múzeum). The country's main collection of foreign works of art. Heroes' Square; tel. 343-6755. Yellow underground to 'Hősök tere'. 10.00–17.30 ex. Mon; bookshop and pleasant café in basement; free tour in English Tues–Fri 10.30 (check in advance); see p 150.

Museum of Hungarian Agriculture (Magyar Mezőgazdasági Múzeum), Vajdahunjad Castle in the City Park; tel. 343-0573. Yellow underground to Hásók tere. 10.00–17.00 ex. Mon; free on Tues; small snack bar; limited w/a; see p 154.

Museum of Literature (Petőfi Irodalmi Múzeum). In the former Károlyi Mansion, devoted to Hungarian literature with special display on the Károly family. V. Károlyi Mihály u. 16, tel. 117-3611. Blue metro to Ferenciek tere. 10.00–18.00 ex. Mon; no café; w/a very difficult; occasional concerts in courtyard; see p 95.

Transport Museum (Közlekedési Múzeum), Városligeti krt on the far side of the City Park; tel. 343-0561. Trolleys 70, 77 and 74 to Hermina út. 10.00–18.00 ex. Mon; free on Wed; snack bar; see p 155.

Other museums

Ady Memorial Museum (Ady Emlékmúzeum). The writer and poet Endre Ady's last home. V. Veres Pálné u. 4–6. Blue metro to Ferenciek tere. 10.00–18.00 ex. Mon and Tues; see p 97.

Aeronautical Museum (Repülési Múzeum). The transport museum's exhibition of air and space flight. Petőfi Csarnok in the City Park. Trolleys 70, 74 and 77 to Hermina út. 10.00–18.00 ex. Mon; April to mid-Oct only.

Ambulance Service Museum (Kresz Géza Mentőmúzeum). Hungary has one of the oldest ambulance services in the world. Founded in 1887, it moved here in 1890. V. Markó u. 22. Blue metro to Nyugati tér. 9.00–14.00.

Aquincum Museum. Ruins of the Roman civilian town and museum of Roman finds. III. Szentendrei út 139; tel. 250-1650. HÉV railway from Batthyány tér to 'Aquincum'. 10.00–18.00 ex. Mon; (see p 000). For access to the Roman Baths Museum, Roman Camp Museum and Hercules Villa (see 'Roman Budapest') telephone 250-1650.

Attila József Memorial Room (József Attila Emlékszoba). Birthplace of the working-class poet. IX. Gát u. 3; tel. 117-3143. Tram 30 from Ferenc krt. 10.00–16.00; Sun 10.00–15.00.

Banknote and Coin Collection (MNB Bankjegy-és Aremgyűteménye). Inside the National Bank, V. Szabadság tér 8-9 (Bank u. entrance). Blue metro to Arany János u. Thurs only 9.00–14.00; see p 111.

Bartók Memorial House (Bartók Emlékház). Former home of composer Béla Bartók. II. Csalán u. 29; tel. 176-2100. Bus 5 to Pasaréti tér then short walk. 10.00–18.00 ex. Mon; free on Sat; shop; no w/a; see p 176.

Bible Museum (Biblia Múzeum). In the building of the Ráday Calvinist College. IX. Ráday u. 28; Blue metro to Kálvin tér, then short walk. 10.00–17.00 ex. Mon.

Csepel Local History Museum (Csepel Hélytörténeti Gyűtemény), XXI. Szent Imre tér 3; tel. 276-7343. HÉV railway from Boráros tér. 10.00–18.00 ex. Mon, closed July and August; see p 172.

Csepel Works Museum (Csepel Művek Múzeum), XXI. Gyepsor u. 1. Transport as above. Access only by prior arrangement, tel. 277-6347; see p 171.

Commerce and Catering Museum (Kereskedelmi és Vendéglátóipari Múzeum), I. Fortuna u. 4; tel. 175-4031. Castle bus from Moszkva tér. 10.00–18.00 ex. Mon; free on Friday; children free; w/a reasonable; see p 58.

East Asian Arts Museum (Hopp Ferenc Kelet-Ázsiai Művészeti Múzeum), VI. Andrássy út 103; tel. 322-8476. Yellow underground to Bajza u. 10.00–18.00 ex. Mon; see p 148.

Electrical Engineering Museum (Magyar Elektrotechnikai Múzeum). In a former 1930s sub-station, the history of the electricity industry in Hungary. VII. Kazinczy u. 21; tel. 122-0472. Trolley 74 from Erzsébet krt or walk from Károly krt. Tues–Sat 11.00–17.00; no admission charge; short video in English; no w/a.

Fire Service Museum (Tűzoltómúzeum), X. Martinovics tér 12; tel. 157-2190. Tram 28 from Népszinház u. to Liget tér. Tues–Sat 09.00–16.00, Sun 09.00–13.00; limited w/a; see p 173.

Foundry Museum (Öntöndei Múzeum), II. Bem u. 20. Two stops on bus 11 from Batthyány tér. Mon–Fri 09.00–16.30, weekends 10.00–16.30; w/a good after three steps; see p 78.

Geological Institute Collection (Földtani Intézet Gyűteménye), XIV. Stefánia út 14; tel. 251-0999. Tram 44 or 67 from Keleti Station. Access by prior telephone arrangement only; see p 178.

György Ráth Museum (Ráth György Múzeum). Collection of Chinese and Japanese arts. VI. Városligeti fasor 12. Trolleys 70 and 78. 10.00–18.00 ex. Mon; free on Tues; texts in English; see p 180.

Jókai Memorial Room (Jókai Emlékszoba). Very small collection of belongings of the novelist Mór Jókai. XII. Költő u. 21. Cog-Wheel railway to 'Városkút', or bus 21 from Moszkva tér; Wed–Sun 10.00–14.00; see p 164.

Kassák Memorial Museum (Kassák Emlékmúzeum). Life and work of avant-garde writer, publisher, painter and 'constructivist' designer Lajos Kassák. III. Fő tér 1; tel. 168-7021. HÉV railway to 'Árpád híd' 10.00–18.00 ex. Mon; see p 161.

Kodály Museum (Kodály Múzeum). Former home of musicologist, music teacher and composer Zoltán Kodály. VI. Kodály körönd 1; tel. 322-9647. Yellow underground to the 'körönd'. Wed 10.00–16.00, Thurs–Sat 10.00–18.00, Sun 10.00–14.00; see p 147.

Kun Collection (Lakásmúzeum). Folk art and crafts of collector Zsigmond Kun. III. Fő tér 4. HÉV to 'Árpád híd'. Tues–Fri 14.00–18.00, weekends 10.00–18.00; see p 162.

Laki Collection. Private folk art and crafts collection of Károly Laki. XVI. Kalitka u. 1; tel. 271-7909. HÉV railway from Örs vezér tere to 'Mátyásföld repülőtér'. By prior arrangement only.

Liszt Memorial Museum (Liszt Ferenc Emlékmúzeum). Former home of the composer. VI. Vörösmarty u. 35; tel. 322-9804. Yellow underground to Vörösmarty u. Mon–Sat 10.00–18.00; small snack bar; free concerts usually on Sat morning; see p 146.

Marton Galéria. Private exhibition on the works of contemporary sculptor László Marton. I. Tigris u. 55; tel. 175-0985. By prior arrangement only.

Matthias Church Ecclesiastical Collection, Szentháromság tér, Castle District. Castle bus from Moszkva tér. 09.00–19.00 every day; see p 54.

Meat Processing Industry Museum (Húsipari Múzeum), IX. Gubacsi út 6/b; tel. 215-7350 ex. 178. Tram 2 to 'Közvágóhíd'. For access ask at the library (könyvtár) here.

Medical History Museum (Semmelweis Orvostörténeti Múzeum), I. Apród u. 1–3; tel. 175-3533. Bus 78 from Ferenciek tere to Szarvas tér. 10.30–18.00 ex. Mon; no w/a see p 72.

Medieval Jewish Prayer House (Középkori Zsidó Imaház), I. Táncsics Mihály u. 26. Castle bus from Moszkva tér. Tues–Fri 10.00–14.00, weekends 10.00–18.00, Nov–April closed; see p 57.

Medgyaszay Memorial Museum (Medgyaszay Emlékhely). In the former villa of architect István Medgyaszay (1877–1959). Specialist collection of drawings and photos. XI. Ménesi út 59/b. Bus 27 from Villányi út. Access in the afternoons with prior arrangement; tel. 185-3644.

Milling Industry Museum (Malomipari Múzeum). On five floors of the 1868 Concordia Flour Mill in a still-working warehouse area. Emphasis on Budapest's hey-day as a European milling centre in the late 19C. IX. Soroksári út 24. One stop after Boráros tér on tram 2. Mon–Fri 09.00–14.00; free entrance; no w/a.

Museum of Pipe-laying (Csatornázási Múzeum). Drainage and sewage exhibits in an actual water-treatment plant built in 1912-17. II. Zsigmond tér 4. Tram 17 from Margaret Bridge. Mon–Fri 08.00–14.00, Sat 08.00–12.00. The Trinity Column in the square nearby is one of the oldest still-standing statues in the city (Bernado Feretti, 1706). It was most recently restored in 1994.

Music History Museum (Zenetörténeti Múzeum]) I. Táncsics Mihály u. 7; tel. 175-9011 ex. 164. Castle bus from Moszkva tér. Mon 16.00–20.00, Wed–Sun 10.00–18.00; labelling in English; good w/a; concerts usually on Mondays, in the courtyard in summer; see p 56.

National Jewish Museum (Országos Zsidó Vallási és Történeti Gyűtemény), VII. Dohány u. 2, next to the central synagogue; tel. 342-8941. Red metro to 'Astoria'. Mon–Fri 10.00–15.00, Sun 10.00–13.00; see p 106.

National Lutheran Museum (Evangélikus Országos Múzeum), V. Deák tér 4; tel. 117-4173. All metro lines to Deák tér. 10.00–18.00 ex. Mon; see p 98.

Natural History Museum (Természettudományi Múzeum). At the time of writing there are plans to move the museum to the former Military Academy building on Ludovika tér. Check with Tourinform, tel. 117-9800.

Palace of Wonders (Csodák Palotája). This is a new 'hands-on' science museum being planned at the time of writing. Check with Tourinform or tel. 201-9483.

Pátzay Collection. Permanent exhibition on the work of sculptor Pál Pátzay (1896–1979). Budapest Galéria Kiállítóháza, III. Lajos u. 158. Near the Buda end of Árpád Bridge. 10.00–18.00 ex Mon.

Pharmacy Museum (Arany Sas Patika Múzeum), I. Tárnok u. 18. Castle bus from Moszkva tér or bus 16 from Pest. 10.30–18.00 ex. Mon; children and students free; w/a possible; see p 49.

Physical Education and Sport Museum (Testnevelési és Sportmúzeum).

History of both in Hungary. XIV. Dózsa György út 3. Red metro to 'Népstadion'. 10.00–18.00 ex. Mon.

Postal Museum (Postamúzeum). History of postal services in Hungary. VI. Andrássy út 3; tel. 342-7938. Yellow underground to 'Bajcsy-Zsilinszky út' or walk from Deák tér. 10.00–18.00 ex. Mon; free on Sun; w/a possible via lift; see p 140.

Róth Memorial Museum (Róth Miksa Emlékmúzeum). A new museum on the life and work of Miksa Róth (1865–1944), a prolific crafstman of stained glass work and mosaics. VII. Nefelejcs u. 26. 300m from Keleti (Eastern) Station on the red metro line.

Sewage Museum. Another new museum, planned at the time of writing to open in a district sewage treatment plant. Check with Tourinform, tel. 117-9800.

Stamp Museum (Bélyegmúzeum), VII. Hársfa u. 47, on corner of Dob u.; tel. 142-0960. Tram 4 or 6 to 'Wesselényi utca'. 10.00–18.00 ex. Mon; children and students free; see p 122.

Technical Museum (Országos Műszaki Múzeum). Exhibition of items showing the development of techincal and engineering achievements. Planned to open in the second half of the 1990s in the so-called Palme House on Olof Palme sétány in the City Park.

Telephone Museum (Telefonia Múzeum). In a former exchange. I. Úri u. 49; tel. 201-8188. Castle bus from Moszkva tér. 10.00–18.00 ex. Mon; free on Wed; w/a good; see p 60.

Theatre Museum (Bajor Gizi Színészmúzeum). On the history of theatre and actors in Hungary. XII. Stromfeld Aurél út 16; tel. 156-4294. Bus 112 from Pest. Tues 12.00–16.00, Thurs 14.00–18.00, Sat & Sun 10.00–18.00. Closed July.

Tomb of Gül Baba (Gül Baba Türbe). Gül Baba, which means 'Father of Roses', was a Muslim Dervish who took part in the capture of Buda in 1541 but died soon after in the same year. Yahjapashazade Mehmed, the third Pasha of Buda, had an octagonal sepulchral chapel with hemispherical dome built in the 1540s. Although it has been rebuilt several times and for a while was used as a Christian chapel, it was reconstructed as original in 1962. Apart from Gül Baba's tomb, there are items recalling his life and religious order. For centuries this has been a place of pilgrimage for Muslims, in fact the only such place in Hungary. II. Mecset u. 14. Tram 4 or 6 to Buda end of Margaret Bridge. 10.00–18.00 ex. Mon; closed Nov–Apr.

Underground Railway Museum (Földalatti Múzeum). Small exhibition on Europe's second underground. V. Deák tér underpass; tel. 342-2130. All metro lines meet here. 10.00–18.00 ex. Mon; see p 97.

Varga Collection (Varga Imre Gyűjteménye). Metallic work of contemporary sculptor Imre Varga. III. Laktanya u. 7; tel. 250-0274. HÉV to 'Árpád híd'. 10.00–18.00 ex. Mon; see p 162.

Vasarely Museum (Vasarely Múzeum). Work of the Hungarian-born 'father of op-art', Victor Vasarely. III. Szentlélek tér 1; tel. 250-1540. HÉV as above. 10.00–18.00 ex. Mon; w/a good; see p 161.

Veterinery Science Collection (Állatorvosttörténeti Gyűjtemény), VII. István út 2, in the university building; tel. 322-0849. Trolleybus 74 from Károly krt or walk from Keleti station. Mon–Thurs 09.30–16.00, Fri 09.30–13.00.

Waxworks (Budavári Labyrinthus). In the caves under Castle Hill. Figures from Hungary's past. I. Úri u. 9; tel. 175-6858. Castle mini-bus from Moszkva tér, or bus 16 from Pest. 10.00–18.00; no w/a; see p 61.

INDEX

People's names are given in *italic* and the most important page references are given in **bold**.

A NOTE ON BLUE GUIDES

The Blue Guide series began in 1915 when Muirhead Guide-Books Limited published 'Blue Guide London and its Environs'. Findlay and James Muirhead already had extensive experience of guidebook publishing: before the First World War they had been the editors of the English editions of the German Baedekers, and by 1915 they had acquired the copyright of most of the famous 'Red' Handbooks from John Murray.

An agreement made with the French publishing house Hachette et Cie in 1917 led to the translation of Muirhead's London guide, which became the first 'Guide Bleu' – Hachette had previously published the blue covered 'Guides Joannes'. Subsequently, Hachette's 'Guide Bleu Paris et ses Environs' was adapted and published in London by Muirhead. The collaboration between the two publishing houses continued until 1933.

In 1933 Ernest Benn Limited took over the Blue Guides, appointing Russel Muirhead, Findlay Muirhead's son, editor in1934. The Muirhead's connection with the Blue Guides ended in 1963 when Stuart Rossiter, who had been working on the Guides since 1954, became house editor, revising and compiling several of the books himself.

The Blue Guides are now published by A & C Black, who aquired Ernest Been in 1984, so continuing the tradition of guidebook publishing which began in 1826 with 'Black's Economical Tourist of Scotland'. The Blue Guides series continues to grow: there are now more than 50 titles in print with revised editions appearing regularly and many new Blue Guides in preparation.

'Blue Guides' is a registered trade mark.

If you would like more information about
Blue Guides please complete the form below and
return it to

Blue Guides

A&C Black (Publishers) Ltd

Freepost

Eaton Socon

Huntingdon

Cambridgeshire

PE19 3BR

or fax it to us on

0171-831 8478

Name. . . . .
. . . .
Address. . . . .
. . . .
. . . .
. . . .
. . . .
. . . .